Becoming Mobius

The complex
matter of education

Dr Debra Kidd

Independent Thinking Press

First published by
Independent Thinking Press
Crown Buildings,
Bancyfelin,
Carmarthen,
Wales, SA33 5ND, UK
www.independentthinkingpress.com

Independent Thinking Press is an imprint of Crown House Publishing Ltd.

Images p. 9 © oscity, fotolia; p. 13 ©MC Rendered Artwork, fotolia; p. 14 © Liebstoeckel,
Wurzel, fotolia; p. 15 (top) © blueringmedia, fotolia; p. 15 (middle) © deviantART, fotolia;
p. 15 (bottom) © Ellerslie, fotolia; p. 34 © risto0, fotolia; p. 103 © Delphotostock, fotolia;
p. 116 (top) © Annykos, fotolia

British Library Cataloguing-in-Publication Data
A catalogue entry for this book is available from the British Library.

ISBN Print 978-178135219-9
ISBN Mobi 978-178135225-0
ISBN ePub 978-178135226-7
ISBN ePDF 978-178135227-4

Edited by Ian Gilbert

Printed and bound in the UK by
Gomer Press, Llandysul, Ceredigion

To my boys.
For letting me roam and then pulling me home.
For always making me feel like I matter.
For making me laugh and making me proud.
I love you all very much.

CONTENTS

FOR(E)WARDS AND BACKWORDS

A map does not converse in sentences. Its language is a half-heard rumour, fractured, fitful, non-discursive, non-linear … It is many tongued, a chorus reciting centuries of accumulated knowledge in echoed chants … A map provides no answers, it only suggests where to look.

Miles Harvey, *The Island of Lost Maps* (2000)

This book started its life as a thesis for my professional doctorate which was awarded in December 2013. Without the kind and humorous support of my supervisors, Rachel Jones and Cathie Pearce and Manchester Metropolitan University, it would never have emerged in any form at all. While I worked on my first book in the early months of 2014, *Teaching: Notes from the Front Line*, my editor, Ian Gilbert, asked me to send him a copy of the thesis. I sent it with a warning. It was not like my blog. It was not like my other book. This was a different, more complex beast altogether. We would not be looking at a bestseller. He wanted to publish it anyway because he's like that. He likes to think differently.

It's taken another year to get it to this point. Very little of that time has been spent writing, but it needed incubation. A thesis is never finished; there is just a deadline at which point you hand it over and hope for the best. The same is true of a book. But to move from thesis to book, this text needed to evolve, to take into account the fast changes happening in the world of education, to live a little and to learn more. There are new voices now in this text that never appeared in the original – the most important belongs to Gert Biesta. Both Ian Gilbert and my external examiner, Dr Phil Wood, told me I must read him – that he would enrich my life and my book. And he has.

This is a text about living with uncertainty. This is a state of being that many people struggle with in day-to-day life and in education; being uncertain has almost become a sin. We are told that children are on a trajectory of certain progression from their baseline tests at 4 to leaving school at 18. We are sold a narrative that this course is fixed and certain, and that only poor teaching can knock it off course. And to make sure that this happens, we are policed. And judged. And berated. And punished. It is a lie, and the protection of the lie carries a cost paid not only in the form of a vast amount of funding and energy from politicians, but in the haemorrhaging of teachers from the profession. If we are truly to have an education system that 'works', we need to accept that learning and life are not simple, and we need to engage with difficult and complex ideas.

I was not always comfortable with uncertainty myself. I arrived at my first professional doctorate session back in 2007 as a newly appointed initial teacher training (ITT) tutor with a plan. I knew what I knew. I was going to 'do' action research. I was going to 'prove' that my preferred pedagogy 'worked', and it was simply a matter of doing my time until I was able to submit. I had a bike; I knew how to ride it. I had a roadmap; I knew where I was going. As a result, my first assignment was a polemic full of certainty. Over the course of the next six years, that certainty waned until it became my doctoral thesis – a more tentative text.

This point was arrived at via a meandering route of experimentation. By 2009 (I blame post-structuralism) my bike was in pieces on the floor. Instead of going forwards and reaching a destination, I had systematically dismantled all that I thought I knew. Nothing was what I thought it was; I was only certain of not being certain. I had the assemblages of a bike; I could no longer ride it. I had an out-of-date roadmap; I had no idea where to go. Post-structuralism had offered me a way of unravelling assumptions and had been instrumental in shifting my thinking, but I was looking for something more – a way of not so much reconstructing but assimilating and making sense of what I could now see was a complex relationship between the human and non-human; between the certain and the uncertain; between the complex and the simple.

I now know that what I needed to do was to embrace the inherent weakness of education, but I hadn't at that point read the book that Biesta had not yet written![1] I had been drawn to exploring emotion in the classroom from the start, but now I began to see how our feelings and sensations are impacted not only by power but also by desire, space and time. It has always been my belief that we teach (or should teach) in order to make the world a better place – to see it anew. (Or else what is the point? Do we teach to maintain a status quo? To return to an idealised past?) To this end, the idea of education as a democratic process with a strong moral purpose has always been my goal. This remains – that foundation has not been shaken by uncertainty. But it has been reframed, re-examined, re-evaluated along the way. There are markers of social justice through-out this text and, above all, these stories have the notion of justice at heart. But they are framed in philosophical lenses through which we explore the nature and purpose of education.

During those six years, I stumbled off roads altogether. Wandering here and there, relaying between left, right, forwards, backwards, in-between. Getting lost, finding new ways, foraging and gathering – in my wander-ing I had become wonderer. A nomad. This book posits the possibility that wondering and wandering teachers might impact greatly on a child's ability to live with and thrive among uncertainties. It suggests that while things might be complex, they don't have to be complicated. It asks of us, not only as teachers or researchers, but simply as human beings, what are the things that affect us, and how can we remain attuned to all their possibilities while still functioning?

On this little wander, I found a sturdy pair of shoes: science and phil-osophy. I found science to be working with the same sorts of ideas that I found in the philosophy of Deleuze and Guattari. Long before neuro-scientists started thinking of the brain as an emergent system, Deleuze was moving towards this possibility by describing the brain in rhizomatic rather than arboreal terms. I was also drawn to science and by science – the pioneering, experimental, uncertain science at the edges, and not what Furedi calls the empirical 'scientism' of certainty.[2]

Both Deleuze and Guattari altered my thinking, giving me both a lan-guage and navigational tools. Their conceptual frameworks – that life is lived at the edges, that it is complexly and rhizomatically connected, that it is constantly shifting shape and form, that it is brim-full of possible becomings – really resonated with my experience of the classroom. I found that both these scientific and Deleuzian concepts allowed me to better understand why it was impossible to fully understand a learning process and why it was so important to keep on trying.

This book is my attempt to present and map that journey. It is where we step off the road. There is no transport. I'm afraid you have to walk, and it is not a stroll in the park. A former adviser to Michael Gove once told me that he refused to read Deleuze because he was 'wilfully obtuse'. But just because something is difficult does not mean that it's not worth the effort of engagement. The content *is* difficult, but there are, hopefully, enough signs to ensure that you don't get too lost. The opening chapter is long and theoretical – bear with me – but it's important to frame the discussion and explore the ideas underpinning the rest of the text. I hope it provokes new thinking.

This is a journey through a landscape of education. You will see children on plains surrounded by beautiful and terrible distractions; shepherds and lost lambs; dams and roadblocks, streams and passageways. The data consists of stories, and these tales have been drawn from a number of contexts. Primary, secondary and higher education – I have taught in all of them. Some of these narrative landmarks were collected as part of my consultancy work in schools. It has all been selected because of its pull on memory. It is not what was sought, but what was most powerfully present either in the moment or at a point of recollection in the future. This is not, I grant you, the usual means of collecting data, but it's an honest one and one that seeks not to tell truths but to open doors to further questions.

By 2010, I had returned to work in school – in a secondary setting, employed as an advanced skills teacher (AST). Some of this book explores the difficulty of the return from higher education to a full-time teaching role and my frustrations in that role. And how, eventually, those frustrations spilled over into a resignation. I stand here now, outside of school, but wholeheartedly inside the education system. A nomad, still figuring out where to go next. But the focus in this book is not on the here and now of my context. It is on the process of learning and teaching; the attempts to find the middle and to stay in the middle, resisting linearity. The middle way is not the easy route. It is not a straight route. It is not a cop-out. It is a means of living in, with and through complexity and multiplicity. It is an attempt to bring forward something new – to find ways of making education anew. I have no final solution, no silver bullet, but I have a map of an emerging world, and it keeps on growing.

Notes

1. G. Biesta, *The Beautiful Risk of Education* (Boulder, CO: Paradigm, 2013).
2. F. Furedi, *Authority: A Sociological History* (New York: Cambridge University Press, 2013).

Chapter 1

A MATTER OF
THE MIDDLE:
INTRA-DUCTION

Intra-duction
In.tra – prefix *within; inside*
In.tro – prefix *in, into or inward*

Oxford English Dictionary

But Mousie, thou art no thy lane,
In proving foresight may be vain;
The best-laid schemes o' mice an' men
Gang aft a-gley,
An' lea'e us nought but grief an' pain
For promis'd joy!

Robert Burns, 'To a Mouse' (1785)

Little of what follows is what I thought it would be. There were times when I sat with head in hands, bemoaning the plans that 'gang aft a-gley'. Times when, like St Pierre, I found myself 'stopped, stuck – dead in the water',[1] not noticing at first the nibbling nudges at the edges of consciousness attempting to tell me that all was not lost, that the outcomes were simply 'other'. It was in the process of learning to allow those nudges / gut feelings to find their ways into thoughts, or to lie fallow until another experience pinged them into a resonant life, that this thinking would really begin to take form. I had intended to write about children's experiences of learning, and then I became lost in methodology, and gradually the two fused in a complex intra-relay between theory, practice, self and other.[2] All experience mattered. All experience became matter. It has been a messy, sticky process. It is still messy, still sticky, still half-formed and half-emerging. What follows is not a completed act, but a point in time – an intra-duction.

An intra is, of course, a 'middle' and not a beginning, and in many ways this book is a series of mid-points or conjunctions, inspired mostly by the work of Gilles Deleuze and Felix Guattari. They conceptualise experience as rhizomatic – think of a strawberry plant or grass. The rhizome is always in the middle, in places where affects, ideas, assemblages converge and become other: 'The middle is by no means an average: on the contrary, it is where things pick up speed ... a stream without beginning or end that undermines its banks and picks up speed in the middle.'[3] Both men challenge the traditional modes of thought that life and ideas are arboreal (tree-like), that thoughts and experiences follow a linear progression from root to fruit. Instead, they argue that human life is not tree-like, but a much more messy tangle of rhizomatic root structures, complexly and unpredictably connected. They conceptualise time as similarly complex – not linear at all, but a mishmash of pasts, presents and imagined or possible futures pressing in on moments and decisions and actions.

Deleuze separates out the functions of time into two types – aion and chronos (more on these later). Inspired by this, my work is nothing less, or more significant, than a selection of story-streams, which oscillate in aion time in which pasts press upon and fragment the present in arcs towards potential futures.[4] The fracturing nature of time, as explored by Deleuze, has created a fractal element to the work, and therefore there are leaps and lines of flight which are deliberately enmeshed and which may confuse or tax the reader. They are connected by resonance, by theory and by concepts that have emerged from my lived experiences of working with children. The writing leaps about, connecting ideas in a way that is not entirely linear, although, of course, you are more than likely to read this in a linear way. But thoughts and resonances have been left largely where they occurred and, to that end, this is a piece of writing that, instead of a road, is more of a plateau. Dahlberg and Moss describe working in plateau as:

a continuous, self-vibrating region of intensities whose development reac-
tivated or between which a number of connecting routes could exist. This
avoids any idea of moving towards a culminating point or external end
– the antithesis of the dominant discourses in today's … education with
their fixation on predetermined and sequential outcomes. Instead we are
always inbetween, with many possibilities open to us.[5]

The plateau is a useful geographical term here. It represents both a physical flattening and a flattening of time – a place which has been formed
by geophysical pressure, but one from which there is a flattened view.
From a distance it looks like a uniform and simple structure; close up,
there are folds and layers of complexity.

We can stand in/on a plateau and follow the markings and lines that
have formed this place – an assemblage. Each plateau (or chapter) in
the text represents a 'line of flight' with none dependent on or entirely
detached from the others.[6] There is no 'finale' in this text, no chronology.
It is my attempt to write as an assemblage, and one that deliberately
disrupts. There is, nevertheless, content (education) and there are participants (teachers, researchers, an AST and children) and, inevitably,

issues relating to power and justice emerge throughout. By working in this way, I hope to add to and develop ways of working with and through multiplicity in educational settings, but always with a sense of social justice in mind and heart.

As teachers, we often bemoan the role of ideology in education. But we all have an ideology. Our values and beliefs as practitioners are always enacted in classrooms. Often this is done subconsciously – we re-enact the education we value, which is often that which worked for us. It is far more helpful, however, to step back and consider who you want to be and what you want to stand for. This can involve reading. It certainly involves reflecting on what you see, feel and experience. It demands that you find resonance, connections; that you try to make sense. For me, that resonance came through Deleuze. But what matters is that you seek to understand why it is *you* do what you do. And that you keep on looking – because first conclusions are rarely the only ones you might draw. Life thrives in multiplicity. And there is always another possibility – or, indeed, many possibilities.

In attempting to let go of the structure of this text, I attempted to reflect the complex nature of teaching, learning, researching and, indeed, of living. I found that Deleuzian frames allowed me to explore complexity anew. Part way through my doctoral study, I returned to classroom teaching from higher education, and then I left it again. In many ways, this work charts a series of returns as I attempt to explore how the past sits within our present; how returns and differences can help us to make anew; how, ultimately, complexity can be navigated (and embraced) without becoming overwhelmingly complicated. It is my contention that while many teachers recognise the complex nature of teaching, the desire to conform, perform and survive, and to push forward binaries, leads some to reject the complex and reach for the simple.[7] Instead, I argue that by engaging with complexity in a playful manner, we can finds modes of resistance which allow us to 'become-Mobius' – to exist in the between spaces of one AND another in order not only to survive but also to thrive.

As I move among my stories – not in forward motion, but in loops and returns – I explore and play with surfaces, rhizomes and middles instead of beginnings, endings and roots. In line with the philosophies of Deleuze and Guattari, this book is predominantly preoccupied with notions of immanence taken from the Latin intra (to remain within) and becoming (moving outwards). Deleuze and Guattari describe the plane of immanence as 'a single wave that rolls [concepts] up and then unrolls them',[8] and it is here, in this rolling and unrolling, that I have found myself working.

For Deleuze and Guattari, there is no attempt to signify: 'writing has nothing to do with signifying. It has to do with surveying, mapping, even realms that are yet to come.'[9] And so this is an attempt to map – to write into being – an educational landscape without attempting to consciously shape or conclude. Yet, inevitably, shapes will be perceived and conclusions drawn. This tension between resisting certainty and stating beliefs is simply something that has to be lived with. It is not a contradiction but an intra-action, and the work will be unsettling to anyone seeking to know 'what works'. In both teaching and research settings, I attempted to survive in a linear culture while subverting the notion of linearity and developing a tolerance for uncertainty. There is no 'one time' underpinning the trajectory of this book or uniting the stories that form its data.

Stories of matter

The 'matter' of the title is both material and emotional – the entanglement of matter in the process of becoming and mattering. 'We are all matter, and we all matter.'[10] The ambiguity of these words has very much preoccupied my thinking process and those of others, such as Karen Barad, who points out the resonances between what we think of as material matter at a scientific level and emotional matter at a human level.[11] These notions of both organic and inorganic material becomings form a significant part of Deleuze's thinking on the non-human dimensions of his work on bodies without organs,[12] 'that thrives in the multitude of its modalities'.[13] The idea of 'becoming' is very much central to Deleuze's work – the means by which we become other. And there are connections here also to the work of Biesta, who argues that education is (or should be), in part, a process of 'subjectification'[14] – in itself a form of becoming. Similarly, the philosophy connects to the world of theoretical physics.

Karen Barad, herself a theoretical physicist, challenges notions of intentionality from both within the human perspective and the more non-organic material perspective at the level of particle physics. Just as 'there is no determinate fact of the matter' in human intentionality,[15] she argues, the same is true of all matter. For the physicist, the acceptance that the conceptual and the real are both material is a given. Niels Bohr argued that his work was not 'ideational' but related to 'specific physical arrangements'.[16] The intra-actions between the physical world and the educational experience are explored throughout – environment and bodies messily enmeshed in learning processes and memories. And underpinning them all is the notion that it is possible, always possible, to become 'other'. That life is not predetermined; that possibility always exists.

I have found myself indebted to Barad's explanation of mattering which resonates with these ideas:

Individuals do not pre-exist their interactions; rather, individuals emerge through and as part of their entangled inter-relating ... matter and meaning, come into existence, are iteratively reconfigured through each intra-action, thereby making it impossible to differentiate in any absolute sense between creation and renewal, beginning and returning, continuity and discontinuity, here and there, past and future.[17]

For Barad, these impossibilities suggest a process of becoming which is better understood through the metaphor of diffraction than reflection. She points out that the use of reflective practices makes assumptions about the nature of reality – a 'right back at you' approach – whereas diffraction focuses on differences, small and minute differences, in order to better understand things and processes. She uses the images of waves in diffractive patterns to show how diffractive methodology might work in visual terms. It is at the points of intra-action where we should focus our attention.

In short, it is at the point where there are differences, outliers, disturbances that the really interesting stuff happens. In education, we too often look for the trend, the pattern, the average. But it is not here that

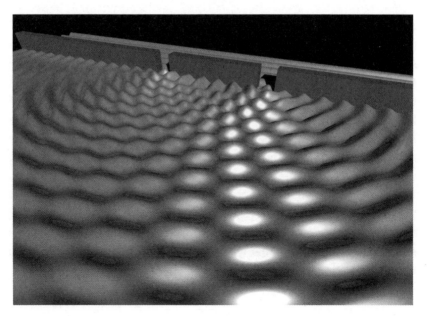

Diffraction in water

challenge is born. It is in the nuance, the not yet, the difficulty. If we focus on the trend, we'll always miss the possibilities sitting just out of sight, at the edges of our experiences.

There are clearly resonances here – in Barad's images of diffraction, where waves of physics and philosophy converge – with the developing understanding of the workings of the mind through neuroscience. Susan Greenfield touches upon the overlaps of the two science disciplines in her writing as she explores the 'assemblies' of consciousness and accepts the limitations of her science:

The big and indeed unanswerable question now ... is what phenomenology can be matched up with this very physiological phenomenon of a neuronal assembly? ... The great question is still the causal, water-into-wine relationship of the physical brain and body with subjective mental events.[18]

Greenfield argues for closer working between biological neuroscientists and quantum physicists, but she also acknowledges the role of philosophy and anthropology. This blurring of the lines between disciplines and ideas is fractal – the point at which one thing converges on/with/ through another. Her view of the brain–mind relationship brings modern-day neuroscience much closer to that explored by Deleuze and Guattari. Indeed, the lines between philosophy and science are blurred in the field of physics too, particularly at quantum level where the notion of lines and outlines is also problematic. As Feynman says in explaining the structure of the atom, 'what is the Outline? ... It is not, believe it or not that every object has a line around it! There is no such line!'[19] Similarly, time and place are differently understood at the subatomic level, drawing scientists into an acceptance of unpredictability: 'it is not possible to predict what will happen in any circumstance'.[20] Neuroscientists use these uncertainties and complexities to warn against reductionist views of the brain,[21] a position that Deleuze and Guattari posited while brain science was relatively new:

The brain is not a rooted or ramified matter ... the discontinuity between cells ... make the brain a multiplicity immersed in its place of consistency or neuralgia, a whole uncertain, probabilistic system.[22]

As I am drawn to the connections between Deleuzian concepts and scientific metaphor, I find myself visualising another natural form – the rhizome. Look at the images below of the plant and of the brain cell:

Rhizome plant structure

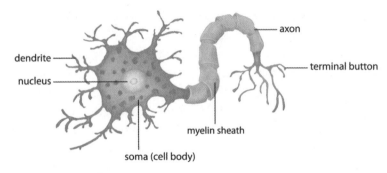

Dendrites and brain cells

And the networks they produce:

Rhizome root network

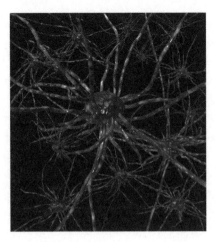

Synaptic link network

Synaptic links, like rhizomes, appear in the 'middles' and are complex assemblages of proteins and hormones; of cells and particles interacting in ways that are unpredictable, and which together create emergent systems which are more than the sum of their parts – or immanent. These developing understandings of the brain bring science closer to Deleuze and Guattari's declaration that the brain is 'grass', that is complexly and rhizomatically interconnected.[23] The fusing of these two worlds through the interdisciplinary reading of images and texts creates new understandings.

Many aspects of my attempts to explain and outline my rationale for the role of exploratory research in my work wrestle with the ideas of 'difference' and 'repetition'. Derrida and Deleuze have used these words in contrasting ways. Barad brings those contrasts closer by conceptualising the Derridian concept of 'difference' through diffractions.[24] Diffractive analysis requires a series of returns – a key element of Deleuze's work on difference. Although these theorists contemplate what seem to be similar concepts, for example repetition, the difference between their positions is marked. It is described by Bearn as, 'simple and deep: it is the difference between No and Yes'.[25] I am drawn to the potential of these and other complexities. For Derrida, the deconstruction of the 'norm' performed strategic reversals, forcing the reader to worm into the roots of discourse and of social constructs to better understand how our identities, values and cultural selves are created and maintained. I am also drawn to his rejection of empiricism.[26]

Deleuze extends the notion of 'difference' in *The Logic of Sense*. Both he and Guattari offer a new way of conceptualising difference, moving from root to rhizome and from language to a broader plane of immanence and affect.[27] For Derrida, the digging into discourse creates 'depth', but for Deleuze it is not depth but width that yields the most interest. Much of the work for this book has been spent 'digging' for roots, but finding along the way that the network is complex and unpredictable, and is spread along or near to the surface. Instead of roots I have found rhizomes. Instead of digging down I have learned to rake across, and this is an important skill for a teacher working in a culture that desires single answers. If we dig down too deeply into one line of enquiry, we are in danger of blinding ourselves to the multiplicity of the width.

In education, this has become evident in the way in which politicians have pursued synthetic phonics as an 'answer' to the complexity of reading, forcing a hard stare at a single solution. Meanwhile, at the edges of our vision, boys in particular are losing a love of reading which impacts on their future success at school and in life.[28] Viewing an issue thinly – looking at the edges for unintended influences and consequences – takes vigilance and patience. It requires returns. It is not shallow to work in the shallows.

These impossible differentiations between time, discipline and creation – the images of intra-related connections which fold in on themselves and become both inner AND outer – have come to dominate my view of matter and mattering. These entanglements have drawn me to notions of complexity and to the points at which philosophy and science become entangled. Ricca explores how complexity theory has developed within a scientific framework,[29] and offers useful parallels for viewing educational experiences in the classroom as complex adaptive systems, characterised by 'growth, mutual influence and non linear connectedness'.[30] Similar connections between complexity, science and social/educational research have also been developed by Barad, Walby, Allan and Turner, among others, and both Protevi and Plotnitsky have written about the connections between the Deleuze–Guattari project and theories of chaos and complexity.[31] This complexity leads Biesta to encourage us to celebrate education as a 'beautiful risk' in which uncertainty and complexity are not to be feared but to be embraced and worked with as tools of hope and possibility.[32] There are striking resonances between the metaphors used by scientists to explore complexity and Deleuzian notions of immanence, folds and rhizomes. As a result, I have become interested in thinking within science about complexity and Deleuzian philosophy as lenses through which classroom interactions might be viewed. I stress here that my interest in, and references to, science do not stem from a positivist frame; instead, I draw from the difference between science and scientism – the former being the pioneering work at the edge of certainty and the latter rooted in a deadening desire for certainty.[33] It is within the former definition that I have found scientists playing with ideas and language in a field of complexity and uncertainty.

The inter- and intra-relationship between ideas and experiences requires a mode of eclecticism in terms of exploring educational ideas driven not by categorisation and linearity but by resonance through emerging connections. There is a flattening of logic, of discourse and of materials in which it is the material at the edges that is most interesting. What is emerging? Where is the potential growth? Where are the intra-actions? How do the seemingly unconnected connect and become more than the sum of their parts, creating emergent systems? As Anderson says:

The ability to reduce everything to simple fundamental laws does not imply the ability to start from those laws and reconstruct the universe … At each level of complexity entirely new properties appear. Psychology is not applied biology, nor is biology applied chemistry. We can now see that the whole becomes not merely more, but very different from the sum of its parts.[34]

Telling tales

This work demands a different way of looking – sideways glances AND full-on stares, soft AND hard focus, zooming in AND zooming out. There is an avoidance of planning, per se, and more focus on setting up a method that leaves the process open to serendipity and chance. As such, rather than bemoaning the disruption of 'best-laid plans', I have learned to accept and embrace the disruptions, and even to seek to disrupt in order to better understand or explore a position. This desire to remain open to exploration, or play, has led to viewing the development of my thinking as a *Gedankenexperiment*. This is an idea borrowed from the world of physics in which a concept is explored outside of laboratory settings. These experiments are described by Barad as 'pedagogical devices – tools for isolating and bringing into focus key conceptual issues … there is no expectation that a *Gedankenexperiment* will be realized as a laboratory experiment'.[35] This book takes place outside of a literal lab, of course, but it also takes place outside of the constructs of a methodological 'lab' – a place of agreed experimental structures. There is no formal methodology, no planned collection of data and the analysis sits within a conceptual realm and not an empirical setting. To this end, I attempted to 'follow' the data – to work with what emerged rather than simply codifying it. This process, as Deleuze and Guattari observe, is 'not the same as reproducing' which is simply a mode of watching a 'flow'.

Following requires an examination of the 'singularities of a matter',[36] and I have attempted to do this not by fixing the data in a single interpretation, but by following a number of possible lines of flight from it.

This is a deliberate attempt to disrupt the dominance of the question, 'What works?', because that question demands 'certain' answers. And certain answers force a reduction in terms of framing the question and validating the evidence. In education, then, in asking the question, 'What works?', we necessarily reduce our focus to test results. What works in terms of securing test results? Even this is not foolproof – there will always be the children who fail, the outliers. But they don't interest the hunters focused on averages. If we can get the vast majority through the tests we can claim to have an education system that 'works'. But only if the purpose of education is to pass tests. Many, Biesta and Egan among them, are demanding that we broaden our question out.[37] Instead of 'What works?', perhaps we need to be thinking about what we want education to achieve in terms of both human and non-human futures. Such questions demand autopoietic thinking which is characterised by growth, emergence and complexity.[38] This is, in itself, a risk as teachers are not encouraged to be emergent; instead, they are told that theirs is a technical role, one by which the adherence to certain sets of habits and practices will make them 'teach like a champion'.

This resistance to technical modes of thought also impacted on my writing process. By allowing both writing and teaching to 'emerge' through diffractive thinking, rather than being forced or structured – by attempting, as Richardson and St Pierre suggest, to 'travel in the thinking that writing produces'[39] – I could play with the idea of allowing the writing to lead, and for both the data and the writing to take on a performative element. This creates a sense of writing as a means of creating smooth nomadic spaces in which the writer sits on the camel of the keyboard and allows the work to emerge. In resisting traditional modes of writing, of research, of teaching, we put ourselves out on a ledge – a precipice from which there is danger of failure and ridicule. But there is also a unique view and a heightened awareness of what is possible. It is a risk worth taking.

There are clearly connections here to post-structuralism in which 'language does not *reflect* social reality, but rather produces meaning and creates social reality'[40] – that is, language acting as a diffractive process. I hope to explore how language, both spoken and unspoken, impacts on learning. But I am not attempting to expose or codify 'social reality', rather to gently uncover possibilities so that we see difference, not necessarily truth. While post-structuralism initially focused on the ways in which language is used to create power dynamics, meta-narratives and discourses, it has, more recently, been used as a tool to defend and even celebrate the blurring of boundaries between genre and notions of truth, and to invite us to 'reflect on our method and find new ways of knowing'.[41] In this later work, what Denzin and Lincoln describe as the 'methodologically contested present' of 'the seventh movement',[42] arguments are formed for the validation of more radical approaches to conducting and interpreting 'research', arguing for the recognition of these alternative forms of knowing. One of these, and the one with which my work is most concerned, sits in the affective dimension, and requires a wider notion of literacy than that which exists within language. This is one reason that Diana Masny's work resonates for me:

Literacies are a construct; a combination of social, physical, economical assemblages … literacies consist of words, gestures, attitudes and ways of listening, speaking, writing, human and non human, ways of becoming in the world … literacies are actualised according to a particular context of time and space … and involve constant movement in the process of becoming other.[43]

This view of the literate human as one who is open to 'reading' intra-actions as 'texts', and viewing them in a non-linear way, requires an openness to serendipity, to chance, to the fleeting moments of affect which vibrate across time and space. It also requires a rejection of norms, a refusal to comply with the expectations of others, while acknowledging a responsibility to at least attempt to explain. Sometimes that which one hopes to explain is so fleeting and momentary that it is hard to justify as 'data'. Yet it is in these moments that strong pivots take place – moments which, while fleeting, are so powerful that they shift a person or a group into a new trajectory of being. It is in these moments that what I would describe as a 'gutterance' occurs – a communication without words, which is nonetheless fully felt and understood. This interests me, for it is in these moments, sometimes less than a second long, that the outcome of a lesson can be decided and which can ignite resentment or joy or hope or anger. I have been drawn, therefore, to exploring concepts of time. These gutterances are calls to 'action', and so other plateaus explore what actions might be and examine different notions of actions, deeds and events.

This exploratory text is both a reaction against and a product of a 'now' time in which it seems, more than ever, that we, as a species, are living with the demand for certainty while the world itself seems more uncertain.[44] Austerity is driving a relentless focus on reliable outcomes, on what works, what is deliverable, and this is mirrored in a demand for research to answer questions about that most complex and unpredictable of human beings – the child. Governments across the world have called for educational researchers to use the same methodologies employed by the medical profession,[45] and in promoting the Education Endowment Foundation's toolkit[46] – a synthesis of Hattie's work[47] – have encouraged the acceptance of large-scale statistical randomised controlled trials, meta-analyses and effect sizes. But as Furedi points out, children are not illnesses and education is not a cure.[48] The move towards this form of research approach is worryingly reductive and ignores the complexity of both human and non-human inter- and intra-action. It exposes what Biesta calls a 'misguided impatience' in which 'children are being made fit for the education system rather than ask where the causes of this misfit lie, and who, therefore, needs treatment most: the child or society'.[49]

Dylan Wiliam puts across well the danger of overly simplistic thinking in this yeast analogy:

A: *When you don't add yeast, bread doesn't rise.*
B: *When you do add yeast, bread rises.*
C: *Therefore, yeast makes bread rise.*[50]

Of course, yeast only makes bread rise in the presence of moisture, heat and so on. He points out that while looking for patterns and trends is a useful thing to do, we must always bear in mind that where there are seemingly simple correlations 'it's usually a bit more complicated than that'. We cannot be as certain as we would like to be.

A map

There are many leaps and lines in this text – it is unsettling and refuses to sit still – so it might be helpful to view the structure of the book as topographical rather than linear. Less of a road and more of a landscape. The features of the landscape are connected and form a whole – there is a map but no directions. Kitchin et al. offer a view of maps as 'unfolding potential: as conduits of possibilities; as the sites of imagination and action in the world',[51] and this is how I hope the text will be read. The creation of each plateau has been intra-dependent – working outwards and returning back in folds and waves. In many sections of this book for example, data which pre-exist the thesis emerge alongside 'new' data, just as long gone glaciers leave valleys on our maps but remain present in a new form. Each plateau is a topographical feature, some connected to methodology, some to experience, some merging both. They are significant not in terms of their separateness but in how they come together to create an intra-active whole. As such, I present a series of cartographies in which lines of thought are depicted in the hope that they add to the emerging literature relating to Deleuze and education.

This plateau, the first of our landmarks, sets out my position – perhaps it is a welcome sign on the border. Like a landscape, we can view each topographical feature separately, but it is not until we step back and take in the whole that we get a full sense of 'where we are'. So, in our landscape, we encounter material conceptual features:

- **A matter of amorphodology.** An exploration of the notion of method and the search for forms and processes that resist linearity and embrace complexity. It aims to open up questions about how complexity might be playfully navigated. How does data appear? How might we embrace serendipity? What can be learned from others experimenting in the field?

- **A matter of space.** Here we encounter gaps and folds, smooth and striated spaces, freedoms and constraints. This plateau aims to explore how spaces can be opportunistic places which offer the potential for change, becoming other. It examines the folded spaces where elements hide – 'pleats of matter' waiting for recurrence and reterritorialisation which make us notice a 'something'. It argues that we, as teachers, can find spaces for play, for investigation, for possibility.

- **A matter of action.** This plateau examines deeds and events, affect and effect from two perspectives – that of Deleuze and Arendt – and asks what new understandings can be gained from examining the two theories not comparatively, but conjunctively. It brings in Biesta's critique of Arendt's assertion that politics and education should be entirely separate, and asks what constitutes action in the classroom, examining the nuances and complexities of the formation of events and actions.

- **A matter of time.** This plateau charts a return to classroom practice framed though the concept of time and travel. It aims to unravel a developing sense of myself as an artisanal nomad and how that position throws up challenges for me working in a school context. It frames this journey as an experience of time, conceptualised through chronos and aion, and examines the impact of our conceptualisation of past, present and future on children's learning experiences.

- **A matter of making sense and taking responsibility.** I examine the multiple meanings of sense by straddling the roles of teacher and researcher. This plateau aims to explore the different ideas of sense – sensations, making sense and being sensible (responsible) – within a Deleuzian model of ethics, one which rejects a notion of morality and yet is rooted in notions of justice.

- **A matter of (r)evolution.** This large plateau explores myriad ways in which systems of linearity might be subverted at macro, micro and nano levels. It examines current educational rhetoric and places this within the notional framework of control societies. It explores what might be done at a micro level in terms of curriculum and pedagogy and, finally, it posits the idea that neither macro nor micro revolutions can be effective without taking into account the nano – the significance of minute and important small classroom interactions.

Taking both Deleuzian concepts outlined in other plateaus and Biesta's work on weaknesses and risks, it asks how the teacher might 'become Mobius' in meeting demands from competing pressures. It asks what might be done, what might 'work', subverting the current notion of work being equated purely with achievement in examinations or inspections. It argues not for revolution, but rather for the idea that teachers form collective and conscious modes of evolutionary practice which could revolutionise education.

- **A matter of hoping.** Finally, I consider the theory and process that have been instrumental in creating what has emerged. This plateau asks what this exploration is in terms of being something of matter, and explores what it can become in terms of making an ongoing contribution to the field of teaching and learning. It returns to other plateaus in this book in order to explore how they, and the process of writing itself, have combined to create, and continue to combine to create, new lines of flight. It also explores the responsibility that writing and remembrance bring.

In attempting to present a meandering process rather than a linear journey, data and themes flit focus – in school/out of school, me/us/them, then/now/future. Some have been informed by looking back; others have emerged seemingly from nowhere. But, of course, this is not true – they have pre-existed in some form or other. The data has acted therefore more as a schizo disruption, as described by O'Sullivan in his exploration of Guattari's work:

First it might come after the accessing of any signifying nuclei. This would be a retroactive recognition, as it were, an 'Ah! So that's what it was!', or even an 'Ah! So that's me!' It might also, however, operate prior to the asignifying nuclei as a kind of platform or catalyst. Here signifying material is predictive, even prophetic.[52]

While I reject linearity, there is no doubt that lines of flight have emerged from my thinking. These lines are presented within the text as interruptions in the form of the data. They chart, or map, as rhizomatically as possible, my battle to be artisan rather than architect in my teaching.[53]

They expose the weaknesses – the many failures – as well as the pressures to comply and hopefully also small triumphs, which offer some scope for improvement and movement while recognising complexity.

Disruptive stories

Just as science grapples with notions of consciousness, so research grapples with trying to pin down that which is hard to prove. Traditional linear notions of research demand a degree of predictability and certainty, which is usually produced in linear and logical form – from what Deleuze refers to as 'denotating intuition' (hypothesis) to oversimplified conclusions of signification.[54] It is difficult to resist the temptation to draw denotative conclusions in outcome even if the process is more fluid. To stand outside of, or to defy, this 'established way of thinking' in which 'a prevailing system of representation is naturalised and seen as the only truthful and correct way' is daunting.[55] Doing so is an act of resistance.

It is this refusal to engage with the simplicity of origins that has made the process of writing this book so complicated. Conformity lives in the margins – described by Norris as 'the powerful normative consensus'.[56] This consensus has haunted me as I have written, as I have attempted to write myself out of norms within a normative form, to unsettle the 'unsettling forces'. This has formed a jostling between the data and the narrative – the latter being the central text and the former an attempt to trouble the centre. The data itself exists not simply as something to be analysed but as an interruption, a disruption, and there has been a great temptation to refuse analysis – to allow it to sit. Yet as a species we are driven to make sense. It is hard to resist the impulse to draw single conclusions; so instead I attempt to suggest possibilities. The 'data' has appeared at the margins of consciousness, as headers and footnotes, and sometimes as images in my emerging thinking. Not so much sought, as niggling their way into the main 'text' and appearing, seemingly innocently, as stories.

These stories concern affects and effects. They have come to me loaded with emotion and have arrived rather than been chosen by virtue of their impact – the impact that tells the mind that 'this matters' even if at that moment it is not clear why or how. They are the ordinary moments, easily missed, that carry the potential – when they connect to others at some future or past point – to become extraordinarily or consciously meaningful. We all experience these pivotal moments throughout our lives, but we tend not to consider them in terms of the impact they have on classroom experience and practice. Anthropologist Kathleen Stewart offers a useful definition of the notion of ordinary affects:

Ordinary affects are the varied, surging, capacities to affect and be affected that give everyday life the quality of a continual motion of relations, scenes, contingencies and emergencies. They're things that happen. They happen in impulses, sensations, expectations, daydreams, encounters and habits of relating, in strategies and their failures, in form of persuasion, contagion, and compulsion, in modes of attention, attachment, and agency and in public and social worlds of all kinds that catch people up in something that feels like something.[57]

Ordinary affects, as defined by Stewart, are distinguishable from Deleuzian 'affect' in that they are wholly concerned with the human experience. (Deleuzian affects exist outside of the lived realm and form part of a number of assemblages.) Ordinary affects are, nevertheless, within the Deleuzian affective realm – they are sensations, not easily defined or identified, and they are problematic for both research and for education. They cannot be planned for and, therefore, the concept of a methodology becomes difficult. They might be conceptualised as a 'non-conscious experience of intensity' that leads to forms of action.[58] They are differently experienced, not only by each participant or witness, but also by the same witness at different points of recall. They are fleeting, emotive, ephemeral, and so do not take kindly to being pinned down in time, in language, in meaning. They connect, in my mind, to the liminal workings within science and philosophy of synapses and rhizomes. They are inextricably linked to multiple literacies and, by implication, to notions of smooth and striated spaces, all of which are concepts I explore more thoroughly in other plateaus. They demand new conceptualisations of time. They are problematic and, as such, are often ignored or subdued in favour of that which can be fixed and defined. But ordinary affects shape our worlds in such powerful ways that to ignore them is to reduce human experience

– even to deny human experience. The fact that exploring, understanding and representing those 'somethings' is difficult should not make us shy away from trying. In the very act of trying, new resonances, understandings and disturbances occur, and the dance goes on.

I believe that by embracing the ephemerality of ordinary affects, of the rhizomatic nature of life and complexity, we start to see the learning process as a nuanced experience which is enacted at a highly individual level. This is in contrast to the mass delusional 'reality' we are presented with in educational policy – of fixed trajectories; of predicted grades; of levels; of high, middle and low ability; of potential (or not); of labelling; of hypothesising; of believing that we know what another is capable of. Throughout this book, I touch upon issues surrounding pedagogy, assessment, context and the content of the curriculum, but all within the frame of relationships and resonance. For it is in these moments that futures are formed, pasts are reformed; presents are all present and possible. It is in these moments that things are done, undone and redone. Throughout, I return to concepts I pursued as a researcher and ask whether it is possible to maintain notions of nomads and non-linearity, artisans and amorphodologies, gutterances and gambles while immersed in the humdrum pressures of a classroom context.

I contend that by attuning to moments of chance and choice – and making explicit the messy unpredictability of those moments, not only to the adult readers of educational research but, crucially, directly to children – we can begin to hope that change is possible, that learning can occur. Not the kind of learning that can be tested in a quiz, but the kind of knowledge that helps us to cope, to adapt, to accept and to challenge as necessary; to become and keep on becoming; to witness, to celebrate, to understand; to accept that understanding is impossible. To survive *and* thrive. It is my hope that, ultimately, this book achieves that aim. There are possibilities and positive futures emerging from the ruins of 'best-laid schemes … Gang aft a-gley' and that, far from leading to 'nought but grief an' pain', these emerging futures carry hope.

Notes
1. E. A. St Pierre, Nomadic Inquiry in the Smooth Spaces of the Field: A Preface, in E. A. St Pierre and W. S. Pillow (eds), *Working the Ruins: Feminist Poststructural Theory and Methods in Education* (London: Routledge, 2000), pp. 279–284 at p. 258.

2. G. Deleuze and M. Foucault, Intellectuals and Power, in D. F. Bouchard (ed.), *Language, Counter-Memory, Practice: Selected Essays and Interviews* (Ithaca, NY: Cornell University Press, 1977), pp. 205–218.
3. G. Deleuze and F. Guattari, *A Thousand Plateaus: Capitalism and Schizophrenia*, tr. B. Massumi (London: Athlone, 1987), p. 25.
4. G. Deleuze, *The Logic of Sense* (London: Continuum, 2004).
5. G. Dahlberg and P. Moss, Contesting Early Childhood – Series Editor's Introduction, in M. Sellers, *Young Children Becoming Curriculum: Deleuze, Te Whāriki and Curricular Understandings* (New York: Routledge, 2013), pp. x–xiii at p. xii.
6. G. Deleuze and C. Parnet, *Dialogues* (London: Athlone, 1987), p. 125.
7. K. Roy, *Teachers in Nomadic Spaces: Deleuze and the Curriculum* (New York: Peter Lang, 2003); G. Biesta, Why 'What Works' Still Won't Work: From Evidence-Based Education to Value-Based Education, *Studies in Philosophy and Education* 29(5) (2010): 491–503.
8. G. Deleuze and F. Guattari, *What is Philosophy?*, tr. H. Tomlinson and G. Burchell (New York: Columbia University Press, 1994), p. 36.
9. Deleuze and Guattari, *A Thousand Plateaus*, p. 4.
10. L. Birke, M. Bryld and N. Lykke, Animal Performances: An Exploration of Intersections between Feminist Science Studies and Studies of Human/Animal Relationships, *Feminist Theory* 5(2) (2004): 167–183 at 178.
11. K. Barad, *Meeting the Universe Halfway: Quantum Physics and the Entanglement of Matter and Meaning* (Durham, NC and London: Duke University Press, 2007), p. 21.
12. G. Deleuze, *The Fold* (London: Continuum, 2006).
13. S. Zizek, *Organs without Bodies* (London: Routledge, 2012), p. 108.
14. G. Biesta, *The Beautiful Risk of Education* (Boulder, CO: Paradigm, 2013).
15. Barad, *Meeting the Universe Halfway*, p. 109.
16. N. Bohr, Causality and Complementarity, *Philosophy of Science* 4 (1937). Reproduced in J. Faye and H. Folse (eds), *The Philosophical Writings of Niels Bohr*, Vol. 4 (Woodbridge: Ox Bow Press, 1998), quoted in Barad, *Meeting the Universe Halfway*, p. 109.
17. Barad, *Meeting the Universe Halfway*, preface (no page number).
18. S. Greenfield, *You and Me: The Neuroscience of Identity* (London: Notting Hill Editions, 2011), pp. 69–70.
19. R. Feynman quoted in Barad, *Meeting the Universe Halfway*, p. 153.
20. R. Feynman, *Six Easy Pieces: The Fundamentals of Physics Explained* (London: Penguin, 1998), p. 35.
21. A. Damasio, *The Feeling of What Happens: Body, Emotion and the Making of Consciousness* (New York: Vintage, 2000); V. Ramachandran, *The Emerging Mind* (London: Profile Books, 2003); Greenfield, *You and Me*.
22. Deleuze and Guattari, *A Thousand Plateaus*, p. 15.
23. Deleuze and Guattari, *A Thousand Plateaus*, p. 15.
24. Barad, *Meeting the Universe Halfway*.
25. G. Bearn, The University of Beauty, in P. Dhillon and P. Standish (eds), *Educating After Lyotard* (London: Routledge, 2000), pp. 230–268 at p. 241.
26. J. Derrida, *Writing and Difference* (New York: Routledge, 1967).
27. Deleuze and Guattari, *What is Philosophy?*; G. Deleuze and F. Guattari, *Difference and Repetition* (New York: Continuum, 2004 [1968]).
28. National Literacy Trust, *Boys' Reading Commission: The Report of the All-Party Parliamentary Literacy Group Commission* (London: National Literacy Trust,

2012). Available at: http://www.literacytrust.org.uk/assets/0001/4056/Boys_Commission_Report.pdf.

29. B. Ricca, Beyond Teaching Methods: A Complexity Approach, *Complicity: An International Journal of Complexity and Education* 9(2) (2012): 31–51.

30. Ricca, Beyond Teaching Methods, 32. See also I. Prigogene, Thermodynamics of Evolution, *Physics Today* 25(12) (1978): 38; I Prigogene, *Order out of Chaos* (New York: Bantam, 1984); M. Alhadeff-Jones, Three Generations of Complexity Theories: Nuances and Ambiguities, *Educational Philosophy and Theory* 40(1) (2008): 66–82.

31. Barad, *Meeting the Universe Halfway*; S. Walby, Complexity Theory, Globalisation and Diversity. Paper presented to the British Sociological Association, University of York, 2003. Available at: http://www.leeds.ac.uk/sociology/people/swdocs/Complexity%20Theory%20realism%20and%20path%20dependency.pdf; J. Allan, Staged Interventions: Deleuze, Arts and Education, in D. Masny and I. Semetsky (eds), *Deleuze and Education* (Edinburgh: Edinburgh University Press, 2013), pp. 37–57; D. Turner, *Theory and Practice of Education* (London: Continuum, 2009); J. Protevi, *Political Physics: Deleuze, Derrida and the Body Politic* (London and New York: Athlone, 2001); A. Plotnitsky, Chaosmologies: Quantum Field Theory, Chaos and Thought, in Deleuze and Guattari, *What is Philosophy?*, *Paragraph: A Journal of Modern Critical Theory* 29(2) (2006): 40–56.

32. Biesta, *The Beautiful Risk of Education*.

33. F. Furedi, Scientism in the Classroom: Opinion Masquerading as Research. Paper presented at ResearchEd, Dulwich College, London, 7 September 2013.

34. P. Anderson, More is Different, *Science* 177(4047) (1972): 393–396 at 395.

35. Barad, *Meeting the Universe Halfway*, p. 100.

36. Deleuze and Guattari, *A Thousand Plateaus*, p. 372.

37. Biesta, *The Beautiful Risk of Education*; K. Egan, *The Future of Education – Reimagining Our Schools from the Ground Up* (New Haven, CT and London: Yale University Press, 2008).

38. F. Guattari, *Chaosmosis: An Ethico-Aesthetic Paradigm* (Sydney: Power Publications, 1995); N. Denzin, *Performing (Auto)ethnography: The Politics and Pedagogy of Culture* (Thousand Oaks, CA: Sage, 2003).

39. L. Richardson and E. A. St Pierre, Writing: A Method of Enquiry, in N. Denzin and Y. Lincoln (eds), *Collecting and Interpreting Qualitative Materials* (Thousand Oaks, CA: Sage, 2008), pp. 473–501 at p. 476.

40. Richardson and St Pierre, Writing: A Method of Enquiry, p. 476.

41. Richardson and St Pierre, Writing: A Method of Enquiry, p. 477.

42. Denzin and Lincoln, *Collecting and Interpreting Qualitative Materials*, p. 27.

43. D. Masny, Rhizoanalysis: Nomadic Pathways in Reading, Reading the World and Self. Paper presented at the third International Deleuze Studies Conference, Amsterdam, July 2010. Available at: http://www.youtube.com/watch?v=CNTcuhdVeek/.

44. M. Bassey, *Education for the Inevitable: Schooling When the Oil Runs Out* (Brighton: Book Guild, 2011); H. Jun, Deleuze, Values and Normativity, in N. Jun and D. Smith (eds), *Deleuze and Ethics* (Edinburgh: Edinburgh University Press, 2011), pp. 89–108; J. Schostak, *Maladjusted Schooling: Deviance, Social Control and Individuality in Secondary Schooling* (London: Routledge, 2012); A. Gore, *The Future: Six Drivers of Global Change* (New York: Random House, 2013).

45. B. Goldacre, *Building Evidence into Education* (London: DfE, 2013). Available at: http://media.education.gov.uk/assets/files/pdf/b/ben%20goldacre%20paper.pdf.

46. Education Endowment Foundation (EEF), Teaching and Learning Toolkit. Available at: http://educationendowmentfoundation.org.uk/toolkit/.

47. J. Hattie, *Visible Learning: A Synthesis of Over 800 Meta-Analyses Relating to Achievement* (London: Routledge, 2009).

48. Furedi, Scientism in the Classroom.

49. Biesta, *The Beautiful Risk of Education*.

50. D. Wiliam, Why Education Will Never Be a Research-Based Profession. Paper presented at ResearchEd, London, 6 September 2014.

51. R. Kitchin, C. Perkins and M. Dodge, Thinking about Maps, in M. Dodge, R. Kitchin and C. Perkins (eds), *Rethinking Maps: New Frontiers in Cartography Theory* (Abingdon: Routledge, 2009), pp. 1–25 at p. 18.

52. S. O'Sullivan, Guattari's Aesthetic Paradigm: From the Folding of the Finite/Infinite Relation to Schizoanalytic Metamodelisation, *Deleuze Studies* 4(2) (2010): 256–286 at 273.

53. C. Groves, The Living Future in Philosophy. Working paper. Available at: http://www.cardiff.ac.uk/socsi/futures/wp_cg_livingfuture121005.pdf.

54. Deleuze, *The Logic of Sense*, p. 17.

55. T. Trinh, *Framer Framed* (London: Routledge, 1992), p. 125.

56. C. Norris, *Derrida* (Cambridge: Harvard University Press, 1987), p. 19.

57. K. Stewart, *Ordinary Affects* (Durham, NC and London: Duke University Press, 2007), pp. 1–2.

58. E. Shouse, Feeling, Emotion and Affect, *M/C Journal* 8(6) (2005). Available at: http://journal.media-culture.org.au/0512/03-shouse.php.

Chapter 2

A MATTER OF AMORPHODOLOGY

And then, a moment occurs that disturbs me into 'wide-awakeness'.

Maxine Greene, *The Dialectic of Freedom* **(1988)**

Becoming method

I have always struggled to decide what I want to be when I grow up. I'm still deciding. No one thing has drawn me – there has been no 'plan'. Yet out of these nothings have come somethings. When I was writing my thesis, it was expected that I would include a chapter on methodology. But my thinking was emerging in such a way that there was madness in method. It was hard to argue for chance and serendipity while setting out a plan. So, instead, I argued that this way of thinking demanded less of a methodology and more of an amorphodology. The same is true of teaching. You can plan a lesson, but unless you are open to possibility – able to seize opportunities as they arise, recognise misconceptions, misunderstandings, disengagement – you are lost. We are always in a process of leaving a plan behind.

In a sense, my life has been a series of abandoned plans. While my identification of self as teacher is core to who I feel I am, I have refused to conform to the notion of specialist. I have taught aspects of English, drama, maths, history, science, geography, RE, ICT and PHSE in both primary and secondary schools. I have taught 4-year-olds, 14-year-olds and 40-year-olds. I liked all of it. I'm still not sure what I'll do when I'm grown up though. As Colebrook and Bell ask of thought: 'at what point do we begin or cease to imagine a future?'[1] It is as if my whole professional life has been a series of improvisations where I stand in front of possibilities and try to embrace as many as possible. There are always those that got away; not far away, but away for now. And I am beginning to believe that this is what we can offer children – the ability to embrace improvisation as a means of becoming who we might be. Even if we never quite get there.

It is perhaps not surprising, then, that I struggled to commit myself to the notion of a methodology. In my experience, new discoveries have a tendency to be pulled back within the already known, and the already known will arc out towards the new in a constant movement. As Deleuze and Guattari point out, for as long as 'one steps outside of what's been thought before … thinking becomes … a perilous act',[2] putting us not only in the firing line of others who seek to protect their own paradigms and beliefs, but also one 'whose first victim is oneself'. As I outlined in the For(e)ward to this book, there had been peril in dismantling my own belief systems, a danger that I might be left with nothing: 'Thinking is always experiencing, experimenting … and what we experience, experiment with, is … what's coming into being, what's new, what's taking shape.'[3] It is hoped that, from this thinking process, a shape is emerging in the form of my writing and my teaching, but it is always not-quite-yet. Always perilously close to collapse.

The process of establishing a methodological position is to aim and fire, which suggests a linear trajectory. In such ways does research blind itself to that which lies outside of itself. For example, in 2013, the highly respected and very personable academic, Professor Robert Coe, published his inaugural speech for the Centre for Evaluation and Monitoring at Durham University.[4] Entitled *Improving Education: A Triumph of Hope Over Experience*, it made the case for GCSE grade inflation based on a comparison of data between the country's teenagers' performances in those exams and in international tests such as TIMSS and PISA. Because the rate of improvement at GCSE was not matched in the international tests, the conclusion, logically, was drawn that there must have been grade inflation at GCSE. Another alternative may simply have been that, while we have become more adept at getting children through GCSEs, by teaching them examination techniques specific to those particular papers, the content taught does not transfer to other contexts. In fact, it may be that the *only* use for the GCSE is to pass the GCSE. Beyond that there is no transferable purpose. This throws up a much messier and more complex set of questions surrounding the purpose of education and the need to radically rethink assessment of learning. But the methods and aims of Coe's research did not allow for these questions to be addressed. I don't give this example to undermine the original enquiry, but rather to draw our attention to the fact that looking for broad strokes or single answers forces us to ignore the details that would make the most radical differences to our system. We can have methods, but without an amorphous mentality which seeks out possibility, change, nuance and difficulty of interpretation, we will not find alternative modes of becoming. To do this, we have to resist simplicity and move beyond. Normal structures are suspended.

Working in this nomadic way requires a broader view of reading. If we want to explore education as a process deeply rooted in the whole human experience – emotion, thought, knowledge, body and intra-actions with the rest of the world – then we need to look beyond narrow fields of reading too. The references in this book are drawn not only from research methodology and educational research but also from philosophy, anthropology, neuroscience, cognitive psychology, physics and art – from across the breadth of human experience and endeavour. In the same way that it is nonsensical to separate the impacts of complex factors (e.g. teacher/child relationships, child/child relationships, the physical environment of the classroom, the home life (of the teacher and the child), the time of day, the temperature, other creatures like flies – you'll meet him in Chapter 7) from judgements about the effectiveness of pedagogy or progress in education, it seems equally foolish to imagine that all that is relevant to our study is what is written in our field. We are all (teachers, learners, researchers, readers) complexly intra-related.

In attempting to resist the fixing of method, of meaning and of measuring, I have also resisted the tradition of drawing from just one well in search of methodological literature. Instead, I am interested by the commonalities in inter-/intra-disciplinary writings and what can be learned by one from the other – working in fields of play in which 'there is no such thing as getting it right, only getting it differently contoured and nuanced'.[5] At this moment in time in education, I argue that a great deal could be learned from others working at the edges of social and methodological research; in what Richardson and St Pierre call a 'post-post' period where 'messy, uncertain … experimental texts become more common'.[6] In this world, research requires not only deconstruction and analysis but also playfulness. Playfulness as a state of mind – a mind in which readiness, responsiveness and an ability to recognise the extraordinary in the ordinary are matched by a willingness to improvise with the representation and presentation of data.

It may feel to the reader that this is a breathless text with little space to sit and pause, but it is intentionally so. This is a book that attempts to unsettle. It attempts to rake surfaces, work at edges. It is surface tension work, and we – reader and writer – work like a pond skater, seemingly resting, but perilously positioned.

The teacher/researcher is always in pond skater mode if they are to be truly attuned to what is going on in the classroom. It is a perilous balance between conformity and rebellion; between doing and waiting; between succeeding and failing. In this state, Barad's notion of diffraction – a mode of finding the differences in the return – can be really helpful.[7] Going back over material in ways that seek out new interpretations and possibilities allows us to see the alternative viewpoints that may exist in our work. It allows us to challenge our assumptions and reframe them in different ways. To this end, I have tried to look for retellings of my data that 'theorize[s] the ethics of such tellings and that work[s] the limits of a narrative "I"',[8] and which resist an attachment to 'normal hierarchies, clarities, tyrannies'.[9] I have tried to work the differences, to reframe them so that the narratives are plugged into theory to create a 'something else'.

As such, these stories are not so much about me and them, but are more intra-active – where the separation between the 'I' and the 'they' becomes blurred. Every account has more than 'I' present. There are others – children, adults, elderly people on benches – weaving an intra-active web. I recognise that I can't speak for them, or properly represent them, but I can be mindful of them. While there are certainly a lot of 'I's in the text, and although I have found that my own learning has been inextricably connected with that of the children represented here, my aim has shifted from recount and represent – which suggests simple repetition and reinforcement – towards disturbances through returns marked by difference. This involves engaging with the complexity of the 'I' telling the tales being told – an identity situated in a 'complex site of thoughts, attitudes, affects, beliefs and values'.[10]

The pond skater sits, perilously positioned but highly attuned, waiting for the 'something' to make the danger worthwhile. So it has been with this book – avoiding methodology while waiting for nudges to settle and become has been perilous. The temptation to dive in, to break the surface tension – to break faith – has been overwhelming. But I have trusted to the Deleuzian concept that the interesting stuff is in the thin material – the edges of tension – and this has driven the work forward and has created, if not a comfort with uncertainty, then an acceptance of it. It is this acceptance, if not comfort, that I ask of the reader. I find myself sitting (with you), waiting (for you), seemingly poised with 'infinite humour to take an impossible voyage with an improbable crew to find an inconceivable creature'.[11] We are at the edge, peering and fiddling; dealing with paradoxes between seeing, being and telling:

Could this relation be, perhaps, essential to language, as in the case of 'flow' of speech, or a wild discourse which would incessantly slide over its referent, without ever stopping? [...] Or further still, is it not possible that there are two distinct dimensions internal to language in general – one always concealed by the other, yet continuously coming to the aid of, or subsisting under, the other?[12]

These possibilities and tensions have driven my thinking and helped me to better understand why it is so hard to teach and so hard to monitor learning. Working in this way, as both teacher and researcher, is experimental – we do not know in advance what we will find.[13] The dimensions of language; the words and the stops; the said and the nearly said; the intended and the received; the referent and the idea are in a constant mode of slippage, and language can only function as a crude tool of improvisation which attempts to perform outcomes. This is not to suggest that one should give up, but instead that living within the multiplicities – learning to see the classroom and processes of research as 'multiple literacy texts' forming complex adaptive systems – has been useful.[14] Multiple literacy theory is a theory of complexity which seeks to 'shift the educational terrain by rendering collective desire into a productive pedagogical force'.[15] Such thinking means that I've had to view both classroom practice and data as more than the sums of their languages; to explore the slippages – those 'lateral sliding[s] from left to right',[16] the connections, the emerging diffractive patterns of difference and repetition; to examine the layers of text pressed so finely together that only regular and gentle returns can tease out the threads. This forms a mode of 'flexion',[17] a duality in which the data can be liberated of that which 'conceals' it, even as it appears apparent. This requires patience and an attempt to view the data from different angles and perspectives.

In her multiple literacy theory, Masny posits that there are many 'texts' being read at any one time, and that as they jostle into focus – rise into consciousness, as it were – events occur. One example she offers is a smell of coffee, tempting one from an initial purpose (a deterritorialisation) into a new one (reterritorialisation) in which the smell is one of many of the 'texts' being encountered, each one with the potential to create a new line of flight.[18] In such multiple texts, the notion of reading becomes much more complex. In the same way that Masny paints the picture of the coffee acting as a tempting text, distracting the subject into the kitchen and away from wherever it was he or she was heading, there are distractions in everyday interactions and classrooms. We will meet them in other plateaus – smells and flies and animals in fields – where they press upon the moment, disturbing and deterritorialising purpose. This theory, situated as it is within a notion of experience and being rhizomatic, has allowed me to consider what is or might be 'there', beyond that which is seemingly obvious.

Meandering at the edges

Sometimes what I have been looking for has not appeared and what is there has not been immediately apparent. Sometimes it is there but not there – another unimagined future event will bring it into being, but it is still as yet, not yet. A connection will not be made until one moment, some time later or earlier, prompts a new reading of another. This requires watchfulness across the *width* of experience, for the resonances do not always occur where you expect them. It has been helpful to turn to Deleuze who, in *The Logic of Sense*, uses the work of Lewis Carroll to explore the value of width rather than depth when investigating possibility.

In some strands of research, the tradition has been to dig deep, to mine a narrow field in order to find new hidden insights – the discourse analysis of Foucault and Derrida is rooted in this tradition, even within their rejection of tradition; so too is constructivism.[19] One builds and another deconstructs – towers and archaeological pits, columnic or quarried. Instead, Deleuze explores the wisdom of width – the thin places where events occur at the edges. He and Guattari describe concepts as 'columns' but place them within a flattened plane of immanence which is a 'breath', and 'which implies a groping experimentation'.[20] Later, writing alone, Deleuze uses the playing cards in *Alice's Adventures in Wonderland* as an example, and also points to the idea that only a thin layer of the earth is fertile, but that area extends across most of its surface. I have taken this idea to heart in raking through a wide range of sources for my literature; in recognising that it's that which is not clear which is most intriguing and that the edges are never fixed – that the finer the edge, to borrow from classical physics, the more affective the forces on the atoms at the edges become.[21]

As such, I use a broad range of surface data – not sought but discovered and examined at its edges. I look not for deep roots but for tentative rhizomes, and I begin to link these methodological processes to educational ones. I would argue that it is the ephemeral and the indefinite that influence learning and relationships in and out of the classroom, and that in order to challenge educational orthodoxy, we need to be working at the messy edges of pedagogy as well as methodology.

Events and improvisations

For Deleuze, the rhizome is a 'multi-dimensional system of thought'[22] – a system of multiplicities which offer opportunities for events to emerge; the plane of immanence acting as a 'sieve'[23] from which events may be produced from complexity and chaos. Deleuze's 'events' create 'life as a work of art'[24] – an act of creativity out of chaos[25] in which knowledge emerges from and within an intra-active and haphazard process. Here and in other chapters/middles, I attempt to introduce some significant happenings in relation to the connections they spawn; perhaps this writing forms a screen or 'space' through which they can be interpreted. This screen is amorphous. It shape shifts to better frame or view that which is seeking to be understood. These elements are not complete or whole, but their parts, when put together, create new understandings. As John Rajchman puts it:

The bits don't work together like parts in a well formed organism or a purposeful mechanism or a well formed narrative – the whole is not given, and things are always starting up again in the middle, falling together in another looser way. As one thus passes from one zone or 'plateau' to another and back again, one thus has nothing of a sense of a well planned itinerary; on the contrary, one is taken on a sort of conceptual trip for which there preexists no map – a voyage for which one must leave one's usual discourse behind and never be quite sure where one will land.[26]

These connections cannot be planned because they are, by their nature, spontaneous. Once in consciousness they prompt other resonances, tuning the brain to the possibility that other moments might have similar themes – but this is a matter of tuning in, not of planning. This realisation led me to coin the phrase 'a-tune-meant', a tuning in for meaning and resonance, something which I think is a key researcher trait if we are to work at the edges of certainty, for we can never know where the data might come from and what form it might take. A-tune-meant requires us to be ready, open, mindful, flexible, hopeful and opportunistic. It is not enough to identify the tune; we need to listen for its potential for meaning, even when the tune is not what we wanted or expected to hear. It is not simply a question of tuning in, but of trusting in the capacity for meaning to emerge through this process of tuning. It is simultaneously passive and active, accepting and probing, relaxed and alert. It is playful work, requiring a spirit of adventure, an openness to improvisation and an ability to explore 'what lies between our consumptions and communications, memories and sense'.[27] For example ...

What's in a wink?

I am in role as a despotic king of Ancient Argos – the grandfather of Perseus. My role allows me to behave rudely towards my advisers, who are normally my PGCE students. I have demanded from them advice and they are presenting to me possible solutions to a problem identified by the Oracle. Most of the group have engaged in the role and are presenting probable solutions. One group of three girls tests the fiction by making a lewd suggestion. I have a choice – to remain in role or come out of it. If I come out, I will have to adopt my teacher role, which I have carefully crafted to be nurturing, supportive and kind. In this role I can't say, 'What a stupid idea' and 'Look – you've spoiled it now'. I would have to say something in a jovial tone like, 'Hmmm, I don't think that would happen in that time and culture, would it? But this is interesting because it's what children might do to test you. If you were the teacher what would you do?' Instead, I stay in role as the despot king. I can vent my frustration without fear, 'What?! What did you suggest? And you are supposed to be my advisers. Guards, take them to the dungeons and cut off their heads!' The girls laugh for a moment – they look at me and there is a hint of challenge behind their eyes as briefly we are out of role. I wink at them. Then, in a moment, we're back in role – I am frowning, glaring at them, and they drop to their knees. 'Please your highness, forgive us, what we meant to say was ...'

(Journal, 2008)

What is a wink? What does it do? It is of the body, of the flesh, the nerves, the muscles; the biological. It is almost always unexpected – an element of surprise – and so is psychological. It can be playful or seductive. It is communicative and affective. It can encourage complicity – the sharing of a lie or deception – thus including some and excluding others. It can reassure and unsettle. It can be many things and yet, in that moment, a decision has to be made by the recipient of the wink as to which of these many interpretations might be the one intended. So, the wink (a swift and present action) is dependent on a multiplicity of past and present time. The past time presses in, bringing with it concepts of trust – what do I know of her? Is she trustworthy? Is this play? At the same time, there is the future – what are the implications of accepting or rejecting the wink? Decisions are made, so the wink is complexly connected to time and to sense. It cannot be seen as a single entity, and neither can the analysis of its intention and impact.

The relationships in this data extract are complex, and the power is shifting all the time. The challenge for the diffractive researcher is to bring forth not a future 'truth', but to return to the moment to find the 'immanent truth of an entangled phenomenon'.[28] 'It is not about engaging in pure interpretation to establish what thoughts mean; it is about engaging with what thinking does; it is about how things work.'[29] There are multiple layers of thought and matter in this encounter – my own assemblages, as I struggle with the desire to assert power while maintaining an image of myself as a kind and patient teacher. I find myself slipping between the two selves and other assemblages, thereby affecting the students, prompting and bringing forth their reactions. My role allows a distance to be created, so that behaviours can be managed in a 'safe' environment. I can come out of role and complain about the king and how terrible 'he' is – no one blames me because they accept the fiction that he is not 'me'. But, in fact, the reaction was more 'me' than the teacher persona they accept as the real person. Emotionally I am angered, yet the role allows me to position the anger outside of myself. This constitutes a slippage, allowing me to step into an in-between space in order to improvise – to wink. In the moment of the wink, a conversation, a 'gutterance' has occurred. If I scripted it, it might look like this:

Students laugh.

LAUGH: That wasn't what I expected her to do.

Teacher winks.

WINK: Come on now – you're forgiven and this is a second chance to play.

Students look.

LOOK: We messed up, didn't we? We'll try again …

This data is a form of improvisation in which a teacher is developing a sensitivity 'to the ongoing life and experiences of themselves and the students in the situation'.[30] Being able to improvise, to slow down a moment in order to choose an action, to be responsive to forms of intra-play, is only possible if the teacher is possibility orientated – that is, open to chance in the present moment. As Barad says: 'the ongoing practice of being open and alive to each meeting, each intra-action, so that we might use our ability to respond, our responsibility to help awaken, to breathe life into ever new possibilities for living justly'.[31] The wink allows justice and kindness to override anger and impatience, while the role gives expression to the anger and impatience – it is this AND that. Or.

AND … A return with a new focus can offer a different view. For example, I have *chosen* to be a despotic king. I have selected the 'regulatory power' of an 'ideal'[32] and have returned to sameness through the choice of maleness and royalty as an expression of that power – 'becoming majoritarian'.[33] I use my inhabited maleness to control the women who are challenging my authority with a gesture that is often used by men to flirt and which can be received uncomfortably by women. Of course, this 'choice' is dictated to some extent by the fact that I am exploring the Greek myth of Perseus, but, nevertheless, the lesson has been constructed to give me that dominant role. I could, therefore, choose to view these assemblages through the ideas of gender and power.

On the one hand, I have created 'a community of consent' where discursive boundaries will be drawn around what is both understood and sought, so my anger is situated in my perceived resistance to this 'consent'. The wink is my alibi – it allows me to simultaneously reject that power at the point I am demonstrating it, to escape 'coded scripts and binary logic'.[34] I wink (Come on, girls, I'm one of you). I am both male and female, separate and part of, dominating and pleading. My students are making similar choices related to their relationships to me (past, present and future), to the material (past, present and future) and to power (past, present and future). Their pasts, pressing in on possible futures (aion) create slippage in the present (chronos). There is an opportunity to select or reject, to comply or rebel. In fact, as Deleuze points out, both are present, slipping over each other, coming to each other's rescue. It is not that one is chosen and one is rejected; they are both present. But one gains temporary dominance over the other – an event takes place. Or.

AND ... This is a moment about (mis)trust and (dis)comfort. I am squirming – my lesson could fall apart. The wink is a plea for trust, an admittance of a need for their cooperation. In the wink there is a communication that we are experiencing similar feelings of uncertainty. The girls are uncomfortable in role. Embarrassment presses in on them – they are afraid of looking foolish. Perhaps there are tensions between them and other members of the group. Perhaps they have had experiences that have made them feel as if speaking is perilous. Perhaps they have never had to take on a role before. Perhaps they are afraid. Sensations pierce them; they are giggling, but the giggles are anxious (are they?). One blurts out the idea that the others thought had just been a joke. There is a fracture. I am on one side; they are now on the other. Stakes are raised. They look at me – and I see a challenge. Is it a plea? Rescue us? Can the wink form a bridge? It is a possibility I can only see in return.

There is no straightforward interpretation of this data. The lenses I choose will dictate the interpretation, and I use it now only to demonstrate the multiplicity of interpretation – an issue I return to when I examine the interpretations of accountability in 'A Matter of (R)evolution' (Chapter 7). It is my role now, in writing, to choose, but to select in the knowledge that I present only a possibility. This resistance to straightforward representation and its complexity, in terms of what is given/received/read, is what interests me and it pivots in affect and in the ability for the participants to be able to 'read' and appropriately respond to a situation outside of language.

In such ways as this has data appeared – not because it has been sought but because it has niggled. This example is tied to the notion of 'mattering' – matter as something significant (i.e. the content or idea of power and gender) and as something abstract (i.e. the emotional). But there are also minute physiological, or material, elements to this exchange. My heart beats faster, my skin tingles, my throat goes dry in the second when I try to 'decide' how to react. The matter matters and becomes entangled with different concepts of time (which is explored in Chapter 5). The whole assemblage creates the spring of the middle – the surging reterritorialisation of an event. There is a palpable possibility in the air – it is present and received and yet unseen. It is as material as the air but as invisible.

Whichever of the three interpretations (and more) we see above, there is a becoming in the form of the wink – the wink becomes both the material evidence of an action / event and a cause of future events. It is both a line of flight and the source of new lines; a moment of becoming in chronos and an arcing in and out of aion. It forms a moment of 'radical potential',[35] a 'niggling at the margins',[36] in which an event becomes a 'future history'. These futures / pasts / presents – these temporal and semantic layers – become matted in the working with data, the academic and emotional visits which compress and make new something that once was – and still is and will be – as those people are encountered again and as new people encounter the same material again. Each 'again' is both new and old simultaneously. Such is the complexity of teaching.

The language of amorphodology

To work in this way requires trust and patience as well as an almost ruthless opportunism which is able to seize the moment when it appears. It requires a hoarder mentality when applied to data. Since the spark which will connect one piece to another is unpredictable and unknown, we cannot plan for the collection of material that might be relevant. This form of teacher / researcher work requires an acceptance of uncertainty and change. It demands amorphodology – a process of becoming which is in perpetual flux.

In the dictionary, 'morph' means an organism which is open to change. Etymology borrows the concept and lends it to the parts of words which alter meaning – morphemes such as prefixes, suffixes and roots. I apply the idea to methodology because this kind of data and meaning-making needs a process in which it has the freedom to adapt, alter, change, respond. Experiences undergo metamorphosis, and that which is initially amorphous – lacking in structure and identity – eventually takes form. To bring these formless, sometimes wordless, moments into something that holds meaning, form and clarity, even for a moment, requires a fresh language. Amorphodology is the unfixed, shifting methodology of change. The very word 'morph' has shifted semantically through time. The 1986 Collins dictionary simply lists it as a noun – a unit or organism. By 2010 it had also been added as a verb meaning 'to change'. These subtle but important shifts in etymology demonstrate not a breaking down or debasing of language, but rather the human struggle to find the 'right' words to explain and express their experiences. We are all striving to be understood. We are all striving to understand.

Charting this intra-related process is difficult and complex. There is never a point where the data is 'collected' and 'stored', ready for use. It is always folding in on itself – what some describe as a process of decomposition.[37] There is never a point where the meaning is clear and fixed. Never a point where conclusions are drawn. Nothing is proven. Instead there is a constant recomposition and decomposition of meaning; not entropy but rather renewal in aion time in which there is a 'power to create something continuously new',[38] a self-organising autopoietic system or an act of becoming. Within research, these complexities in representing that which is felt or experienced, and the attendant issues of how best to document and record these experiences, are well documented.[39] But, in education, their validity is largely ridiculed. Instead, teachers are encouraged to be researchers, but only insofar as to reinforce and enact the dominant pedagogies believed to improve test results.

The teacher/researcher as an explorer of human development – a facilitator of what Biesta terms 'subjectification',[40] an artisan of hope and possibility – is to be very much discouraged. It is a mess we have to live with for the moment, but there are still aspects of freedom within this culture of constraint – freedoms afforded by play and by acts of resistance in the form of writing. In Chapter 8, I write about the importance of blogging and social media as forms of subversive and (r)evolutionary practices that offer us freedoms. And to find these freedoms, we have to explore possibilities in terms of space, time and deeds. We also have to be playfully subversive. This playfulness is serious. It is 'serious fun' because it acts as a disruption to expectation and assumption.[41] It is a fractal device.

It is also a form of resistance – resistance to norms and pressures of expectation – and a way of bringing forth newness into sight. When a new idea comes to mind – 'this something new at the edge of arrival',[42] a 'thing' not yet brought to light but sitting in that half-formed, half-light – language is sought. Often we struggle to find the 'right' word, so we make do with the wrong ones, or, if we are to avoid binaries, ones which simply don't feel quite right. This feeling of 'not rightness' is difficult. We make do, working under pressures of time to communicate our thoughts to others. We live with the frustration – a frustration that is well-expressed by Barad who declares that 'language has been given too much power'.[43] However, the inadequacy of language, and our frustration with its supremacy, is useful *if* we accept that the uncertainty lies in the fact that the writing or expression does not need to be anything more than a marker in time. That is, if we do not become hung up on notions of proof or truth or authenticity, accepting that these things are illusionary. In this case, we give ourselves permission to play, challenging the 'substantialising' nature of language.

Thinking our way out of the trappings of the past, out of what we thought was 'true' and into that gossamer state of sharing new thoughts – even as they pop half-formed into being – sometimes requires new words. The newness of the word represents the uncertainty, the intangible quality of what we are attempting to explain or describe. It allows us to invent, to experiment, to chance language rather than simply to choose it. Chancing with language is one way of celebrating the serendipity of affect, while recognising our responsibility to move into modes of interpretation of/in experience. Derrida tells us that 'in its relation to Being, the attempt-to-write is the only way out of affectivity'[44] – in effect, we write ourselves into being. In this sense, writing as a creative, dynamic process allows us to write not only our researcher self into being, but also the content, for as we write, the past and possible futures vie for attention, 'popping' into our head. One word resonates and connects with a dormant event in the past, creating a possible new question or enquiry for the future. In order to present an idea, which has been formed in what Deleuze terms as 'affect', we need to find a language to do so. This is a tricky manoeuvre, as Deleuze points out. The temptation to denote or to manifest, rather than suggest, is increased by the inadequacy of our language to express implications without allowing freedom for possibilities to remain. As such, a playfulness with language at least attempts to avoid fixing too tightly the meanings that have already shifted as they were being written.

New words allow us to provide 'unconditional hospitality' – an openness to chance, to possibility/ies – while recognising the charge of power and responsibility as the host. A host of ideas; of other's lived moments, combed for meaning; of the acceptance that not only is 'writing without citation ... impossible', as Derrida said,[45] but so is the thinking into existence – the connecting and forming of ideas. All require citation – appearing not afresh, but already connected to and partly formed by past events and experiences. Every gesture, every word carries citation. This process of citation forms the basis of culture, of human interaction and understanding. We recognise a wink to be more than a rapid closing and opening of one eye, or a nod to be more than a physical move of the head because of this citation. This collective language allows us to tune in and understand the significance of affect. Moreover, the nod, or indeed the wink, works as acceptance or permission and is rooted in the citation of what is and is not acceptable – the tangled and multiple nodes of behaviour that we learn as we grow, often without ever speaking of them.

The problem with fixing and recording leads to questions about modes of presentation and representation. An amorphous methodology requires an amorphous form, but the creation of the form itself is a process of metamorphosis – a process of becoming something, a morph or fixed organism in its own right. This cannot be avoided. But to see our writing as a morph – an organic, living thing with all the potential of the living to grow and change upon reading (and, of course, to die) – is more comforting and more in keeping with its intentions than for it to be viewed as static. Nevertheless, if we do not wish to fix the meaning too tightly, then the presentation itself needs to lend itself to interpretation and reinterpretation.

Playing with form requires rethinking truth and representation. I come to these issues in more detail elsewhere, but every choice leaves something out. The picture data analysis paints is never whole – it is but an impression of 'truth', an image. Pretending to be reliable, to be 'true', is a form of self-deception – a deception that continues to pervade social research, particularly in the field of education.[46] It is underpinned by a fear of uncertainty that drives a 'call to order, a desire for unity, identity, security, popularity (in the sense of *offentlichkeit*, finding a public)' in public policy and in research that inhibits experimentation.[47] Yet if we accept, as others do, that we live in a performative society in which our language is 'cinematic'[48] and loaded with metaphor and image; if we accept that our perceptions of private have become public via a media obsessed with the confessional in which the private is publicly performed; if we accept, like Derrida, that there is no 'outside text' and that there is no innocence, then writing becomes playful and performative.

Playing with data

In such processes, data is not so much collected as encountered – it is acting as a 'system of relays within a larger sphere'.[49] An amorphic methodology accepts that data is tricky and can appear at any moment. This flitting between the data of then and another then draws me towards the metaphor of a wormhole (or Einstein-Rosen Bridge), a concept drawn from physics which posits the theory that the folds in time and space might allow for a form of time travel, in that shortcuts through the fabric of space could theoretically allow an object to move faster than the speed of light and therefore arrive at its destination before it left.[50] I draw upon this image for my data as I find that I revisit myself in metaphoric form, returning to the body through various wormholes at different times, raking the data for other possible meanings. Something happens, a wormhole is created and, suddenly, that which I saw one way I now see differently in relation to a new or re-remembered experience. Memories flow in and out of the present, reforming the past, reconstructing future understandings, future realities. Data blows in from all over the place, sometimes whooshing the 'collected data' off the table altogether, but more often mating with it and creating new offspring. Nothing is nothing, to quote Lear; it is all a potential something.

This is a problem if you take a forensic view of educational research methodology – a logical, chronological view that data is pure and should be reliable. This is currently the dominant view in education and policy, and it is finding its way into the language of lobby groups, think tanks, government[51] and the blogs of young teachers.[52] But the data in this book is necessarily emotive, situated in memory, in resonance, in 'affect', in identity. It will never be innocent and it will never be still. It is an organism – a morph which is open to change, metamorphosis, and which is initially amorphous. It represents the complex reality of human interaction and learning – a reality that will never be reliable enough to be captured with empirical data, no matter how much policy-makers try. To quote Massumi, 'the question is not: Is it true? But: Does it work? What new thoughts does it make it possible to think? What new emotions does it make it possible to feel?'[53] Massumi argues that the 'concreteness incarnate' which underpins the desire for 'truth' is 'reductive' in its 'dismantling of the absolute'. He argues that the inseparable elements of empiricism – 'analysis and synthesis' – seek simply to dissemble and reassemble that which is 'unsplittable'. At least, it can be split, but not without becoming a 'generality'. It is this tendency to attempt to find general truths from a mass of complexity that drives educational policy into difficulty, as I explore in greater detail in other sections. These are difficulties that matter and which create material effects.

Resonance and relevance

I recognise that this is a dense text, and, in many ways, focusing on the tiny, seemingly inconsequential but niggling moment of maybe-something can seem frivolous. For many teachers, such work is difficult to retain in the frenetic nature of day-to-day activity. These moments are continually lost, at least consciously – displaced by pressures for measurements, for pace, for certainty of outcome. Rarely would a teacher have the time or thinking space to reflect for a split moment beyond a brief sense of relief. A moment of 'phew'. But its importance will resonate throughout her future encounters with this class, perhaps with others too. It might shape a whole host of future outcomes without anyone quite knowing where that learning pivoted, or how it might not. Nevertheless, a space in the moment opens up – a moment of hope, the possibility of remembrance, a rhizome. It is as yet amorphous but it is bubbling with the possibility of meaning, of form. For my part, the constant intra-play between the reader / theory / researcher / teacher demands that this writing pauses to say hello to that other self, processing and interpreting that work in the classroom day by day. It acts as a marker to remember, to take note, to take hold. The amorphic method sits within the teacher – it is material to her identity – shaping her as it shapes the thesis.

Teaching is an internally and externally collective process – thoughts, feelings, memories collate and are intra-dependent. In the room we breathe in and exchange each other's air; my matter becomes your matter. Similarly, we exchange thoughts, ideas, looks and gestures, and a complex system of memory is laid down. Experiences morph and merge, events are created, becomings are stimulated as the learning and the actions are deterritorialised and reterritorialised in the smooth and striated spaces of intra-action.

Throughout it all, it is important to keep on relating back to the material of the matter. Materials and senses carry the capacity to change events – they form texts of deterritorialisation. In the classroom, both sensory and emotional charges can affect processes more deeply than policy-makers admit. Education policy assumes an individualised experience, but beyond platitudes of 'good relationships' and 'high expectations' it does not really engage with these complexities. Grossberg claims that any meaning and significance has to be affectively charged 'for it to constitute your experience … it can be affectively charged through forms of social machinery. It can be affectively charged subconsciously.'[54] Charging describes a metaphoric jolt at which point a connection is made or laid down for future making. It is a spark of creation, of becoming, yet these moments often slip into the subconscious, shaping and forming us without being known. As both Stewart and Massumi point out, these connections often stem from the small and ordinary affective moments that have momentously accumulative effects.[55] An amorphous process attempts to bring forward these moments into knowing, while accepting that the point of looking, of attempting to understand, is simply that – a mid-point, but not an end. Attempting to bring into knowing requires a sharing of the moment through talking or writing, which creates distance and problems.

At the point of sharing, a moment becomes fixed in another moment and movement – arcing backwards and forwards. When we look back on the moment in time, we may feel disappointment or betrayal of our past recognition or understanding, because the moment is now remembered differently in connection with other newer and older moments of experience – a point of difference. If we accept that this is just the way it is, then there is no problem. But if we cannot, or if others attempt to fix us based on that one moment of sharing – with all the impurity that moving into language brings to experience – then alternatives are lost, and the problem gets away instead of getting more interesting. At the same time, however, the sharing creates new alternatives – it affects others. In 'The Politics of Becoming', four writers share memories and reflect on what happens to the memory of another when it resonates with their own:

As one of us reads, it is not Matthew she sees, but another 5 year old – a familial connection recreating a fictional Matthew, generating empathy, but also making assumptions, which allows sorrow to be shared – fusing of two times, two children, two memories so that there is a moment of 'that reminds me.' Discourses can make and unmake sense, but they cannot sense and we are interested here in searching for the potential for change. Sensing requires impromptus – there is something not quite given, not quite known.[56]

Almost, but not quite. Recognition of these difficulties is not enough in itself. As Deleuze reminds us, it is not enough to recognise our entanglements, for recognition alone enslaves us to pre-given images of thought. Cole writes:

Deleuze and Guattari's project has a wider scope than creating a buffer zone around the social constructions in the classroom and reflective critique. Their idea is to utilise all the forces present in the learning arena and to create an intensive experimental field where any possibility may become apparent.[57]

Utilising the forces present requires a belief in change and possibility – it requires hope and a capacity to think as a 'perilous act'. The seeming paradox between hope and peril is a further example of the 'in-betweenness' of Deleuzian thought – being both this AND that. Peril is as inherent to the adventure of improvisation as hope, which 'lives in the spaces between our lived realities and how things could be otherwise'.[58] When one teaches, one does so with peril in tentative partnership with hope. Improvisation helps to navigate the teacher through the adventure. Not going well? Improvise. What emerges? A wink. What happened? Break it down, explore all the possibilities. Find that which may be salvaged – often the flotsam of disaster is an opportunity. Gather the pieces. Trust them. Give it time. Immerse, engage, forget, return.

Method and data are inseparable entities of the experience of becoming teacher and becoming researcher in an affective dimension. Any act of planning is a form of method, and any assessment of process and outcome is both a collation and a reflection of data. But both demand attention in return – a coming back to the cadaver again and again, and not looking for sameness but for difference. What do I understand anew? How is the data altered for the 'me now' as opposed to the 'me then'? How can it improve the 'me to be'? An amorphodology allows for a connection to be made between these returns as well as between methodological positions. It creates a bridge between post-structuralism and action. It refuses to be wed, however, to one model or another. It is heuristic in spirit but not in process. It uses then discards bricolage, montage, narrative, reflexivity, rhizoanalysis, ethnography. It is perilous, promiscuous, fertile and shameless. It is whatever it needs to be.

Notes

1. C. Colebrook and J. Bell (eds), *Deleuze and History* (Edinburgh: Edinburgh University Press, 2008), p. 29.
2. G. Deleuze and F. Guattari, *What is Philosophy?* (New York: Columbia University Press, 1994), p. 103.
3. Deleuze and Guattari, *What is Philosophy?*, p. 104.
4. R. Coe, Improving Education: A Triumph of Hope Over Experience. Inaugural lecture to the Centre for Evaluation and Monitoring, Durham University, 18 June 2013. Available at: http://www.cem.org/attachments/publications/ ImprovingEducation2013.pdf.
5. L. Richardson and E. A. St Pierre, Writing: A Method of Enquiry, in N. Denzin and Y. Lincoln (eds), *Collecting and Interpreting Qualitative Materials* (Thousand Oaks, CA: Sage, 2008), pp. 473–501 at p. 478; see also L. Richardson, *Fields of Play: Constructing an Academic Life* (New Brunswick, NJ: Rutgers University Press, 1997).
6. Richardson and St Pierre, Writing: A Method of Enquiry, p. 478.
7. K. Barad, *Meeting the Universe Halfway: Quantum Physics and the Entanglement of Matter and Meaning* (Durham, NC and London: Duke University Press, 2007), pp. 71–94.
8. A. Y. Jackson and L. A. Mazzei, Experience and 'I' in Autoethnography: A Deconstruction, *International Review of Qualitative Research* 1(3) (2008): 299–318 at 299.
9. L. Berlant, Cruel Optimism, in M. Gregg and G. J. Seigworth (eds), *The Affect Theory Reader* (Durham, NC: Duke University Press, 2010), pp. 93–117 at p. 116.
10. R. Holmes, Risky Pleasures: Using the Work of Graffiti Writers to Theorize the Act of Ethnography, *Qualitative Inquiry* 16(10) (2010): 871–882.
11. M. Gardner, *The Annotated Snark* (London: Penguin, 1974).

12. G. Deleuze, *The Logic of Sense* (London: Continuum, 2004), p. 4.
13. H. Lenz Taguchi, A Diffractive and Deleuzian Approach to Analyzing Interview Data, *Feminist Theory* (13) (2012): 265–281.
14. D. Masny, Learning and Creative Processes: A Poststructural Perspective on Language and Multiple Literacies, *International Journal of Learning* 12(5) (2006): 147–155; see also B. Ricca, Beyond Teaching Methods: A Complexity Approach, *Complicity: An International Journal of Complexity and Education* 9(2) (2012): 31–51.
15. J. Wallin, Get Out From Behind the Lectern: Counter-Cartographies of the Transversal Institution, in D. Masny (ed.), *Cartographies of Becoming in Education* (Rotterdam: Sense, 2013), pp. 35–52 at p. 36.
16. Deleuze, *The Logic of Sense*, p. 11.
17. Deleuze, *The Logic of Sense*, p. 326.
18. D. Masny, Multiple Literacies Theory: Exploring Spaces, in I. Semetsky and D. Masny (eds), *Deleuze and Education* (Edinburgh: Edinburgh University Press, 2013), pp. 74–93.
19. K. Tobin (ed.), *The Practice of Constructivism in Science Education* (Washington, DC: AAAS Press, 1993); M. G. Jones and L. Brader-Araje, The Impact of Constructivism on Education: Language, Discourse and Meaning, *American Communication Journal* 5(3) (2002). Available at: http://ac-journal.org/journal/vol5/iss3/special/jones.pdf.
20. Deleuze and Guattari, *What is Philosophy?*, p. 36.
21. R. Feynman, *Six Easy Pieces: The Fundamentals of Physics Explained* (London: Penguin, 1998).
22. M. Sellers, *Young Children Becoming Curriculum: Deleuze, Te Whāriki and Curricular Understandings* (New York: Routledge, 2013), p. 11.
23. Deleuze and Guattari, *What is Philosophy?*, p. 36.
24. G. Deleuze, *Negotiations 1972–1990* (London: Continuum, 1995), p. 94.
25. E. Grosz, *Chaos, Territory, Art: Deleuze and the Framing of the Earth* (New York: Columbia University Press, 2008).
26. J. Rajchman quoted in C. Pearce, The Life of Suggestions, *Qualitative Inquiry* 17(7) (2011): 631–638 at 637.
27. Pearce, The Life of Suggestions, 632.
28. Barad, *Meeting the Universe Halfway*, p. 73.
29. Sellers, *Young Children Becoming Curriculum*, p. 18.
30. T. Aoki, Sonare and Videre: A Story, Three Echoes and a Lingering Note, in W. Pinar and R. Irwin (eds), *Curriculum in a New Key: The Collected Works of Ted A. Aoki* (Mahwah, NJ: Lawrence Erlbaum, 2005 [1991]), pp. 367–376 at p. 370.
31. Barad, *Meeting the Universe Halfway*, p. x.
32. J. Butler, *Bodies That Matter: On the Discursive Limits of 'Sex'* (New York: Routledge, 1993), p. 1.
33. Deleuze and Guattari quoted in L. Jones, Becoming Child/Becoming Dress, *Global Studies of Childhood* 3(3) (2013): 289–296 at 294.
34. Jones, Becoming Child/Becoming Dress, 292.
35. C. Colebrook, *Deleuze: A Guide for the Perplexed* (London: Continuum, 2006), p. 35.
36. C. Pearce, D. Kidd, R. Patterson and U. Hanley, The Politics of Becoming ... Making Time ..., *Qualitative Inquiry* 18(5) (2012): 418–426 at 424.
37. G. Deleuze, He Stuttered, in C. V. Boundas and D. Olkowski (eds), *Gilles Deleuze and the Theatre of Philosophy* (London: Routledge, 1994), pp. 23–28; Pearce, The Life of Suggestions; M. MacLure, R. Holmes, L. Jones and C. Macrae, Silence as Resistance to Analysis. Or, On Not Opening One's Mouth Properly, *Qualitative Inquiry* 16(6) (2010): 492–500; R. Holmes, Fresh Kills: To (De)Compose Data, *Qualitative Inquiry*.

Special issue: Analysis After Coding. Guest co-editors E. A. St Pierre and A. Y. Jackson (forthcoming).

38. F. Guattari, *Chaosmosis: An Ethico-Aesthetic Paradigm* (Sydney: Power Publications, 1995).

39. C. Ellis and A. P. Bochner, Autoethnography, Personal Narrative, and Reflexivity: Researcher as Subject, in N. Denzin and Y. Lincoln (eds), *The Handbook of Qualitative Research* (Thousand Oaks, CA: Sage, 2000), pp. 733–769. See also N. Denzin and Y. Lincoln, *Collecting and Interpreting Qualitative Materials* (Thousand Oaks, CA: Sage, 2008); N. Denzin, The Reflexive Interview and a Performative Social Science, *Qualitative Research* 1(1) (2001): 23–46.

40. G. Biesta, *The Beautiful Risk of Education* (Boulder, CO: Paradigm, 2013), pp. 17–19.

41. R. McDermott and M. McDermott, 'One aneither': A Joycean Critique of Educational Research, *eJournal of Educational Controversy* 5(1) (2010). Available at: http://www.wce.wwu.edu/Resources/CEP/eJournal/v005n001/a018.shtml.

42. L. Fels, Coming into Presence: The Unfolding of a Moment, *Journal of Educational Controversy* 5(10) (2010). Available at: http://www.wce.wwu.edu/Resources/CEP/eJournal/v005n001/.

43. Barad, *Meeting the Universe Halfway*, p. 133.

44. J. Derrida, *Writing and Difference* (New York: Routledge, 1967), p. 14.

45. Derrida, *Writing and Difference*, p. 14.

46. R. E. Slavin, Evidence-Based Educational Policies: Transforming Educational Practice and Research, *Educational Researcher* 31(7) (2002): 15–21; R. Plant, *Analytic Review: Data Systems* (London: Department for Education, 2013). Available at: https://www.gov.uk/government/uploads/system/uploads/attachment_data/file/193912/00047-2013PDF-EN-02.pdf.

47. J. F. Lyotard, *The Postmodern Condition: A Report on Knowledge* (Manchester: Manchester University Press, 1986), p. 4.

48. Denzin, The Reflexive Interview, pp. 23–46.

49. G. Deleuze and M. Foucault, Intellectuals and Power, in D. F. Bouchard (ed.), *Language, Counter-Memory, Practice: Selected Essays and Interviews* (Ithaca, NY: Cornell University Press, 1977), pp. 205–218 at p. 206.

50. A. Einstein and N. Rosen, The Particle Problem in the General Theory of Relativity, *Physical Review* 48(73) (1935). Available at: http://prola.aps.org/abstract/PR/v48/i1/p73_1.

51. Department for Education, New Randomised Controlled Trials Will Drive Forward Evidence-Based Research, press release (3 May 2013). Available at: https://www.gov.uk/government/news/new-randomised-controlled-trials-will-drive-forward-evidence-based-research.

52. J. Kirby, The Research-Practice Paradox, *Pragmatic Reform* (29 March 2014). Available at: https://pragmaticreform.wordpress.com/2014/03/29/research-practice-paradox/.

53. B. Massumi, *Parables for the Virtual: Movement, Affect, Sensation* (Durham, NC: Duke University Press, 2002), p. 164.

54. L. Grossberg, Affect's Future: Rediscovering the Virtual in the Actual (An Interview with Gregory J. Seigworth and Melissa Gregg), in M. Gregg and G. J. Seigworth (eds), *The Affect Theory Reader* (Durham, NC: Duke University Press, 2010), pp. 309–339.

55. K. Stewart, *Ordinary Affects* (Durham, NC: Duke University Press, 2007); B. Massumi, *Parables for the Virtual: Movement, Affect, Sensation* (Durham, NC: Duke University Press, 2002).

56. Pearce at al., The Politics of Becoming, 419.
57. D. Cole, MLT as a Minor Poststructuralism of Education, in D. Cole and D. Masny (eds), *Multiple Literacies Theory: A Deleuzian Perspective* (Rotterdam: Sense, 2009), pp. 167–180 at p. 172.
58. Pearce, The Life of Suggestions, p. 633.

Chapter 3

A MATTER OF SPACE: PERILOUS CLASSROOM SPACES

Fool: Can you make no use out of nothing, Nuncle?
Lear: Why no, boy, nothing can be made out of nothing.

King Lear, Act I, sc. iv

This plateau is concerned with space, with gaps and folds, with what Deleuze and Guattari conceptualise as smooth and striated spaces, with freedoms and constraints. It aims to explore how spaces can be opportunistic places which offer potential for change – becoming other; but also that these places are potential sites of terror and peril. It examines the folded spaces where elements hide – 'pleats of matter'[1] waiting for recurrence and reterritorialisation – and which make us notice a 'something'. It picks up, but does not depend on, the notion of serendipity outlined in 'A Matter of Amorphodology' (Chapter 2) and outlines moments in which such stops have occurred in educational settings.

Space cannot really be separated from time, even though I have attempted to do this by dealing with them in separate plateaus. Here I am more concerned with the potentiality of spaces, particularly the open, nomadic spaces of smooth space – an experimental space of improvisation and possibility. This chapter seeks to explore how smooth spaces of possibility might be created in classrooms and what their impact might be. This shifting from being (smooth) to examining requires a return to striated space – a space of order – and, of course, the teacher must coexist in both modes, living between the two.[2] The clock is always ticking, but I argue that we can stall, wait, highlight and extend time by occupying and generating smooth space and by examining and unravelling folds. In doing so, we move towards a better understanding of how we might be able to operate complexly in our classrooms. But we have to be brave; we need to hold our nerve. We are, in these plateaus, gathering the tools that will help us to resist and effect changes in our classrooms. One such tool involves conceptualising space.

Smooth and folded space

For Einstein, the concept of space/time as a continuum was relative to the movement of the observer, and as such there was an impact on the way that time might be experienced. While this was a radical position in the way it challenged Newtonian concepts of linearity, Bohr went even further, challenging the assumption that Einstein made that the observer and the object being observed were fixed entities. In his work on quantum physics, Bohr sees the object and observer not as separate entities, as Einstein does, but as interrelated entities.[3] According to Barad, he questions the 'ontological assumptions and their epistemological implications'.[4] The idea that space and time might not only be experienced relatively, but also multiply connected with the object/subject forms the basis for much theoretical physics. In my opinion, it also forms a key element of Deleuze's concepts of body without organs, space/time and rhizomes. It makes possible a reconceptualisation of the space of experience as flexible and multiply positioned and experienced. In a sense, this is 'smooth' space.

More recently, the hypothesis that the matter we have been able to identify, and which lives by the laws of gravity and relativity (at least at a macro level), is outnumbered by an unidentified form of dark matter, which influences the movement of galaxies,[5] creates a metaphor in my mind of the difference between the smooth and striated spaces and the inside/outside elements of the Deleuzian fold – that is, what is known is not all that is there. Both modern science and modern philosophy are conceptualising space, time and matter in terms of complexity. They are finding that significant changes take place at a nano level – in thinness – and their impacts are vast. Modern education has not yet embraced this type of thinking, at least not at policy level. At research levels, however, there are interesting developments emerging from many fields where attempts are being made to explore complexity in the classroom through

Deleuzian and post-structural lenses. One common strand of this work is finding the freedom to work in what Deleuze and Guattari describe as smooth space.

Smooth spaces are characterized by passages and passaging in between, with points becoming relays to be passed through in mo(ve)ments of speed and slowness; the nomad is always in the middle, in-between, with points passing through constituting a relay or trajectory – a line of flight.[6]

This contrasts with striated space, the space we most commonly find ourselves bound to in education. Striated space is ordered space – the space of the lesson plan, the objective, the certainty of progress. When a teacher 'delivers' a lesson (on a plate, served cold), she is marching to the tune of striated space, but smoothness lies beneath. It is not a question of one or the other – both exist simultaneously. In the smooth space that which cannot be planned or anticipated is gathering. Choosing to work nomadically is not to choose to be in one or the other, but to shift attention from one to the other. To work in-between. To retune.

In *The Fold*, Deleuze explores spaces through folded entities, investigating how these 'folds' or 'springs' represent 'an innate form of knowledge [which] when solicited by matter … move into action'.[7] He speaks of matter triggering 'oscillations' which allow movement into the chambers 'above' where action might occur. The creation of these oscillations depends on 'some little openings' through which possibility can develop, and it is the entrance of possibility into the folds that allow the smooth spaces, which he describes in *The Logic of Sense*, to emerge.[8] However, smooth spaces are not empty – they are brimming with matter, taut with possibility:

Matter thus offers an infinitely porous, spongy or cavernous texture without emptiness, caverns endlessly contained in other caverns: no matter how small, each body contains a world pierced with irregular passages … the totality of the universe resembling a 'pond of matter in which there exist flows and waves.'[9]

It is in the interactions and connections of these possibilities that becomings and events can take place. These becomings transcend time in a linear sense. The image of the wormhole, as data fast-tracking across time, sits well with the notion of experience as folded, fabric-like, layer upon layer. This resonance between the Deleuzian image of the fold and Einstein's notions of space as a folded entity, in which it is theoretically possible for holes to allow the transporting of experience from one 'time' to another almost simultaneously, is fascinating.[10] It is through such passages that serendipity travels.

It is my belief that by opening up smooth spaces we allow ourselves to teach in ways that accelerate learning when it is required. We can teach children to question, challenge, stretch, feel, experiment and make mistakes in smooth space and, in doing so, we allow them to gather the tools they need to function and perform in the striated structures of examinations. While I think that we, as a profession, should seriously push and question the validity and purpose of examinations, we do not have to sacrifice striated outcomes in order to create smooth authentic learning experiences for children. What is required is a purposeful shift of focus.

Space and voids

This entire thesis is bound up in time and space, in recounting moments in which things become more than repeated habit – the moments in which there is a 'something' occurring (what Stewart calls 'ordinary affects'[11]). For it is in these moments that we experience the 'stop': in the moment 'between closing and beginning lives a gap, a caesura, a discontinuity … it is neither poised nor unpoised, yet moves both ways … It is the stop.'[12] The moment of the stop is a diffractive space, a place where flow meets an obstacle and a decision has to be made. It is a hosting site for the old, the fragmented, the not-yet-formed, the 'tip of the tongue'. It is a space in which anything can happen – a myriad of possibilities sit, awaiting action. It is a void. If language and action are matter, then the void is the dark matter of the universe – not a holding place, but a place of becoming.

The notion of a void or a stop has been explored in several forms. Trinh writes that, for some, 'void' is the counterpart of 'full', but she also offers an alternative view:

As an absence to a presence or as a lack of a center, it obviously raises a lot of anxieties and frustrations because all that is read into it is a form of negation. But I would highlight the difference between that negative notion of the void, which is so typical of the kind of dualist thinking pervasively encountered in the West, and the spiritual Void thanks to which possibilities keep on renewing, hence nothing can be simply classified, arrested, and reified. There is this incredible fear of nonaction in modern society, and every empty space has to be filled up, blocked, occupied, talked about.[13]

Here, the notion of the void is full of possibility. It is a serendipitous event, something that can be learned from or simply experienced, but too often it is feared. This resonates with the concept of the void as outlined by Deleuze and Guattari, where the void is taut with possibility and from which events emerge. Void spaces are holding places for time, places where time slows down, which can feel uncomfortable. The void acts as a dam, slowing the flow while simultaneously building pressure, leading to a 'rush' – the creation of something or a process of becoming. Our language is full of such moments, usually described under the umbrella term of 'awkward'. In teaching, awkward moments, pauses and stops are difficult, especially in observed lessons, where we fear they may lead to the impression that the pupils are not making progress. In art, there are no such constraints. For Perec, the void was an absence of something deemed to be essential – the letter 'e' 'not as a handicap, but as a spur to the imagination'.[14] In their explorations of art in *What is Philosophy?*, Deleuze and Guattari conceptualise the void as a summoning 'force'.[15]

In the world of counselling, the void is sometimes described as existing within the 'third' space – a dimension in which the relationship, the matter, the understanding of the matter and of the relationship – is shaped, negotiated and renegotiated with and without words. The word 'space' becomes less about place and more about less tangible qualities such as 'ethos'[16] or 'contact rhythm'.[17] This space can be created in response to words, but often it is in response to the body; to the environment; to the nuances of speech, tone and gesture; to resonances with past experience, memory, associations, values and beliefs; and, importantly, to silence. In the third space, these affective 'conversations' are spontaneously and almost subconsciously reflexive. A small gesture will encourage another exchange, and so the 'conversation' is complex, multilayered, rhizomatically constructed. It is also multiply timed – the now time is resonating with a past time, and together they are forming future possibilities. In the void time, there is a freedom of possibility, for nothing is fixed until an action is taken. There are connections here to Barthes' concept of the 'third meaning'[18] – meanings which emerge as they pass through strata of experience and which may, in their emergence, offer a form of method and reflection which may attempt to capture, but not contain, actions and consequences.

It is in these nuanced, sometimes tiny, moments that connections often appear – a memory pops into the mind. These 'wormhole' moments create new meanings. Once those meanings are made, the stop turns to go. Action may follow – although, from a Deleuzian view, it is possible for affects to remain inactive yet still vibrate with potential.[19] Where actions emerge, they create reterritorialised spaces – becomings. For the teacher there is fear in the void – a lack of certainty. For the researcher there is interest. But for all – teacher, researcher, child – there are possibilities both for action and for a-void-ed actions. Void space is smooth space, and powerful nomadic actions can emerge in these pedagogically rich spaces.

There are ways out of the void, but the purpose is not to escape the void but to recognise it as a place of potentiality, frustrating and fearful as that may be. These resulting (intra-)actions – moments of decision – are varied and multiply possible. Some will result in writing – the act of writing brings into being, into citation, all the players in the stop. The void is characterised by choice because multiple possibilities exist in the moment before decision. This is a form of freedom, one that Foucault would describe as a paradox, for once the action is chosen, the freedom to choose is lost.[20] In the void moment, then, there is possibility. This is not necessarily a still or silent place – as Deleuze makes clear, it is taut with matter. Neither is it an 'empty space',[21] but a very 'busy site of agency'.[22] Externally there may be silence – pregnant pauses. Internally there may be a cacophony of thought. Often there is movement – the hand on the chin, the fingers covering the face, tapping, scratching the head. These are subconscious actions connoting thinking; stalling while conscious actions have not yet taken place. Allowing the void to exist, and recognising its value and potential, is vital in allowing human beings to have agency over their actions. But it is an uncomfortable space. Especially for those in positions of authority or in charge of a group. Education policy and practice have created an ethos in which the seeds of pausing, waiting, watching, reflecting, engaging with the unknown – in other words, playing – have little space to grow. For the void is a garden in which the gardener must stand and wait a while. Sometimes, what comes up is not what we thought we had planted.

Void data

While working in the education department of Manchester Metropolitan University, I had grappled with these moments of uncertainty and frustration in a number of ways after the notion of the 'void' had first occurred to me within the context of a teaching experience. This led to a conference workshop presentation in which the notion of the void was set up as an experimental space.[23] In the data extracts below, I contrast that space with the void in school space, and the attendant notions of risk attached to both. The extracts show examples of the 'stutterings'[24] which form 'conjunctions' within Deleuzian concepts of space.

The void is an uncomfortable space for a teacher or workshop leader. It is a place where fear grows at an exponential rate. The fear that our gift is about to be rejected. The fear that we are unclear, vague, wishy-washy – a bad teacher. The fear that no one understands, or that they understand but don't like it/you. It is a scary place. We frequently rush to fill it. In education, we try to anticipate it and avoid any possibility of a void by issuing a lesson objective at the start of the session, success criteria, detailed planning for every ability/eventuality/moment. A-void strategies. Any question of 'Why are we doing this?' or 'What is the point?' is an accusation of failure – a failure to make clear your intentions, your aims, your purpose. A failure to maintain the illusion that we can control learning, experience and success by meticulously planning it and ensuring that our plans are explicitly shared with the learners. We view these questions as disruptions rather than genuine attempts to understand or engage. We are controlled by the belief that no good learning comes of nothing. Why, nothing can come of nothing! Yet the void – a smooth space – allows *something* to emerge.

These stuttering communications are difficult to pin down. The language may be subtle, sometimes even 'like silence, or like stammering … something letting language slip through and making itself heard',[25] or it may appear in its extra-linguistic mode of functioning as the various regimes of signs. Such a mode of communication is indirect and operates in order 'to bring this assemblage of the unconscious to the light of day, to select whispering voices, to gather the tribes and secret idioms from which I extract something I call my Self'.[26]

The experimental void

CARN Conference presentation, Athens. Two workshop leaders stand in an open space, facing 35 people they have never met. Some look anxious. Some look bemused. They may be neither. The participants are all action researchers. The leaders have never been to a research conference before. They are afraid.

Rebecca: Make a restaurant.

There is a very brief silence then people begin to move. And almost immediately, they begin to talk.

Eminent Researcher: I'm a cash register!

He leans against a wall, pushing his bottom out. He thinks and turns around, leaning his back against the wall, putting his arms out in front and spreading his fingers.

Eminent Researcher (beaming): Ker-ching, ker-ching!

Doctor One: I'm a wine bottle. What are you?

Professor: I'm not playing.

He is standing straight, in the middle of the group. His arm is cocked in front of his waist as if holding a cloth. He denies his part in the play, but he does so in the midst of the players, while adopting a physical pose.

Researcher One: I'm a chair – can you tell? Come and sit on me.

Researcher Two: Waiter! This food is cold. Take it away!

Professor: I'm not a waiter.

Doctor Two: I am. I'll take it to the chef and get it warmed for you.

(Journal, 2009)

For us, the void in the data sits in the moment between issuing an instruction 'Make a restaurant' and the first actions. It is the perilous space in which we fear rejection, scorn, misunderstanding AND it is the positive space of possibility. It is both. The void persists – that fear does not dissipate. It drives the analysis, giving impetus to the need to make sense of the risk. The void is a moment of peril from which lines of flight emerge. The words and actions are matter. The motivations, possible interpretations, beliefs, values and power systems – they are the heavier, dark matter of the moment; shaping and pulling with gravitational force which exceeds that of the matter which can be seen and heard. If we are lucky, the tribes will gather; if not, they will rebel or war with each other. Opening the void is a perilous act, but a necessary one.

We, the instigators of the action, stand and observe, like Newtonian scientists exploring the impact of the force on an object. But we are not separate to the action – we are intra-related both within and outside of the action. We are anxious that we may be judged or ridiculed, but we are essentially safe by virtue of the fact that we have established this as an experiment and by the knowledge that whatever occurs can 'become' data. While we feel a sense of risk, we are protected by academic assemblages that protect us from the kinds of consequences a teacher might face in an observed lesson. There is a buffer zone. Our anxiety, nevertheless, presses in on the space 'like stammering'.[27] It attempts to mask itself, but ultimately manifests itself in shrugs and smiles, open palmed gestures and soothing phrases: 'Let's see what happens …' Our forced smiles, placatory gestures and the redness of our cheeks expose our unease and press into the void. Perhaps the participants feel this, perhaps they are being kind. We see the Eminent Researcher cheerfully taking on the role of a cash register (Ker-ching!) as a sign of this kindness. We like him. We see the Professor's refusal to play as unkindness. We don't like him. Or …

A series of material affects override our presence. We are not relevant. The clock, the scents of lunch-to-come, the sunshine streaming through the window, the open/exposed floor space we occupy press upon the moment, bringing together 'the virtual and the actual'.[28] Does smelling food make the participants feel more connected to the task? It is an accident, but an affect. Does the sunshine make people feel more playful? We are play provocateurs, but there are other assemblages affecting the lines of flight that others choose to take. Or …

This is about the power of language and of presence – the ordering of self in smooth space while attempting to mark territory (to striate). Looking again, we consider how the players assert their material representations through language, not quite trusting in the gestural and physical. And there are power relationships being asserted and averted. The Eminent Professor with the greatest reputation to protect is the most playful, yet he chooses the domain of capital control – a cash register (Ker-ching, ker-ching!). In the moment, all we feel is relief that he is cheerfully participating, but in the return we look anew. Butler might view his actions as a performative act – that the word 'ker-ching' is both a signification and an enactment of the notion of profit, with the attendant constructs of capitalism and power.[29] Or …

We observe how the material aspects of restaurant – objects which constitute the assemblage of a restaurant – are mimed but with declarative language ('I'm a chair – can you tell? Come and sit on me!'). This language asserts position and intent ('I am', 'I'm not'), privileging speech over action. Some are uncomfortable ('I'm not playing'), but they are declarative. There is slippage between the roles of play and seriousness – for example, it is fascinating that the body of the refuser is accepting the task while his voice declares he is not. I wonder, is he aware of what his body is doing? And the question arises: to what extent are we aware of the texts that our bodies create? All interpretations exist as possibilities, and none is truth. There is a dual space in existence, and this is true of any learning environment, making problematic the idea of observation and judgement.

We wanted to test the void – for us, at this time, the place between asking and doing; where decisions are made to take part (or not); where the mind interprets, decides, assesses the situation; but where we also create future histories in which the data becomes a cadaver to be picked over again. These are ways to 'prolong the text'.[30] The returns are marked by differences – the retelling cannot be the same as either the original action or previous tellings.

Diana Masny's multiple literacies theory allows us to layer these multiple interpretations of space onto this event. She speaks of reterritorialising spaces and concepts in order to allow new literacies to emerge:

In the virtual, reading the world is the point at which language and the world meet and sense actualizes in situ. Reading self in the virtual consists of asignifying machinistic encounters in an assemblage that resonates and produces sensations (affects and percepts) within an assemblage. This process is one of becoming, deterritorialisation.[31]

In the examples above, the concepts or constructs of what a conference presentation 'should' be are deterritorialised. But the culturally shared understanding of what a restaurant is allows for a reterritorialisation to take place. However, this is not simply a representation of a restaurant. The idea of a restaurant creates a holding place or vessel for other events to emerge. For some, this is embraced. For others, it is rejected. Personality and power affect the outcomes. Then, and in a series of continuing returns, we stand reading, reading, reading, attempting to stay 'outside' while unable to extract ourselves from the intra-active assemblages – we are Mobius. This experiment sets us on to new lines of flight; new futures and possibilities forged by 'why' and 'I wonder'. I wonder how our bodies and minds interact. I wonder what this void space looks like / feels like in school, where the void takes on a higher level of risk.

The emotional void

It is open evening. Twenty sets of parents have been herded into a room to listen to a group of Year 7s and their teachers talk about a new curriculum model. I am one of the teachers. Because I am in charge of the new curriculum model, I am trying to impress the parents.

Teacher: So, we've used the book to explore the idea of immigration and multiculturalism, but perhaps it's better to let the children tell you about that. Neil, would you like to tell the parents what you think you've learned this half-term?

Neil blinks furiously. His face goes pink. He looks at me. I smile and nod. He clears his throat.

Neil: I've learned …

Long pause … a very, very long pause. Other children start to shoot their hands up and jostle for attention – 'We know, we know!' Other teachers look at me … the parents shift uncomfortably … my heart is pounding. Hold firm, I tell myself, wait. But the imagined voices of all the other people in the room are flooding into my head. 'What is she doing?' I imagine the teachers are thinking. The clamouring children before me are desperate to answer. 'Why is she ignoring us?' I imagine they are thinking. 'Leave the poor lad alone, move on, move on,' I imagine the parents are shouting at me. I feel hopeful, defiant, guilty, fearful, all at once. It feels like an hour, but then Neil speaks.

Neil: I've learned that I … can … that I can cope. I was scared coming here, and I get scared when I'm asked to talk, but I've learned that I can have a go and that I can cope. I am coping … with being at school and all the new things and meeting new people and that I can do it. It's OK.

The relief in the room is palpable. I nearly cry, and I don't know if it's because I'm moved or relieved. I can hear the sighs in the room. The parents smile, some are a little damp in the eye area.

'Miss, Miss!' shouts out one persistent child (keen to get in on the action?).

'Yes?'

'That's what them immigrants might feel when they come to our city, isn't it, like they're coping?'

I think the parents are on the verge of applauding.

(Journal, October 2012)

Here the void is bigger. It carries palpable perilous force, not merely in the threat that one might be embarrassed (as in the conference presentation), but in the fear that one might be inflicting harm. It grows with every second of waiting and, unlike the first data extract, it was not set up to create or test 'void effect' – it emerged violently and unexpectedly. It felt like a violence as I physically reacted – adrenaline pumping, heat rising. But it brought opportunity and forced new becomings. The void was perceived as silence, an awkward silence, but it was deafening. Blood pumping in my ears. Boom, boom, boom. Breaths and strains and creaking chairs. An orchestra of discomfort. Then relief.

Neil didn't impress with the vocabulary I had hoped he would use (plurality, economic migrants, etc.), but he seemed to touch upon something far more profound. Perhaps the sharing of his personal and emotional journey as a human being impacted on others, creating almost tangible new lines of flight for those witnessing the event. This event emerged from a chasmic void – the pause which was taut with material tensions: heat, blushes, breath, quickening heart rates and slowing time – the gathering of the stream in what Lather might term 'rigorous confusion'.[32] From this void, there are tentative sensations of becoming for Neil and for me – not quite yet, we are maybe this and maybe that, but somehow altered. Our relationship is redefined but, more importantly, he was, in that smooth space, something other. In the space of the void emerged an event. Perhaps it came from the long silence in which he made a decision. Perhaps it came from the decision I made to ignore the other children's hands up in the air, jiggling about, whispering 'Miss, Miss!', confident they had the 'right' answer. Perhaps it came from the word 'immigrant' – for, as Cole points out, 'one can never fully predict how a word will be actualized in advance'.[33] Or perhaps from a trust in silence and in waiting, and once out, we all recognised, even those who couldn't articulate the recognition through anything other than 'Ahh' that a 'something' had happened. It was a stuttering form of becoming which 'itself ushers in the words that it affects'.[34] It is what Dewey would describe as a 'total organic resonance'.[35] The breathlessness, the sweaty palms, the widening pupils, the furrowing brow, the blush ... all organically resonating and bringing forth the language, and that which sits beneath the language, into being. Neil becoming immigrant. Not sitting outside of and explaining immigrant, but in the pause, the alienation, the discomfort, the fear of judgement, the transformation of the idea into the tension of the moment, in all of this was the possibility that Neil became immigrant and the idea of immigrant was viewed through Neil. Viewing Neil in this way allows me to reframe him from the assemblage of a learner to another, more vulnerable self – a newcomer being folded into a new culture. I see both him and immigrant differently, and they alter me.

I cannot return to this data and play with it in the same way that I can with my king of Argos data (see Chapter 2) and Athens conference data. In both of those instances, there was a separation that allowed for a space to open up between the emotional investment of the moment and the curious return. But Neil is still present in/with me. Still being processed. It will be some time before I can see this data anew. Another place; another space.

In both of these examples, the spaces created by the void have allowed for events to emerge. In this sense, void space is event space in which the pedagogical aim has not been 'the transmission of the same, but the creation of the different'.[36] Although the teacher, or workshop leader, is not 'doing' with the participants in these two cases, they are intra-actively connected, and there is the potential for learning for both teacher and learner, working together as emitters of signs.[37] These events are linked to choices and possibilities, and as soon as a choice is made, other possibilities are lost. Maybe another child would have said something wonderful too. Maybe something else would have happened. But this happened. It became fixed in the moment and then was released to resonate with its witnesses. In that moment in time, there would have been other moments present in the minds of every observer – times when they too had felt acutely embarrassed – and their own personal experiences of how those moments were resolved would have impacted on the lens through which they viewed this moment. Once witnessed, the memories of their own times are infused with the now time of this moment. They are never again the same, and all future similar moments have been affected. The time folds into this now space.

For Neil, there may have been a transformation, an 'event of life', in which an assemblage was created – 'creations that need to be selected and assessed according to their power to act and intervene in life'.[38] In this sense, Neil's choice to speak of his personal learning, and not the content of the curriculum, while simultaneously 'becoming' the curriculum, represents a selected and assessed creation – a re-creation of self. And witnessing this as an event is emotionally powerful for those present:

We witness the incorporeal power of that intense matter, the material power of that language ... Gestures and things, voices and sounds, are caught up in the same 'opera', swept away by the same shifting effects of stammering, vibrato, tremolo and overspilling.[39]

Recording these 'void' moments is difficult. Once captured they can become sentimental, feel somehow false. Once out of the context of affect and the resonating emotions in the room, they become just pieces of black ink on white pages, unless there is a new connection made with the personal experience of the reader. That moment becomes this moment – the removed moment of reading about another's lived moment. That data may resonate, may connect to the reader's own experiences, and time folds in again. Or they may not, and time moves on. As I write, I worry about my representation of this moment. I can't recreate the flushed faces, the palpable heat rising in the room, the physiological and physical conditions of the moment. The language attempts to represent a process of manifestation and signification, but at the point at which it is fixed it becomes what Deleuze calls 'denotative'.[40] Here it is – just words. It can only find affective freedom or space in the way it stimulates and impacts upon a reader – a process I cannot witness. The physical world is such a crucial aspect of affectivity that it can be frustrating to write about, and I am drawn again to questions of 'Why?' and 'What?' What is happening here?

Body as space

I touched upon the resonances between science and philosophy in 'A Matter of Amorphodology' (Chapter 2), and here I would like to introduce some of those scientific ideas into my explorations of data explored above, in terms of conceptualising spaces as places situated in the matter of body and mind, as sites of learning and of being. As scientists draw on philosophical concepts, so too have philosophers explored elements of science. Guattari was drawn to those working at the edges of science and technology in what he termed 'operational modelisations that stick as closely as possible to immanent empiricism'[41] – that is, working at the edges of science and philosophy. Synaptic links are themselves rhizomatic and multi-sensory. Think of how a scent can wormhole you immediately into a past memory – inorganic matter becoming fused with organic memory. Once there, the present moment and the past moment become fused, and a complex system of connections expands. It is not surprising, then, that the language and metaphors of science are merging with those from philosophy. Claxton draws our attention to the fields of cognitive science and neuroscience and, in particular, work exploring the implications of new discoveries to education.[42] He challenges the traditional TOD (The Official Doctrine) model of cognition,[43] which has evolved over centuries in a trajectory from Plato to Descartes to Freud, in which there is thought to be a close relation between intelligence, conscious thought and human identity – an arboreal version of intelligence.

Claxton outlines the TOD principles in an acronym: CLEVER.

Clear-cut (not vague)
Logical (dispassionate)
Explicit (well-justified and not heart-felt)
Verbal (not manifest in gesture or expression)
Explanatory (not manifest in action or perception)
Rapid (requiring neither patience nor contemplation)[44]

Both Claxton and Greenfield explore how this dominant model of intelligence has been discredited by current research into the brain, which has revealed that there are no points of locus, rather a series of complex junctions and connections which are poorly understood.[45] Despite this, education is rife with claims that the brain is, indeed, understood and that there are logical steps that can be taken to control learning – beliefs which have formed a collection of neuromyths.[46] Clark also expresses concern about how these myths and traditional models of thinking permeate our discourses and assumptions about education.[47] He argues that we should move away from the model of mind as manager and towards the mind as an extended, embodied, active (complex) system. The desire to simultaneously declare and dispute 'truths' about the brain and how we learn is leading to declarative wars about what we 'know' works, without any sensible exploration of the reality that what we know most reliably is that we know very little. For example, one of the difficulties in the fields of both cognitive science and neuroscience is that the more senior the expert, the more narrow their field of study. So someone working on working memory, for instance, is not in a position to connect those findings to other discoveries in the areas of, say, embodied cognition, or movement, or the development of language. Such diversions are seen as distractions. As a result, we get pockets of isolated information with few connections. Our obsession with certainty forces a blindness on us, and so we place great stock on these snippets of knowledge. But the reality is that what is known is folded into all that is not yet known. We are always in a state of 'not yet'.

Claxton points to a series of studies which show a complex and interrelated system of knowing in which the physical, emotional and intellectual are mutually dependent and variably expressed. In the traditional view, the body can be seen as what Claxton describes as 'distracting, disruptive or unreliable',[48] and yet, as Greenfield points out, 'below the eyebrows, there's a whole body with incessant feedback to and from the brain'.[49] These physiological elements of thinking and communicating are aspects of immanence – they form texts and are part of the process of reterritorialisation and deterritorialisation.

Yet, even as education moves towards an interest in thinking skills and emotional literacy (evident in the national curriculum's Personal, Learning and Thinking Skills (PLTS) grid), an epistemological paradigm has persisted in its view that thinking is rooted in language, that it can be taught and learned, and that it is inextricably connected to logical modes of intelligence. This model has strengthened further in recent years as the rhetoric has shifted back towards the importance of knowledge domains.[50] Many have challenged this notion of intelligence[51] – for example, Claxton's work explores a more intuitive 'tortoise minded' mode of unconscious and intuitive thinking which requires time to ferment.[52] In 'A Matter of (R)evolution' (Chapter 7), I consider the implications of this work in the classroom and its attendant implications for research, referring again to past/present/future time and how this impacts on identity and motivation. But, for now, I am drawn to the high levels of activity occurring in what sometimes feel like moments of stillness and silence – in the event/void/smooth spaces I have explored above.

As teachers, we need to do more in order to look beyond the obvious and to explore the power of gesture and silence as a means of demonstrating ways of knowing. Some of these revolve around the differences between language and image. Language, of course, is not the only form of expression which attempts to make meaning out of experience. Higgins points out Socrates' error in assuming that because an artist cannot articulate in words what (s)he has attempted to represent in art, that (s)he is in some way lacking in intelligence or understanding of the very thing (s)he has created:

If the artist could have said what she was trying to say just as well in words as in sax solos or paint, then she would have ... [Socrates] conflates intelligence with reflectiveness, reflectiveness with articulateness and articulateness with expository, meta-discourse. In contrast, some of the most valuable types of knowledge are embedded and mute.[53]

In *Matter and Memory*, Bergson asserts that the image is folded between 'representation' and 'thing', neither completely objective nor purely dependent on the perceiving subject. 'By an "image",' Bergson writes, 'we mean a certain existence [of matter] which is more than which the idealist calls a *representation*, but less than that which the realist calls a *thing* – an existence placed halfway between the "thing" and the "representation"'.[54]

We know from recent developments in neuroscience that this 'gap' between the thing and the representation is complex. It is a complexity that interests Deleuzian educationalists. Cole picks this up by connecting it with developments in neuroscience which suggest that learning 'is mostly a function of novelty' which operates by making connections between the 'visual, numerical, linguistic and the gestural', thereby creating a Deleuzian 'educational life form'.[55] Many 'conversations' take place in non-verbal space, and they are conversations which can shape the mood of the participants powerfully.[56] Current thinking in the field of neuroscience suggests that it is almost impossible to separate the emotional, motor and higher order thinking processes, and where it is possible there is damage to the brain.[57]

Barad, Deleuze and Guattari would add external non-human matter to this entanglement – the body acting in and with matter. The body's motor system reacts to metaphor and imagination as quickly and effectively as it does to reality, but that 'memory' depends on matter. In my book, *Teaching: Notes from the Front Line*,[58] I point to the literature review into embodied cognition in which Claxton cites studies from Masson, Bub and Newton-Taylor and Glenberg in which physiological responses occur in sentences such as 'Anna had forgotten her BlackBerry' (listeners primed their motor cortex to make small pressing motions with their thumbs), and even in more abstract modes such as 'Judith delegated the responsibility to Sheena' where the motor cortex indicates a gesture of giving (open palm handed out).[59] It is tempting to focus on the human elements of these findings, but to do so ignores the material. The reflexive pressing of an imaginary phone is dependent on the material existence of the phone having been present at some point in the past. The phone is pressing in on the present – it is materially present in the thinking process. While we linguistically accept that metaphors such as 'kicking habits' or 'pushing up daisies' mean other things, our brains still react literally to them, priming our legs and hands to kick and push. Words form affects which 'transpierce the body like arrows'[60] and create physical effects, and yet this power is little understood and rarely analysed by teachers.

These findings – the complex intra-actions between language, gesture and matter – connect to Deleuze's notion of teacher as emitter of signs and learning spaces as assemblages of multiple texts. If, as seems to be the case, metaphor exerts such a powerful influence on our motor-physical and cognitive processes, then it stands to reason that it forms a 'text' within a multiple literacy space. That these gestural, silent and metaphorical influences act as assemblages within these spaces. And as such, they contribute to acts of learning as an intra-active process.

I knew it but I didn't know I knew it …

I am teaching Year 9 and trying to get them to identify metaphor. I ask, can they tell me what a metaphor is? One boy is bouncing, hand in the air, but when he tries to say it, he falters.

'I thought I knew, it's ... No, I can't explain it.'

Normally I would move on, but I've just read an article on embodied cognition and I look at the boy's hands.

'Look at your hands – what are they trying to tell you?'

He looks. His hands are making a curved shape – a bit like the shape men make of women, a bit like a vase. I'm not sure which, but his hands are moving in this shape without him knowing. He looks.

'Oh, it's like a vase ... a vessel ... Is a metaphor a vessel – like a container for a meaning? Oh, I can't say it!'

'You did – you found a metaphor for your metaphor.'

(Journal, November 2012)

As I think about Billy now, I am reminded of how fragile that moment seemed – it felt like trying to hold a butterfly. 'I thought I knew ...' I didn't have habit to fall back on – I had to watch for signs. But being ready, being prepared to both improvise and remain open to signs meant that I could see the pre-definition[61] – the physical sign of emerging understanding. Tuning in to pre-definition is a form of the sensitivity or improvisation that Aoki speaks of in becoming sensitised to self and other.[62] This sensitivity is considered to be important in the scientific community – it is not an ephemeral concept. Claxton states: 'Teachers who are more sensitive to the meaning inherent in children's gestures are more likely to sense when a student is on the cusp of learning something new and to intervene appropriately.'[63] This reading is a form of teacher literacy that is often ignored and missed – it sits in the third space. How easy it would be to miss Billy's gestures in the classroom, but also as data here. I would have missed it in an earlier form of myself. I have learned that it is vital to tune in and engage in the attempt to respond to signs:

[The] response to another's act involves contemporaneous response to a thing as entering into another's behaviour, and this upon both sides ... It constitutes the intelligibility of acts and things. Possession of the capacity to engage in such activity is intelligence.[64]

Semetsky draws our attention to the correlating points between Dewey's pragmatics and the philosophy of Deleuze in her book, *Deleuze, Education and Becoming*. She brings together what Dewey describes as the 'intelligibility of acts and things' with a Deleuzian notion of reterritorialising in the act of becoming. For Dewey, learning to recognise, even to facilitate, the opening up of these spaces – smooth spaces – constitutes intelligence. This intelligence, in which relationships are constructed and in which dialogue sits as a democratic process, leads Biesta to declare that Dewey's philosophy is not so much 'child-centred as communication-centred'.[65] This would probably be too tight a definition of becoming for Deleuze, but, nevertheless, the capacity to read, to improvise, to be sensitive to 'another's behaviour' is an important part of learning to teach in partnership with serendipity. It allows Billy to 'become teacher'. 'We learn nothing from those who say: "Do as I do". Our only teachers are those who tell us to "do with me" and are able to emit signs to be developed in heterogeneity rather than propose gestures for us to reproduce.'[66]

Billy, like Neil, is inhabiting a smooth space, a 'virtual and intensive'[67] space from which becomings emerge. Lars Marcussen, following Deleuze, argues that the very spaces inhabited by nomads – steppes and deserts – are smooth, and the same is true of the ice desert inhabited by Eskimos, and of the sea roamed by seafaring peoples.[68] In these spaces, orientations, landmarks and linkages are in continuous variation. Deleuze and Guattari observe:

> *There is no line separating earth and sky; there is no intermediate distance, no perspective or contour; visibility is limited; and yet there is an extraordinarily fine topology that relies not on points or objects, but rather on haecceities, on sets of relations (winds, undulations of snow or sand, the song of the sand, the creaking of the ice, the tactile qualities of both).*[69]

It seems to me that Billy and Neil are (possibly) exploring these 'sets of relations' between language (immigrants and metaphors) and being. Recasting and reforming in smooth space in order to engage with and externalise the learning – becoming intra-related with content. In both cases, this requires patience from the teacher and trust between teacher and child; patience and trust are key elements of working in smooth space.

In contrast to this fluid state, the spaces inhabited by sedentary peoples – which are state spaces – are striated with walls, enclosures and roads that exhibit constancy of orientation and metric regularity. While we can never suspend striated spaces indefinitely, it seems that in these moments of void, the sedentary spaces of school classrooms are temporarily suspended and, for a moment, there is the possibility of otherness of place and space that can transcend the limits of regularity to create moments of becoming. Children shifting between these smooth and striated spaces can develop a sense of agency. According to Deleuze, 'agency is the double of a contemplative self that surveys the thousands of interactions required to integrate tiny actions within a more complex apparent action',[70] and such agency requires watchfulness.

These becomings are tentative and essentially private. I, on the outside of them, cannot say 'they are' or 'this is', but merely 'perhaps' and 'maybe'. This is not a deliberately experimental space, which the Athens conference 'restaurant' was intended to be, but an accidentally created smoothness, facilitated by my ability to wait and to trust. Nevertheless, the openness to a-tune-meant creates dynamic enquiry within which I have to accept that there is no single locus of meaning or 'crossing point', but rather a 'multiplicity of transversal communications between different lines'.[71] This is not something that was inherently part of my character. As I explain in 'A Matter of Hoping' (Chapter 8), it has been a part of my own development – a constant intra-action between the smooth and striated spaces I have inhabited: 'passages between the striated and the smooth are at once necessary and uncertain, and all the more disruptive'.[72]

In all of the void moments in this plateau, there are private and communal processes taking place and the forging of new public spaces. Void spaces bind people in a common experience by creating events. These are not sought but discovered, and they take place on a plane of immanence, a space-place which Deleuze, borrowing from Arendt, describes as a body without organs.[73] Arendt describes this plane as it occurs in action (a notion I consider further in 'A Matter of Action' (Chapter 4)):

It may be stimulated by the presence of others whose company we wish to join, but it is never conditioned by them; its impulse springs from the beginning which came into the world when we were born and to which we respond by beginning something new on our own initiative.[74]

While the 'beginnings' of birth present an anthropocentric view of the world that Deleuze would reject, I am nevertheless drawn to the notion of actions and the idea of impulse as natality, perhaps a natality growing from chaosmosis in which subjectivities emerge from a 'groundless ground'.[75] The groundless ground is the space from which such events can emerge. Of course, the tasks and contexts were different in the void spaces I presented here, but I wondered, as I explored them, whether there was room to allow these impulses and improvisations to emerge more forcefully in my day-to-day teaching. It is not a matter of creating them – these spaces open up frequently. It is more a matter of embracing them – allowing pauses to settle – and then to return, with the children, to the moment of the void and ask, 'What happened there?', in the hope that such conversations make pupils more willing to play with uncertainty, to become risk-takers. I wonder if the void opens up the possibility of helping children to step back from what Mazzei describes as 'the barrage of speech-acts [which] blur[s] identity to the point that subjects themselves disappear'.[76] Opening up spaces which allow for a focusing on gesture and other affects subverts the dominance of the speech-act pressing upon the moment ('Miss, Miss …') and allows for a more profound intra-action, or set of assemblages, to emerge. These emerging moments of slowing and speeding, of disrupting the flow of time, are interesting but also disturbing. There are no handbooks for teachers which allow them to conceptualise time and space as a plastic commodity – a place in which time really is relatively experienced rather than simply conceptually understood. Yet it is here, in the middle of the stream, that the rhizome pops up.

Ultimately, these experiments with space have made me think about whether or not such skills – or perhaps attitudes – can be learned and taught, or whether they pre-exist and are simply in danger of being lost. These and other questions bring me back to the notion of natality. I wonder what natality might be, viewed through the Deleuze / Guattari project, and how it might connect to the notions of space, events and becoming. I consider further what it is to act, and how these acts can be forces for change – thoughts form the basis of Chapter 4.

Notes

1. G. Deleuze, *The Fold* (London: Continuum, 2011), pp. 3–14.
2. I. Semetsky, *Deleuze, Education and Becoming* (Rotterdam: Sense, 2006).
3. N. Bohr, Causality and Complementarity, *Philosophy of Science* 4 (1937). Reproduced in J. Faye and H. Folse (eds), *The Philosophical Writings of Niels Bohr*, Vol. 4 (Woodbridge: Ox Bow Press, 1998).
4. K. Barad, *Meeting the Universe Halfway: Quantum Physics and the Entanglement of Matter and Meaning* (Durham, NC and London: Duke University Press, 2007), p. 437.
5. M. G. Walker, On Dark Matter in Dwarf Spheroidal Galaxies, *EAS Publications Series* 48 (2011): 425–434.
6. M. Sellers, *Young Children Becoming Curriculum: Deleuze, Te Whāriki and Curricular Understandings* (New York: Routledge, 2013).
7. Deleuze, *The Fold*, p. 4.
8. G. Deleuze, *The Logic of Sense* (London: Continuum, 2004).
9. Deleuze, *The Fold*, p. 5.
10. M. Visser, *Lorentzian Wormholes: From Einstein to Hawking* (New York: American Institute of Physics Press, 1995).
11. K. Stewart, *Ordinary Affects* (Durham, NC and London: Duke University Press, 2007).
12. D. Applebaum, *The Stop* (New York: SUNY Press, 1995), pp. 15–16.
13. T. Trinh, *Women, Native, Other: Writing Postcoloniality and Feminism* (Bloomington, IN: Indiana University Press, 1989), p. 222.
14. G. Perec, *A Void* (London: Random House, 2008), p. 281.
15. G. Deleuze and F. Guattari, *What is Philosophy?*, tr. H. Tomlinson and G. Burchell (New York: Columbia University Press, 1994), p. 181.
16. J. McLeod, *Counselling Skill* (Berkshire: Open University Press, 2007), p. 93.
17. B. Krietemeyer and G. Prouty, The Art of Psychological Contact: The Psychotherapy of a Mentally Retarded Psychotic Patient, *Person Centred and Experiential Psychotherapies* 2(3) (2003): 151–161 at 155.
18. R. Barthes, The Third Meaning, Research Notes on Some Einsteinian Skills, in *The Responsibility of Forms: Critical Essays on Music, Art and Representation*, tr. R. Howard (Berkeley, CA: University of California Press, 1985).
19. C. Colebrook, *Deleuze: A Guide for the Perplexed* (London: Continuum, 2006).
20. M. Foucault, *The Archaeology of Knowledge* (New York: Routledge, 2002).
21. M. Serres with B. Latour, *Conversations on Science, Culture and Time* (Ann Arbor, MI: University of Michigan Press, 1995), p. 48.
22. E. A. St Pierre, Nomadic Inquiry in the Smooth Spaces of the Field: A Preface, in E. A. St Pierre and W. S. Pillow (eds), *Working the Ruins: Feminist Poststructural Theory and Methods in Education* (London: Routledge, 2000), pp. 258–284 at p. 260.
23. D. Kidd and R. Patterson, Something of Nothing – A-Voiding Action in Action Research. Presentation at the Collaborative Action Research Network Annual Conference, Athens, Greece, 20 October to 1 November 2009.
24. I. Semetsky, *Deleuze, Education and Becoming* (Rotterdam: Sense, 2006), pp. 63–64.
25. G. Deleuze, *Negotiations 1972–1990* (London: Continuum, 1995), p. 41.
26. G. Deleuze and F. Guattari, *A Thousand Plateaus: Capitalism and Schizophrenia* (London: Athlone, 1987), p. 98.

27. Deleuze, *Negotiations 1972–1990*, p. 41.

28. D. Masny, Multiple Literacies Theory: Exploring Spaces, in I. Semetsky and D. Masny (eds), *Deleuze and Education* (Edinburgh: Edinburgh University Press, 2013), pp. 74–93 at p. 76.

29. J. Butler, Burning Acts – Injurious Speech, in A. Parker and E. Kosofsky Sedgwick (eds), *Performativity and Performance* (New York: Routledge, 2005), pp. 197–228 at p. 198.

30. K. Roy, *Teachers in Nomadic Spaces: Deleuze and Curriculum* (New York: Peter Lang, 2003), p. 47.

31. Masny, Multiple Literacies Theory, p. 76.

32. P. Lather, Drawing the Line at Angels: Working the Ruins of Feminist Ethnography, *Qualitative Studies in Education* 10(3) (1997): 285–304 at 290.

33. D. Cole, Affective Literacies: Deleuze, Discipline and Power in Spaces, in I. Semetsky and D. Masny (eds), *Deleuze and Education* (Edinburgh: Edinburgh University Press, 2013), pp. 94–102 at p. 101.

34. G. Deleuze, He Stuttered, in C. V. Boundas and D. Olkowski (eds), *Gilles Deleuze and the Theatre of Philosophy* (London: Routledge, 1994), pp. 23–28 at p. 23.

35. J. Dewey quoted in I. Semetsky, *Deleuze, Education and Becoming* (Rotterdam: Sense, 2006), p. 63.

36. I. Semetsky, Deleuze, Edusemiotics and the Logic of Affects, in D. Masny and I. Semetsky (eds), *Deleuze and Education* (Edinburgh: Edinburgh University Press, 2013), pp. 215–235 at p. 216.

37. R. Bogue, The Master Apprentice, in D. Masny and I. Semetsky (eds), *Deleuze and Education* (Edinburgh: Edinburgh University Press, 2013), pp. 21–37.

38. C. Colebrook, *Understanding Deleuze* (London: Unwin, 2002), p. xiiv.

39. Deleuze and Guattari, *A Thousand Plateaus*, p. 109.

40. Deleuze, *The Logic of Sense*, p. 18.

41. F. Guattari, *Chaosmosis: An Ethico-Aesthetic Paradigm* (Sydney: Power Publications, 1995), p. 106.

42. G. Claxton, Turning Thinking On Its Head: How Bodies Make Up Their Minds, *Thinking Skills and Creativity* 7(2) (2012): 78–84.

43. G. Ryle cited in Claxton, Turning Thinking On Its Head.

44. Claxton, Turning Thinking On Its Head.

45. S. Greenfield, *You and Me: The Neuroscience of Identity* (London: Notting Hill Editions, 2011).

46. U. Goswami, Neuroscience and Education: From Research to Practice?, *Nature Reviews Neuroscience* 7 (2006): 406–413; S. Dekker, N. Lee, P. Howard-Jones and J. Jollies, Neuromyths in Education: Prevalence and Predictors of Misconceptions Among Teachers, *Frontiers in Psychology* 3 (2012): 429. Available at: http://www.ncbi.nlm.nih.gov/pmc/articles/PMC3475349/.

47. A. Clark, Where Brain, Body, and World Collide, *Daedalus* 127(2) (1998): 257–280.

48. Claxton, Turning Thinking On Its Head.

49. Greenfield, *You and Me*, p. 62.

50. See Michael Gove's contributions: I Refuse to Surrender to the Marxist Teachers Hell-Bent On Destroying Our Schools, *Daily Mail* (23 March 2013). Available at: http://www.dailymail.co.uk/debate/article-2298146/I-refuse-surrender-Marxist-teachers-hell-bent-destroying-schools-Education-Secretary-berates-new-enemies-promise-opposing-plans.html; Keynote address to the Sunday Times Festival of Education, Wellington College, 21 June 2013; Education Reform: Schools. Written Statement to

Parliament (8 July 2013). Available at: https://www.gov.uk/government/speeches/education-reform-schools.

51. For example: S. Greenfield, *The Human Brain: A Guided Tour* (London: Basic Books, 1997); H. Gardner, *Intelligence Reframed* (New York: Basic Books, 1999); L. Resnick, Making America Smarter, *Education Week Century Series* 18(40) (1999): 38–40; S. Goldin-Meadow and S. Wagner, How Our Hands Help Us Learn, *Trends in Cognitive Science* 9(5) (2005): 234–241; S. Goldin-Meadow and M. W. Alibali, Gesture's Role in Speaking, Learning, and Reading Language, *Annual Review of Psychology* 123 (2013): 448–453.

52. G. Claxton, *Hare-Brain, Tortoise-Mind* (London: Fourth Estate Press, 1997).

53. C. Higgins, *The Good Life of Teaching: An Ethics of Professional Practice* (Chichester: Wiley-Blackwell, 2011), p. 67.

54. H. Bergson, *Matter and Memory* (London: Lightning Source, 2011 [1896]), p. 9 (original emphasis).

55. D. Cole, *Educational Life Forms: Deleuzian Teaching and Learning Practice* (Rotterdam: Sense, 2011), pp. 32–33.

56. T. Goksun, S. Goldin-Meadow, N. Newcombe and T. Shipley, Individual Differences in Mental Rotation: What Does Gesture Tell Us?, *Cognitive Processing* 14 (2013): 153–162.

57. A. Damasio, *Descartes' Error: Emotion, Reason and the Human Mind* (London: Vintage, 2006).

58. D. Kidd, *Teaching: Notes from the Front Line* (Carmarthen: Independent Thinking Press, 2014), p. 107.

59. Claxton, Turning Thinking On Its Head.

60. Deleuze and Guattari, *A Thousand Plateaus*, p. 356.

61. Goldin-Meadow and Wagner, How Our Hands Help Us Learn.

62. T. Aoki, Teaching as Indwelling Between Two Curriculum Worlds, in W. Pinar and R. Irwin (eds), *Curriculum in a New Key: The Collected Works of Ted A. Aoki* (Mahwah, NJ: Lawrence Erlbaum, 2005 [1986]), pp. 159–165.

63. Claxton, Turning Thinking On Its Head.

64. J. Dewey, *Experience and Nature* (New York: Dover, 1925), pp. 179–180.

65. G. Biesta, *The Beautiful Risk of Education* (Boulder, CO: Paradigm, 2013), p. 32.

66. Deleuze, *The Logic of Sense*, p. 23.

67. Masny, Multiple Literacies Theory, p. 80.

68. L. Marcussen, *The Architecture of Space: The Space of Architecture* (Copenhagen: Danish Architectural Press, 2008).

69. G. Deleuze and F. Guattari, *Difference and Repetition* (New York: Continuum, 2004 [1968]), p. 382.

70. See D. Hoy, *The Time of Our Lives: A Critical History of Temporality* (Cambridge, MA: MIT Press, 2009), p. 158.

71. Deleuze and Guattari, *A Thousand Plateaus*, p. 11.

72. Deleuze and Guattari, *A Thousand Plateaus*, p. 493.

73. Deleuze, *The Fold*.

74. H. Arendt, *The Human Condition*, 2nd edn (Chicago, IL: University of Chicago Press, 1998), p. 177.

75. S. O'Sullivan, Guattari's Aesthetic Paradigm: From the Folding of the Finite/Infinite Relation to Schizoanalytic Metamodelisation, *Deleuze Studies* 4(2) (2010): 256–286 at 258.

76. L. Mazzei, Thinking Data with Deleuze, *International Journal of Qualitative Studies in Education* 23(5) (2010): 511–523 at 518.

Chapter 4

A MATTER OF ACTION: RELAYS BETWEEN THOUGHT AND DEED

There is nothing either good or bad, but thinking makes it so.

William Shakespeare, *Hamlet*

At this point in time, it may seem that there has been a dismantling of what the reader may feel they have relied on in terms of being able to judge the effectiveness of their teaching, and in that process of dismantling there may well be frustration and a feeling of hopelessness. Certainly, as I started to grapple with these thoughts, I began to feel like I was falling and had no way of catching myself. It was only in recognising the value of the fall that I was able to reassemble some actions – to move out of the void. This chapter explores this movement out of voids and smooth spaces into actions that impact on practice and how that practice can be unintended and rhizomatic – praxis growing from 'its extremities or limits'.[1]

This plateau examines two philosophical positions on the notion of becoming, Deleuze's events and Arendt's deeds, and essentially seeks to explore the concepts of events and actions within these frames. It is not intended that they will be seen as convergent ideas. I am not trying to force a connection between the two, and nor am I attempting to prove or disprove one or the other. As Deleuze said in conversation with Foucault, 'no theory can ever develop without encountering a wall'[2] – and, to some extent, Arendt's notions of deeds and natality meet a wall in Deleuze. Furthermore, 'to compare Deleuze with another thinker is already to proceed in counterpoint to Deleuzian practice',[3] in that Deleuze resists comparisons, working instead with conjunctions. But, like Nesbitt, I proceed not regardless of but in the hope that a comparison does exist between ideas, and that the spaces between the ideas offer a return to the plane in which Deleuzian thought sees anew through difference.

I have argued in 'A Matter of Amorphodology' (Chapter 2) for a level of promiscuity in the selection of material, relying not on what is deemed 'proper', but instead on what resonates. Flitting from flower to flower, rather than sticking to one species allows a richer cross-fertilisation of readings to emerge. I contend that promiscuous cross-pollination enables new understandings. For me, reading Arendt created a resonance, and as a promiscuous amorphodologist I cannot ignore the nudge. I hope that what follows exceeds whim and allows me to work in the in-between spaces of one idea AND another. I am interested in conceptualising action in order to move towards understanding classroom practice as 'phronesis', thereby creating 'communicative action'.[4] Working in the stammering spaces of AND helps to do this. This chapter aims to explore action through a set of returns to past data, in an attempt to set out a position on the idea of action, in particular, political action.

The title, 'A Matter of Action', refers to the elements or assemblages leading to actions which reframe and reterritorialise the classroom space, and rather than focusing on the possibility of action, which was a key focus in 'A Matter of Space' (Chapter 3), here I explore actions as performed outcomes. The word 'outcome' is loaded in educational discourses, denoting linear certainty leading from objectives to tested outcomes,[5] but, as I will discuss, there are many outcomes or emerging events in human interactions, most of them unplanned, and it is the multiplicity of these that interest me in terms of their potential for agency and action.

This process allows me to navigate the unease that used to haunt me as a researcher, situated in resistance to 'inaction', to the feeling of dandling about with theory at the expense of practice,[6] and, more particularly, at the expense of justice through action. I have learned to resist binaries, but guilt nevertheless presses in asking 'So what?', and this leads me to consider the *what* through theoretical lenses, allowing me to adopt the Deleuzian view of practice as 'a set of relays from one theoretical point to another' just as 'theory is a relay from one practice to another'. The only way to pierce the wall of theory that Deleuze mentions in his conversation with Foucault,[7] is through its relay with practice, through perception-in-action[8] and by putting philosophy to work. I needed to find ways of enacting the kind of 'doing' – the 'in deed' that Deleuze and Guattari draw out of Nietzsche's *Thus Spoke Zarathustra*;[9] the point at which one seizes the moment to act, to change, to form and to spit out the strangling forces of the past and of convention. In this plateau, I come closer to exploring that notion of doing more fully.

What is action?

What Arendt calls action is closely related to speech; indeed, in some texts she refers to it as speech, but mostly she speaks of speech AND action, deeds AND words, slipping between the two and suggesting there are other forms of representing and continuing action.[10] I was drawn to this interpretation as I looked around for alternatives to language – at least denotative, substantialising language. As my reading developed around language, deed and embodiment, I became aware of Arendt's work and was interested in how it might correlate or contrast with the Deleuzian concepts I was exploring. At the point at which I submitted my thesis, I was unaware that Gert Biesta was also grappling with some of the contradictions and opportunities inherent in Arendt's work. In his book, *The Beautiful Risk of Education*, he explores Arendt's notions of action and freedom within the realm of education, arguing that although Arendt pleaded for the separation of politics and education, the 'forms of human togetherness' that educational spaces create, are the spaces in which 'freedom can appear'.[11] The cracks and spaces between theoretical ideas, between language and gesture, between the known and unknown, force new understandings and new interpretations from which new actions can spring.

At this point, it might be useful to steal a reference from theatre – a place where speech, visual assemblages and movements combine to create sense. Augusto Boal ascribes to the audience the role of 'spectators', the witnesses of actions.[12] In the witnessing, they are participating in the action. The affect is more profound than what we would associate with a mere spectator as there is intra-action between the actor and the spectator, and between the spaces and physical assemblages imposing on the work. This posits the idea of a deed or action coming from within almost of its own accord – 'the deed is everything'.[13] For Arendt and Deleuze, to live a life of deed and action is to live fully, but for Arendt that living is remembered through language, and the deed is dependent on a retelling. Yet she insists that these deeds sit outside the remit of education. Deleuze's events both challenge AND extend that notion so that deeds, or events, can exist outside of language. They can be materially present in a process of becoming, but the power is in their realisation and in the witnessed returns to those moments. This moves the notion of action in education closer to Biesta's challenge to the traditional separation of politics and education that Arendt advocated – one in which there is an assumption that 'once all citizens are properly educated, democracy will automatically follow'[14] (almost as a product of an education, not as a procedural element).

Biesta points out that in denying the role of education in democratic processes, Arendt falls into the trap of placing politics into a psychological frame in which children 'develop' to the point that they are able to understand and articulate the adult realm of politics; thereby creating a belief that notions of childhood and adulthood are developmental, and not social constructs, and that freedom is something that is attained only in adulthood. Such thinking allows us, as adults, to exert a level of control over children – indeed, Arendt views this authority as an adult responsibility – and their experience of education by making assumptions about their capacity to make sense of their experiences and to conserve or protect them from the world, or from what Arendt terms 'the tyranny of the majority'.[15]

It is a frame of thinking that has also penetrated discussions about creativity, in which the ability to create is deemed to follow on from knowledge in a psychological trajectory of development (most clumsily expressed by former Education Secretary Michael Gove on *Question Time* in 2013 when he stated that children could not be creative until they had a firm grasp of reading and mathematics). Arendt, of course, is not so crude or so inaccurate, but the assumption that higher levels of human understanding and interaction with the world come in linear progressions of development permeates much thinking in education. Instead, if we return to Deleuze and think in terms of folds and loops, of multiple lines of flight and assemblages of experience, it is perfectly possible for concepts like creativity and political agency to be developing even before they can be articulated through language or tied down to knowledge.

While Arendt is selective in what might constitute a deed – that which is distinguished by its individuality and its theatricality,[16] and yet produced in togetherness in a mode of plurality, Deleuze allows that an event is 'that to which the power of a thought is devoted, and/or that from which this power proceeds'[17] – that is, an event is the pre-existing state from which becomings emerge – the void space. For Arendt, deeds and actions sit within the public realm; the notion of 'public' is borrowed from Aristotle and requires an audience which is positioned outside of the personal and familial relationships of the actor. For Deleuze, they can exist in either realm since the distinction between public/private/human/non-human is intra-related. Individuality is 'structurally embedded in life' for Deleuze, and so he speaks more of 'singularities'.[18] These singularities occur in the plane of immanence from which multiple possibilities spring forth. Braidotti explains this as, 'not an atomized individual but a moment in a chain of being that passes … nomadically … through multiple becomings'.[19] This Deleuzian interpretation of the deed and the bringing together of the political (for Deleuze, the political is always related to power) and the educational as a process of becoming – or what Biesta would term a process of 'subjectification' – creates an interesting area of potential for the teacher who wants to teach with democratic or empowering intentions.

Arendt accepts the individual as a whole, as a being with the potential to drive action in relation to others. She contests that there is a state of natality – an openness to political possibility that narrows with exposure to the world. The natality is not quite innocence; rather it is impetus and openness to radical possibility, to becoming newly political. It is, therefore, important to her that this potential is not tainted or narrowed by education, but that education provides an incubation period during which the child will gather the developmental, intellectual and psychological skills necessary to put natality to work in the newly found freedoms of adulthood; to make the transition from the home to the public sphere where political action is possible. For it is here where she believes we find the means by which to put our natal possibility to act into deeds – to do something that has never been done before. It is this newness, this constant reinvention through action, that constitutes freedom.

I'm not sure how many teachers feel that they are empowered to be free in this way in the classroom, and perhaps their enslavement is part of the responsibility that Arendt insists is the duty of the teacher: to tell the world as it is, and leaving what it might be to the future acts of the children. But is it possible to create conditions in childhood and early adulthood in which natality and actions can be encouraged and allowed to thrive? There are few environments in our lives, regardless of age, where we are more 'together' in a community than in school. Does Arendt's denial of the role of education in bringing about these acts, which she states are impossible in isolation, close a door on the unique opportunities that a classroom and school community might offer in terms of becoming?

There is resonance in this question with Deleuze's concepts of monads and becoming.[20] Deleuze takes the concept of the monad from Leibniz – the disordered elements of the universe outside of the subject upon which Leibniz claims God imposes predetermined order – and instead reframes the chaosmos as an internal AND external plane of imma-nence through which the nomad wanders – resisting separateness. The monad/nomad image is in many ways indicative of the differ-ences between classical and quantum physics. In the former, there is the order of classification. In the latter, there is uncertainty which, within the frame of our limited understanding, carries the suggestion of chaos. The resulting chaosmos reminds me of the unpredictable and complex nature of subatomic particles like electrons, quarks, bos-ons, photons and so on that act in indeterminate and unpredictable ways and which teem beneath the deceptive majoritarian order of the macroworld.

While drawn to the language of natality and deed, it seems to me that Arendt is offering a similar view to that which is offered in physics teach-ing in the UK – the idea that in order to access the micro (which, let's face it, is the really interesting stuff where anything can happen), the macro should be mastered first. That the mind could not be developmentally ready for the seeming chaos of the quantum world until it reaches a more 'advanced' level of study. Yet to do so closes off physics to many children, removing the magic of what is not known, not certain, not understood. Deleuze, on the other hand, like the quantum physicist, delves into the micro. Moreover, he recognises that even if we bar children from engaging in conversations about this unseen world, it impacts on us anyway – in both macro and micro modes. We are affected by it. If we turn this analogy from physics to education and democracy, it matters not whether we try to remove politics from education – it impinges on the child and teacher's experience all the same.

Deleuze does not question the value of the event emerging from the possible. There are multiple and complex consequences which cannot be separated, but he makes a distinction between three species of monad. He calls the first species 'powers in action', the second 'dispositions' and the third 'the suppression of impediment'. For Deleuze, these monads are individualised – solitary 'souls' or a 'primal force' – but, interestingly, he attributes monads in transition with a collective power.

Badiou defines these assemblages of singularity in terms of events as 'proof' of becomings that form 'the expression'[21] – images which connect (for me, at least) with the idea of the deed arising from the natal. I am interested in how these concepts inform the notion of remembrance: the making memorable of an action or event. In the following data extracts, I am preoccupied with the role of researcher/teacher in this model of deed and action and how one carries the burden of responsibility of remembrance and representation.

To what extent, then, is the role of the researcher/teacher that of the deed recounter rather than the deed maker? In Arendt's view, the educator cannot be the active participant of the deed; she is too entrenched in the habits of the what-has-been, the 'world as it is', and is inextricably tied to the 'single centre', which makes it impossible to think difference or newness into being.[22] Whether or not this is true, the idea that action, real action, springs from fresh eyes, from a mind released from convention and opened up to serendipity, opportunity and difference does resonate. I would argue that natality can spring from retuning – from what I described in Chapter 2 as a-tune-meant – which, like a rhizome, can appear as a 'middle' and is not restricted to birth. I would also argue that it is not age which creates this ability but a state of mind. This brings the notion of natality more closely in line with the Deleuzian concept of becoming:

The event is inseparably the objectification of one prehension and the subjectification of another; it is at once public and private, potential and real, participating in the becoming of another event and the subject of its own becoming.[23]

And, in particular, with 'becoming child' as a 'pre-individual'[24] – a return that can happen to anyone, regardless of age.

Arendt states that, in order to be a deed, the action has to be witnessed and repeatedly recounted – a series of returns. But her returns are marked by sameness, and the act of fully living is entirely dependent upon the connectedness of the actor to the communities around him/her – that is, 'plurality'. While trying to recreate the world, she forces another pattern of repetition onto it. Nevertheless, she resists, like Deleuze, the 'general repression of youth'[25] – she does not see the authoritative and conservative role she ascribes to education as an oppressive one.

Similarly, Biesta observes in her ideas the possibility for facilitating the process of subjectification in education, in which the role of the teacher is not to 'teach' democracy but to create the conditions in which the child might emerge, experience and be immersed in the values and processes of democracy, political agency and responsibility without these being foisted and forced. He suggests that the terms 'adult' and 'child' are in themselves misleading in that they assume a guaranteed transition from one to the other. Instead, he argues that 'the distinction between "adult" and "child" is, in fact, a distinction of definition, in that "adults" are those capable of creating a political space whereas "children" are those who are not capable of this'.[26] From this point of view, maturity is not a matter of age but a matter of attitude and aptitude, and perhaps access to possibility. In the data extracts below, I attempt to put some of these ideas to work in terms of remembrance, agency and eventfulness.

What do children remember about their lessons?

I have been asked to collect evidence for a school that will examine the impact of a curriculum development model in preparation for a governors' meeting. I have been working in a freelance capacity with the school, advising them on the implementation of this model and so I am invested in its success. I have spent the day with focus groups of teachers and pupils, most of whom have said what was expected. Towards the end of the day, a group of Year 7 pupils are sent to me. I have requested children using a 'random selector' tool to ensure that the teachers did not send favourites or those children who they felt could be 'relied' upon.

> Sorrow, outrage, lamentation, acceptance, regret, self-deprecation, indignation, sadness, happiness, apathy, resignation, injuries, wounds, bodily discomfort

Q: Could you tell me one thing that you've remembered from Philosophy for Life [Year 7 curriculum]?

1. I got a DT [detention] and it wasn't even me who was talking.

2. Mr Brown stood on my toe and didn't even say sorry.

3. I said 'Farted' and got a mark in my book that said 'Foul language', and my mum smacked me one.

4. We made a 3D model of an island.

5. Miss White said I was a numpty.

6. We made a monster, but we didn't get to finish it.

7. We did a lot of drama.

8. We labelled this drawing of a man and made a dance.

9. (Shrugs)

10. We built a shelter but mine was rubbish.

11. I kept getting told off.

12. Kyle got moved away from me.

> We *did* together, but I *suffered* alone.

13. We made monsters.

14. Briony stole my picture and pretended it was hers, and the teacher believed her.

15. We did loads of art and made stuff – it was good.

16. Miss called me a star and Matthew called me a geek.

(Transcript of recorded focus group meeting, July 2010)

Of course, had I asked what the children had learned, or even what they had done, the answers may have been different. Indeed, with other children on the same day, when I listened back to the tapes, I realised that I had used the word 'learned' with them, but the answers had focused much more on knowledge. Initially, this extract was not considered to be 'useful' and I almost deleted it, but something about it niggled me and for that reason I kept it. The data created an outlier, which in a statistical sense is an anomaly. Yet it is the anomalous that creates difference. On my first reading, the children had not had their contributions recognised because they did not 'fit' the preconceived notion of relevance that the evaluative research being undertaken would permit. The purpose of the collection of the data was done initially in order to seek relevance and repetition (sameness) – to 'prove' – and so its difference marked it out as deviant. This is an attitude that Arendt sees as problematic in major statistical research:

The laws of statistics are valid only where large numbers or long periods are involved, and acts or events can statistically appear only as deviations or fluctuations ... Yet the meaningfulness of everyday relationships is disclosed not in everyday life but in rare deeds, just as the significance of a historical period shows itself only in the few events that illuminate it. The application of the law of large numbers and long periods to politics or history signifies nothing less than the willful obliteration of their very subject matter, and it is a hopeless enterprise to search for meaning in politics or significance in history when everything that is not everyday behavior or automatic trends has been ruled out as immaterial.[27]

In deselecting their contribution, I was not permitting them to speak – inhibiting their ability to act or have their experiences count as actions. I was imposing my view of what constituted acceptable understanding and development. In the original report they warranted a single sentence. Here, returning, I see anew. I see that I missed something – a new or/and. By accident, or chance, I had changed my word – from 'learned' to 'remember' – and perhaps this 'error' had 'create[d] the conditions that permit the prisoners themselves to speak', as Foucault and Deleuze point out.[28] By refusing to publish or recount the data, I was silencing them – ignoring the outlier. For Deleuze and Guattari, the outlier creates the 'flow' of the minor statistic – the 'quantifiable' difference which separates desire from sensation.[29] Later (now/then), when I consider the data again, it strikes me that while what the children remember most frequently and vividly are moments of intense emotional (sensation) and physical experience, the flow lies not in sensation alone but in the pre-existing (and continuing) desire for justice or recognition.

The data begins to constitute a slow fall through a set of assemblages in which I begin to see and hear, almost for the first time, insults, accidents, acts of sabotage and punishment. Instead of hearing what I wanted to hear, I begin to feel the bruised foot, the hot cheek of indignation. I recoil from the fart. They are bringing me into their sensory world, and it is not a world that teachers often occupy – we tend to fast forward through the awkwardness of their feelings. But the children pause them. The sensations of their emotions have endured for weeks, sometimes months and, long after they have left the memory of the teacher or perpetrator, they resonate with the child. Here is a reminder of emotional matter and its relation to memory. Barad reminds us of this when she speaks of the 'social material enactments that contribute to, and are a part of, the phenomena that we describe'.[30] It is a reminder of the intra-active nature of teaching and both human and material relationships – an 'autopoietic' system in 'a block of space-time'.[31] The emotions themselves are not affects for Deleuze but sensations – affects pre-exist emotions and potential impacts resonating which may (or may not) result in action.[32]

For the children here, the affects took the form of words and actions, piercing their experiences and forming emotions. Their wounds are still present but not attended to – the throbbing toe, the unfinished work, the theft. Perhaps they are telling in the hope that another might take action. Perhaps by telling together they are reclaiming, for that group in that space, a shared memory of a series of separate injustices. Perhaps they are reminding us that if we are indeed charged with conservative authority then we might rethink how we present the world to them. The children are carrying affects and sensations which formed events for them, but they have no agency to act through the telling. Instead, in talking, they are 'making intelligible' their knowledge and exhibiting a form of knowing.

In the return, reframed by the difference of this new interpretation, I remember the way they looked at the recording equipment I carried. I thought at the time that it was with the interest of novelty. I wonder now if it also carried hope. These children are not yet adult. They may not be conscious of the impact of their words (collectively more powerful than individually), but they are deed making, nonetheless, for their words have formed an action in this writing, a retelling, and they have become part of a political reflection. But they are grown and they don't know what they did.

This retelling of the data moves beyond anecdote only if new understandings are explored. This retelling is reflective if I bounce back the normative analysis (the curriculum was successful/not successful, the learning was achieved/not achieved). To me this is 'pedestrian and uninteresting'.[33] It becomes diffractive if we look, instead, at the new patterns created by the interruption of this unexpected data – the new directions thrust upon us. This requires more than reflection, which as I mentioned earlier is simply the same, bounced back. Nor is reflexivity enough. Haraway points out that 'reflexivity, like reflection, only displaces the same elsewhere, setting up worries about the original and the copy and the search for the authentic and really real'.[34] Instead, she and Barad argue for diffraction which is 'marked by patterns of difference'.[35] There is difference in the intra-action I have with the material, the data itself becomes an event for me, but there is also difference in the data itself – fractures. Another or/and emerges.

It seems to me that the children here are recounting awkward, uncomfortable and emotional experiences that are, for them, marked by a notion of difference. They speak of their actions collectively ('We') but simultaneously mark out their separateness as 'I' – in almost all cases, the 'I's carry negative connotations in which the difference is seen as deviance – 'geek', 'numpty', 'foul', 'rubbish'. The collective work is simply commented on in terms of its action – 'We did'/'We made' – with one pejorative judgement of 'good'.

Or/and ... the data presents entanglements with identity and with material ways of knowing:

Making knowledge is not simply about making facts, but about making worlds, or rather, it is about making specific worldly configurations ... in the sense of materially engaging as part of the world.[36]

These children are materially engaging with their world in multiple ways. In one sense, they are engaging with materials – they view making, doing, creating positively. But they are also engaging with the physiological – the stamping of toes, farting, dancing, smacking. In Chapter 3, I explored the impact of active verbs on the body, and it is likely, therefore, that the retelling of these events is accompanied by the contractions of nerves in toes and feet, under the surface of smacked skin and so on. The past becomes present. They cannot divorce learning matter from physical matter. In addition, they seem to struggle to position themselves in that same world without relating to other's perceptions and interpretations of who they are. They demonstrate that they remember what they do, but not why they do it.

If the analysis is diffractive, this conversation becomes an ordinary affect – a 'something' which can lead to action. While I am not using these terms in the way that Deleuze initially intended them, there is resonance here between the 'privileged instant' and the 'any-instant-whatever' nature of representation. 'Data' is often privileged for significance, but here was 'whatever' data creating a void between the expected or hoped for response and the 'reality' of what was created. And this reality is duplicitous – there are many versions. Collectively, however, they hint at multiplicity and complexity. The retellings – theirs and mine – are elements in a process of collective intensification, a return to an examination of a series of Deleuzian events which are, like quantum leaps, both this AND that – 'that which is just happening and about to happen'.[37]

The children remind me of Olkowski's interpretation of *Alice's Adventure in Wonderland*.[38] Contrary to postmodern readings of Alice, Deleuze's in particular, Alice is not the story of a girl who discovers the end of identity and celebrates the absence of sense. Instead, she discovers that she does not want to live in a world where there are no consequences, no identity and no points of reference. The children above are (possibly) recounting a sense of being lost in a world in which the rules they thought existed don't apply – a world where adults say sorry and don't call you names is, in fact, a world where they are thoughtless and careless. This is an abdication of the responsibility that Arendt charges them with, but without giving up their authority either. While the children may not be aware, they are engaging politically with notions of power in their recounts of what mattered to them. In this school-as-Wonderland, anything is possible because propositions can be 'stated as linear and causal hypotheticals … transformed into a series of disjunctions bearing no causal relation to one another'.[39]

And where there is no causality, there are no consequences – whatever learning may have been intended is overridden by the feelings of the children. In order for the teachers and researchers in this project to allow the children to lay claim to a sense of cause and consequence, they need to be attending to *all* the consequences or events converging on the data. Olkowski asks, 'Why organize language so as to escape causal relations, unless to eliminate the possibility that a little girl might grow up and that words and deeds have unpredictable effects?'[40] These two interpretations of the story of Alice reflect debates in education about the levels of influence that teachers should exert on pupils, but there is compromise in Deleuzian notions that both smooth and striated spaces must be navigated in order for events to have worth. As such, rather than recoiling from the mess, as Olkowski claims Alice does, we can, instead, embrace it. But to do so, we cannot reject the data or put it to one side – we must engage with its complexity.

The individual human being, who is different to every other human being, is living a life in the presence of others and other – both organic and inorganic – and is shaped by, and shaping, while also retaining a sense of being essentially individual. For Arendt, the ability of that individual to thrive – to move beyond worldliness, to rediscover natality in a rebirth of action – exists within a community; a community which will witness and judge the action. This notion of community is not unproblematic – who judges? On what basis is the judgement made? Who makes up the community? For Deleuze, it exists within the community of multiplicity and complexity. For both, there is no real separateness, but there are actions which are intra-dependent on others. Educational settings act as Petri dishes for examining this complexity of action, but not all education takes place in a school.

Postcards from Terezín

We sit, all of us, in absolute silent stillness as she speaks. Her voice, echoing in the room, this room, the very room in which she sang as a young Jewish girl to the SS and the representatives of the Red Cross, is distant and present at the same time. Her hands, the same hands that made, as a child, components for military aircraft for the Nazis, are clasped in her lap. Her legs, thin and frail, the same legs that stepped onto a transport to Auschwitz and off again, pressed firmly together. I watch, as she speaks, the faces of the young people sitting on the floor in front of her. Their eyes are open wide, their mouths agape, bodies held still and there is utter silence from them. As she mentions the barbed wire that cut off the Jewish prisoners from the grassy square – where that lunchtime the students picnicked – they lower their heads.

Later, at the end of four days' work here, they present their thoughts and their responses. Some dance, some sing, some draw, some write, some speak – in heart languages – there are more than 20 languages spoken in this room. When they are done there is silence, and then a boy picks up his cello and plays four notes. A violinist joins in. Slowly, clapping, swaying, the rest start to sing. There has been no instruction to do so, but they sing. They sing with tears coursing down their faces, they hold hands, they move. And then, all together and all at once, with no sign or signal, they stop and stand in silence. I realise I have stopped breathing.

Later still, we set up a Facebook page. The children have returned to their home countries, normality restored. But still they write …

'I can't forget her. Her raspy voice, her blunt answers, the moments of silence where you could almost see her train of thought slide from her lips. It all was so emotional. Listening to her speak was so inspiring. It made me want to re-evaluate all the things that are important to me.' (Masha, age 16)

'Going to Terezín, we learnt that bad things happen and we have to learn from them in order to create a better future. We all learnt that bad actions spiral and could eventually get out of control. So stop it while you can. We are the last generation who will have contact with the lived experience of what happened in 1944. What we learnt in Terezín can be used to make a difference. Never forget, but don't dwell on the past – it can't be changed, but the future can. This experience will be forever cherished *in our hearts*. Thank you.' (Guilia, age 15)

'My trip to Terezín was incredible, memories that will last forever. Seeing the cruelty and horror opened my eyes and our final performance just *took my breath away*. I'm determined to make a difference.' (Ryan, age 15)

'I went to Berlin last year and we spent five days visiting places, including concentration camps, but it didn't seem real – sort of external to me. Now, being here, learning in the way we have, it's been incredible. It's like, *it's IN me*. I can't really describe it, but I think I understand here, but in Berlin I just knew facts.' (Mario, age 16)

(Journal entry and selection of Facebook entries from students, March 2012, my emphasis)

Like the Year 7 pupils in the previous data extract, these students also speak of learning with their bodies – 'it's IN me', 'took my breath away', 'in our hearts' – but the experience for them is more affirmative. The retelling of the Holocaust survivor has constituted a deed, but not in isolation from other assemblages – from the material presence of the place, the dust, the barbed wire, the echoes of sound, the rasp. In the student's responses, they are not merely using common metaphor – they are describing a physiological event as well as a psychological one. The intelligence of thought driven by feeling. The physical, material world remains dominant in their retellings and dominant *in* them – this is embodied learning. For these students, there has been a process of 'visiting' – separate to that of tourism. Visiting, for Arendt, is a complex interplay between judging, empathy and imagination – Biesta explains that it is a way of examining the particular. While there are similarities between what they experienced and what the Year 7 pupils experienced, in that each is physically felt and remembered, here the context drives the physiology and both drive a desire to act. They are responding physically and emotionally to that which is being learned. There is a connection between content, context and conceptualisation – the making sense of sensation that eludes Alice in Olkowski's interpretation. And perhaps, as a result of this connection, they are driven forward to declaring actions – that is, this felt learning drives the desire to act. They are adult.

The speech from the Holocaust survivor takes on the qualities of a deed, but it is more than her words that create the quality of action. There is her voice, her physicality, the performativity of place and gesture, memory and words. The space in which she speaks contains multiple texts that are pressing upon the reading of the moment. There is the ticking of a clock, the gentle sound of breathing, the raspiness of her voice, passing traffic outside the window, sunlight making dust motes dance in the air – all combine to both deterritorialise and then reterritorialise the event. Both she and the environment are interacting with the children in opening up possibility. There is a sense of the non-human imposing its own life on the memory, the place itself both lingering and refusing to linger in the past. New paint on the walls settles into old bullet holes. Street names, newly made and mounted, cover the old stencilled numbers of dormitory blocks. Inorganic and organic life – both past and present – is pushing forward, and I am overwhelmed by the vastness of the assemblages pressing in, simultaneously chorusing 'Remember' and 'Move on'. There are no edges, no outlines between then and now, it and us.

The role of memories themselves in shaping futures would be significant, or of value, in Deleuzian terms; but in Arendtian terms they become deeds. The deeds that the children later wish to carry out are not acts of remembrance – or, at least, not only acts of remembrance.

They lead to anti-bullying campaigns in one school, a peer mentoring scheme in another, a community project with elderly residents of a care home in another. These are political actions, born from desires that are not theoretically driven modes of activism but political actions emerging from immanence.[41] They are attempting to change the lived worlds of the children and their peers in the present. And while the impetus to do this did not arise in a school, it was nevertheless a product of an education which is much more than that which Arendt envisages – one which transcends temporal perceptions.

For these children, in contrast to the Year 7 children, there has been an immersion in the suffering of another – the fostering not simply of empathy but of urgency and agency. There has been an understanding which moves beyond knowledge alone, forming this notion of a visitation – a space in which it has been made possible to 'think one's own thoughts but in a story very different from one's own, thereby permitting yourself the "disorientation that is necessary to understanding just how the world looks different to someone else" '.[42] How might we create this disorientation in our classrooms without taking children all the way across Europe? This is one of the key challenges for us as educators: creating conditions in which we might pivot perception. Arendt did not believe that children were capable of such shifts. But they are if circumstances allow.

In contrast, the suffering of the Year 7 children was personal. It happened alone, unwitnessed and unacknowledged. I am not suggesting that having a toe trodden on is comparable to the horrors of the Holocaust, but rather that suffering is memorable partly because of its inseparability from both biological and physical realms – from the human and non-human – and that this, in part, explains its power to persist. Suffering and injustice are active forces on memory, and as teachers we ignore them at great cost to learning. The retelling of an injustice – having it witnessed – forms actions in both instances. Clearly, one has a more positive outcome and a more important injustice underpinning it, but the idea of injustice unites the extracts and brings resonance. The desire for justice is the unifying flow state in both cases, and it is this that fuels my engagement with education. In Chapter 7, I ask whether in order to become more 'just', education needs (r)evolution, but that is the matter of another plateau.

Not every child experiences such an intensive learning opportunity; not all classes can be taken to Terezín. This is an exceptional circumstance. Nevertheless, I believe that it is the responsibility of the teacher who wishes to move the educational experience of the child beyond 'labour' to 'work', and ideally to 'action', to find ways of making education affective, responsive and responsible. This process, when wrestled with consciously, can become paralysing, but if viewed in a more Deleuzian way offers multiple possibilities. Children, on the whole, do not feel like powerful political beings. It is the paradox of their natality that their potential to enact change is inhibited by powerlessness. In a Deleuzian frame, however, futures are always possible and present. Bahnisch is guided by Braidotti when exploring the potentially debilitating effect of reason on action:

A subject identified with reason or the action of drives is frozen in being, and incapable of becoming ... Deleuze/Guattari conceive of desire transcending the inside/outside hierarchy. This enables desire to be thought of in terms of the circulation of affects among bodies. In other words, there is a space for collective, political and ontologically temporal desires which are elided by both psychoanalysis and Cartesian philosophy.[43]

It is the role of the teacher to open up such possibilities for pupils through exposure to a variety of experiences designed to be eventfully possible. This is not an entirely selfless process – such experiences are also described by teachers as 'life affirming'. There is personal gain and self-actualisation here. The teacher is in a state of becoming as much as the children: the 'self becomes itself a sign-event embedded in the complex dynamics of the whole relational system'.[44] For Arendt, this self-actualisation of the teacher was an abdication of responsibility; it was necessary for her to suppress such ideas in the interests of presenting the world as it is to the child. But that depends, again, on the temporal view of the definition of child and adult. In a learning community, it is possible for all to be learning, for all to be involved in political exploration. In 'A Matter of (R)evolution' (Chapter 7), I explore these processes in more detail as political and subversive actions, and ask whether there is room in the ordinary, in the day to day, for more attention to be paid to action and political desire.

Notes

1. A. Amorin and C. Ryan, Deleuze, Action Research and Rhizomatic Growth, *Educational Action Research* 13(4) (2005): 581–593 at 583.
2. G. Deleuze and M. Foucault, Intellectuals and Power, in D. F. Bouchard (ed.), *Language, Counter-Memory, Practice: Selected Essays and Interviews* (Ithaca, NY: Cornell University Press, 1977), pp. 205–218 at p. 206.
3. N. Nesbitt, The Expulsion of the Negative: Deleuze, Adorno and the Ethics of Internal Difference, *SubStance* 34(2) (2005): 75–97 at 75.
4. I. Semetsky, *Deleuze, Education and Becoming* (Rotterdam: Sense, 2006), p. 57.
5. M. G. Jones and L. Brader-Araje, The Impact of Constructivism on Education: Language, Discourse and Meaning, *American Communication Journal* 5(3) (2002): 1–10.
6. C. Rambo Ronai, Sketching with Derrida: An Ethnography of a Researcher/Erotic Dancer, *Qualitative Inquiry* 4 (1998): 405–420.
7. Deleuze and Foucault, Intellectuals and Power, p. 206.
8. A. S. Vazquez, *The Philosophy of Praxis* (Atlantic Highlands, NJ: Humanities Press, 1977), p. 133.
9. R. Bogue, *Deleuze on Literature* (New York: Routledge, 2003).
10. H. Arendt, *The Human Condition*, 2nd edn (Chicago, IL: University of Chicago Press, 1998 [1958]).
11. G. Biesta, *The Beautiful Risk of Education* (Boulder, CO: Paradigm, 2013), p. 102.
12. A. Boal, *Games for Actors and Non-Actors* (London: Routledge, 1992).
13. F. Nietzsche, *On the Genealogy of Morals*, tr. C. Diethe (Cambridge: Cambridge University Press, 1994), p. 28.
14. Biesta, *The Beautiful Risk of Education*, p. 103.
15. Arendt, *The Human Condition*, p. 181.
16. C. Higgins, *The Good Life of Teaching: An Ethics of Professional Practice* (Chichester: Wiley-Blackwell, 2011), p. 94.
17. A. Badiou, The Event in Deleuze, *Parrhesia* 2 (2007): 37–44 at 37. Available at: http://www.parrhesiajournal.org/parrhesia02/parrhesia02_badiou02.pdf.
18. M. Sellers, *Young Children Becoming Curriculum: Deleuze, Te Whāriki and Curricular Understandings* (New York: Routledge, 2013), p. 68.
19. R. Braidotti, Becoming-Woman: Rethinking the Positivity of Difference, in E. Bronfen and M. Kavka (eds), *Feminist Consequences: Theory for the New Century* (New York: Columbia University Press, 2001), pp. 381–414 at p. 404.
20. G. Deleuze, *The Logic of Sense* (London: Continuum, 2004), p. 134.
21. Badiou, The Event in Deleuze, p. 38.
22. P. Hayden, *Multiplicity and Becoming: The Pluralist Empiricism of Gilles Deleuze* (New York: Peter Lang, 1998).
23. Deleuze, *The Logic of Sense*, p. 88.
24. G. Deleuze, *Pure Immanence, Essays on a Life*, tr. A. Boyman (New York: Zone Books, 2001), p. 30. Available at: http://projectlamar.com/media/Pure_Immanence.pdf.
25. Deleuze and Foucault, Intellectuals and Power, p. 212.
26. Biesta, *The Beautiful Risk of Education*, p. 112.
27. Arendt, *The Human Condition*, pp. 42–43.
28. Deleuze and Foucault, Intellectuals and Power, p. 206.
29. G. Deleuze and F. Guattari, *A Thousand Plateaus: Capitalism and Schizophrenia*, tr. B. Massumi (London: Athlone, 1987), p. 219.
30. Barad, *Meeting the Universe Halfway*, p. 26.

31. G. Deleuze, *Cinema 1: The Movement-Image*, tr. H. Tomlinson and B. Habberjam (Minneapolis, MN: University of Minnesota Press, 1986). Available at: http://projectlamar.com/media/Gilles-Deleuze-Cinema-1-The-Movement-Image.pdf, p. 59.
32. C. Colebrook, *Deleuze: A Guide for the Perplexed* (London: Continuum, 2006), p. 54.
33. E. A. St Pierre, Qualitative Data Analysis after Coding. Paper presented at the AERA Annual Meeting, New Orleans, April 2011, p. 5.
34. D. Haraway, *Modest_Witness@Second_Millennium.FemaleMan_Meets_OncoMouse: Feminism and Technoscience* (New York: Routledge, 1997), p. 16.
35. K. Barad, *Meeting the Universe Halfway: Quantum Physics and the Entanglement of Matter and Meaning* (Durham, NC and London: Duke University Press, 2007), pp. 71, 91.
36. Badiou, The Event in Deleuze, p. 38.
37. Badiou, The Event in Deleuze, p. 38.
38. O. E. Olkowski, *Postmodern Philosophy and the Scientific Turn* (Bloomington, IN: Indiana University Press, 2012), p. 117.
39. Olkowski, *Postmodern Philosophy and the Scientific Turn*, p. 105.
40. Olkowski, *Postmodern Philosophy and the Scientific Turn*, p. 117.
41. P. Goodchild, *Deleuze and Guattari: An Introduction to the Politics of Desire* (London: Sage, 1996).
42. T. Disch quoted in Biesta, *The Beautiful Risk of Education*, p. 116.
43. M. Bahnisch, Deleuze and Guattari's Political Ontology of Desire, in P. Corrigan (ed.), *Proceedings of the TASA 2003 Conference* (Armidale: University of New England, 2003), pp. 1–12 at p. 3.
44. I. Semetsky, Not by Breadth Alone: Imagining a Self-Organising Classroom, *Complicity: An International Journal of Complexity and Education* 2(1) (2005): 19–36 at 27.

Chapter 5

A MATTER OF TIME: THE EFFECTS OF TIME ON LEARNING

My dear, here we must run as fast as we can, just to stay in place. And if you wish to go anywhere you must run twice as fast as that.

Lewis Carroll, *Alice's Adventures in Wonderland* (1865)

In previous chapters, I have layered cases (I hope) for the consideration of non-linear processes in both research and education. I have presented data as a serendipitous and resonant force, and I have / am implemented / ing amorphic methodology which forms stops and voids within which to consider implication and affect. I am making a case for spending much of my time and thought in these spaces. In each plateau, there is a sense of pooling – a gathering impetus for action. Perhaps this is what Claxton speaks of when he claims that the 'basic purpose of intelligence is to get things done that matter'.[1] In positing this position, Claxton reinforces the binary of thinking and action, but places greater emphasis on the latter. He argues that conscious thinking can create paralysis. When I worked in higher education, my unconscious and conscious ramblings were re-forming me in many ways. I was becoming more patient, more curious, more observant, more playful and more thoughtful, but I was increasingly removed from classroom practice. As I moved towards the writing up stage of my thesis, I realised that I was only really halfway through – all my methods, musings and ideas were simply preparatory work for something further I felt I had to do, which was to move back into school and into a full-time teaching post. This plateau and another – 'A Matter of (R)evolution' (Chapter 7) explores that transition, but this one does so through the conceptual framework of time. And as time and space are almost inseparable entities, both in Deleuzian thought and as conceptualised by science, there are loops and connections between this and other plateaus relating to space, sense and action.

Whereas in 'A Matter of Space' (Chapter 3), I explored time as stop/ go space, here I explore time in terms of affect and impetus. I aim to examine more closely the Deleuzian concepts of past, present and future times (chronos and aion) and to place these ideas within this new working context. There is, as there is in each of these intra-related plateaus, slippage, and this mirrors the complexity of attempting to separate out concepts that are mutually connected. So, here, time will slip into other notions of being – of nomads and royals, architects and artisans.

A return

I went back to a mainstream state secondary school with the title of AST (advanced skills teacher), which I wore like an albatross around my neck from arrival to departure. The school I was based at is an 11–16 secondary comprehensive with a predominantly mono-cultural intake in a town in which there is a large multi-cultural population. My role in the school was to 'develop' teaching and learning so that children were, in the words of the head teacher, 'empowered and inspired'. Immediately, of course, there was a disconnect between the potentiality of empowerment and the limitations imposed by league tables, Ofsted and examination performance. But more on this elsewhere. The word 'advanced' suggests a movement forward, but my advancement in terms of this study has consisted more of a constant toing and froing. 'Skills' suggests an element of control and certainty, when I have instead been immersed in complexity and uncertainty. As such, I found myself oscillating between feelings of guilt (I worried that I was not doing what I was being asked to do) and rebelliousness (I tried to explain why it was that doing what I was being asked to do was nonsensical). Stepping back into school brought forth the shock of return – I had been a teacher before and I thought I would be the same, but better. I found only difference. Like Alice, musing in Wonderland, I found that 'it's no use going back to yesterday because I was a different person then'.[2] I needed to chart the cartographies of that new place and to reposition myself.

The move 'back' into school felt more like a slow fall – a frantically slow fall, if such a thing is possible. The pace of the day was fast, but the brainwork of the doctorate forced an arrest. As I fell, I noticed absurdity, inconsistency, chaos. Like Alice, I saw the maps and the pictures and the empty jar of marmalade. They were imprinted on my mind as I fell – schemes and charts and vapid promises – a 'thousand little witnesses'[3] paying attention.

I found myself falling, slowly, in an environment in which people seemed to keep running faster and faster in order to stay in the same place. My time streams ran counter to that of others, and also contrary within myself. In arresting, slowing, I began to pluck up courage – the courage to reveal what I believe and don't believe. But these arrests forced a gathering, a pushing up of the stream into rhizome where things gather speed and become other. This pushing and pulling of fast and slow time interests me, and it allowed me to see anew.

An arrest

I am observing a teacher teaching. I have requested that a senior leader jointly observes with me in order to check that there is consistency in the application of the school's observation criteria. The senior observer leans over and points to a boy who is taking part in a task – he is supposed to be listening to another child giving him information from a sheet. It is a focused listening task. The boy is fidgeting. He is slumping in his chair, tapping his fingers on the seat, staring out of the window, his mouth agape. If a casting director had wished to cast the role of 'disengaged child', this child would have been snapped up. My senior observer points to his notes. 'Not all children are engaged', it says. He highlights a section on the observation criteria which states that 'Most, but not all of the children are engaged'. This places the teacher in the box labelled 'requires improvement'.

Minutes later, I walk over to the boy. The class have been asked to recount four pieces of information they can remember from the exercise. He is busily writing down his eighth. Disengaged? It would appear not. Things are not always as they seem.

I creep back to the senior leader. 'He's remembered twice as much as he was asked to,' I say. 'He was listening.' The judgement remains. There is a pause …

'I think she's facilitating thinking here,' I venture.

'The pace is too slow,' is the response.

But learning can be slow, I think. No one looks bored. The questions are probing, but they are taking time. I wonder, is speed more important than depth? But most of all, I am waiting and hoping for an opportunity to challenge without being challenging, to try to point out all the unspoken declamations of understanding – the gestures and the signs that, to me, suggest thinking leading to action – but which, to my co-observer, suggest inaction, a lack of progress.

(Journal, October 2012)

As I examined in 'A Matter of Space', allowing the presence of a void in a lesson is a dangerous strategy for a teacher, because the thinking processes in a void are hidden from the observer. In the instance above, the teacher might have signalled that she knew the child looked disengaged – she might have said, 'Ooh, Luke, I know you are thinking, but you really don't look like you are.' This might have offset the judgement, but in the process she would have interrupted Luke's thinking, possibly disrupting his learning. Perhaps, for Luke, the open mouth was a sign of receptiveness to the information he was receiving. Perhaps the eyes staring into the distance were visualising the matter of the reading – bringing it forward into being. Perhaps his tapping was an engagement with the rhythm of speech – the rhythm of knowledge. Perhaps. We don't know, but we are quick to judge. We rush to see what we think we are seeing, instead of slowing down and examining the possibilities inherent in a highly differentiated environment.[4] It is perfectly possible that we were witnessing the opposite of disengagement – the emergence of imagination from a 'fractal abyss where there was only a hyphen between stimulus and response and canned reaction'; an abyss in which 'imagination takes the body not as an "object" but as a realm of virtuality … as a site for superabstract invention'.[5]

It is easy for me to tut and judge, but for my co-observer it is possible, in this moment, that there is an aionic pressure exerting itself in the form of Ofsted – a future possibility pressing in (and blinding) the observer. He sits, not seeing all the possible present 'maybes' of chronos, but instead imagining a future present – that imagined future where an inspector sits in judgement on a similar situation. Until recently, the criteria for an outstanding lesson insisted that children make 'rapid and sustained progress', and while Ofsted are no longer grading individual lessons, the focus on linear progress remains.[6] To this end then, to be outstanding is to be obvious – to have simplified to a point where there is no uncertainty. Such a simplification can only ever be an illusion. Time in the multiple complexities of the classroom is not rapid and it is not singular. It is bound in prior experience AND future possibility (aionic). It is also, simultaneously and sometimes broodingly, present (chronos). The two fold in on each other, as do the materials of subject matter and the immaterial affects:

Here there is no effort bearing on material forms that does not bring forth immaterial entities. Inversely, every drive towards a territorialized infinity is accompanied by a movement of folding onto territorialized limits.[7]

Sometimes a decision is not made. Sometimes only uncertainty remains. Sometimes progress is not made. Not yet, not then. Or, if it is made, it is made elsewhere – outside the realm of the lesson objective. Sometimes the progress is missed by an observer with tunnel vision. These emerging learning 'becomings' are tenuous and difficult to observe, and they do not fit with the dominant ideology of certainty characterised by the concept of 'progress'.

Over the course of a few weeks in 2013, I see similar judgements being made: 'Sorry. Rule forty-two, you know'[8] – a lesson deemed unsatisfactory because books were not out on the tables for the observer to check. Another because the room was too hot. Arbitrary reasoning deployed to ensure that the school is making rigorous and accurate assessments based on what they think Ofsted might say if they were present in the room. In these early weeks I feel despondent – the Queen of Hearts is ever present in all decisions being made, even though she's miles away and no one has ever actually met her. In the meantime, staff are instructed to keep going, to keep making progress: '"Begin at the beginning," the King said, very gravely, "and go on till you come to the end: then stop."'[9] I feel despondent, but I have places I can go in order to reassure myself. I return to research and tune my mind into being curious, to asking the phenomenological questions that ignite interest and ideas. I read some more and think some more. It seems to me that most of the problems I am encountering are connected to time – to notions of linear progress, to a belief that the present will lead, step by step, to a definable future.

In this view of time, what Groves calls the future of the 'everyday frame of mind', the future is always something yet-to-come – the place where 'we expect our desires to be realised'.[10] Educational policy is rooted in this view – and I use the arboreal image of a root deliberately here, for our education system does not embrace rhizomatic structures. It is necessary to the survival of institutions that there is hope and a belief in meritocracy, otherwise why would anyone attend? Many educationalists have expressed concerns about the economically driven approach to education in which its purpose is rooted in future possibility, in aspiration, in potential outcomes – what Schostak refers to as 'utopia' to which children 'must be pushed, pulled and adjusted until they fit the required categories'.[11] It relies on deferred gratification, though lip service is paid by politicians to the inspirational – to the love of learning.

When schools attempt to create alternatives, through movements such as cooperative trusts or through independent status, there have been battles with Ofsted. One of the most documented has been the legal challenge by Summerhill School to its Ofsted inspection report of 2000; a challenge which led to a change in Ofsted procedure for this school.[12] A school in Cornwall lost its appeal to join a cooperative trust and was forced to convert to an academy in 2012,[13] and there are cases of schools becoming 'free schools' in order to escape the doctrine of government policy.[14] But conversions and trusts do not protect schools from the pervasive effect of Ofsted, and it is unusual for a challenge to Ofsted to be successful. The field may seem open, but there is a shepherd ever present.

The future can become an emotive and potentially frightening place for a child,[15] loaded with discourse markers such as 'if' and 'then' and 'but'. Causality is casually presented as a fait accompli, while on the news we see the numbers of unemployed graduates grow. This model of instantaneity presents to children a future of empty, yet-to-be-filled possibilities, which may seem exciting but are instantly connected to the power principles of work, obedience and an agreed set of cultural codes and values, such as those relating to sustaining a future economy.[16]

Ofsted and other policy-makers or enforcers attempt to bridge the seemingly distant future by breaking it down into a 'specious present'[17] – a series of mini 'nows' which form the impression of a present but which are constantly moving. This flow or motion of time allows for a belief that progress is ongoing, moment by moment; that it can be measured and adjusted incrementally to secure the distant trajectory in a series of steps. It is easy to convince children that this is a linear process. We teach them time connectives from an early age – they appear in the literacy curriculum from Year 2 ('then', 'later', afterwards' and, by Year 5, 'finally', 'eventually' and so on). It is intuitive to see the world in this way, yet Deleuze offers us alternative interpretations of time.

In *The Logic of Sense*, Deleuze presents a dual conception of time as two distinguishable yet interwoven movements: aion and chronos. These concepts trouble notions of chronological, linear time, positing instead an ontological version of time. To someone like a teacher, ruled by the hour-to-hour structure of a teaching day and planning minute-by-minute lessons, such a concept can seem almost absurd, yet we accept ontological notions of time as part of the metaphorical semantic fields associated with the way we experience time – it 'flies', 'drags', 'takes you back', 'stands still'. Human experience of time is such that a second can seem to last for an hour, and vice versa, but our subjective experience of time is often overridden by what we have been taught about the way time is measured – in equal and linear fragments. Orthodoxy prevails over sense.

Thinking in ontological time – that is, the time of experience or being (private time) rather than measured or empirical time (public time) – requires a discourse of excess, which excludes the present and consists of both a past that never took place and a future that can never arrive. This leads us to a reconceptualisation of time through a Deleuzian lens; one which is not dependent on human experience or on the relation between subject/object but, as Hoy says, is more ecological and which transcends temporality.[18] Indeed, it resonates with Bohr's theories on quantum physics (I explore their relation to space on page 56 in terms of the complexity of relationships between object/subject/human/inorganic). Time, like space, is multiply complex. Chronos time is described by Rosethorn as that which is rooted in the reality of the now, in which past and present are illusions.[19] In chronos, intuition is key – there is a sense that now matters and that becoming requires being watchful, in what Deleuze describes as the nowness of 'the greatest present'.[20] My reading of this has led me to think of chronos as 'affect time'.

Aion time, on the other hand, troubles the past and future, and fragments them. I think of this as 'effect time', but effects that both occur and exist as endless potentials. With aion, 'a future and past divide the present at every instant and subdivide it ad infinitum into past and future, in both directions at once'.[21]

For education, there seems to be a presentation of only public time, with constraints and linearity in place. An obsession with linearity and conformity leads to spurious concepts of milestones – points in time by which children should achieve the same goals (i.e. ready for school/ work) – as if, in Robinson's words, 'the most important thing about them is their date of manufacture'.[22] They should all move together, yet are always viewed as being individually accountable and responsible for their progress and behaviours.[23] In setting up the structures that serve this view, educational institutions bring the future into the present. The future exerts its pressure on the present. Future expectations, hopes, ambitions and fears form the basis upon which present decisions are made. The future presses down on these children, and the people holding the pressure pads are their parents and teachers and, above them, the policy-makers. All breathing in time, 'You must succeed'. This leads to a focus in social research policy and funding on the certainty of what works, in terms of 'policy relevant' social research which is concerned with adult anxiety about children, the future and the production of ideal future citizens.[24]

The problem, of course, is that this present future is brought forth in a vision of now – we imagine that the future will be roughly like our present but with more efficient technology.[25] In a sense, we perpetuate our present by planning our future based on a model of now. And we do this, Heidegger would claim, through a process of 'disclosure'.[26] Disclosure is the presentation of the future to us, which is dictated by what it is possible we will become. It is a limited view based on notions of possibility. Depending on the aspirations, beliefs and expectations of influential people around us, disclosure can have both positive and negative outcomes on one's 'to-be' self. Either way, modes of disclosure and those of specious presents underpin both educational and parental habits of mind.

For example:

Parent: Mrs Kidd, could I please have a quick word about this new curriculum?

Me: Yes, of course.

Parent: Don't get me wrong, he's really enjoying it, but I was wondering where the English was?

Me: What are you thinking of when you say 'English'?

Parent: Well, spelling and punctuation and things like that. His spelling is terrible. I was wondering when he'd get spelling tests.

Me: Ah, well we do work on spelling, but on an individual basis, so rather than teaching the whole class the same spellings, when I mark, I target a few for each child and they're written as spelling targets at the end. They're supposed to go away and learn them, and the next time I mark, I check that if they've used that word again, it's been used correctly.

Parent: But there are no tests?

Me: No.

Parent: Right. It's just that when I was at school, we had tests every week and I think it helped me … I'm just worried that if he can't spell he won't get his exams or a job.

Me: I know it's a worry, but these things develop with time – he's only 11. You could really help me by checking those targets in his book and making sure he takes them on board. Perhaps you could test him on them at home?

Parent: (with relief) Yes, yes, I'll do that, thank you.

> (Notes written ethno-dramatically after a Year 7
> 'Settling in Evening', October 2012)

In this conversation, there was little point in me pointing out the other hugely important skills we were covering in English, or directing the parent to the research which questions the impact of spelling tests on learners. In her mind, her current success had depended on her spelling tests at school. Her vision of her son's future was being shaped by her own past, and his present was pressured by this parental belief and fear. For this child, both past (another's) and future (imagined) were exerting considerable pressure on views of present, and this was impacting on his confidence and self-image. He wrote a poem on arrival at school in which there were these lines:

> I play rugby well, but
> I wish I could spell.

In self-assessment sheets, he regularly writes that he needs to improve his spelling. In fact, his spelling is average for his age and is improving, but it exerts considerable influence on his sense of self and his hopes for the future. To help him I need to show him his current skills more clearly (imagining, for the moment, that there is a present and not simply a series of disappearing nows). The next time he writes, instead of highlighting his mistakes, I highlight all the words he spelled correctly. The page is fluorescent: 324 words highlighted, 11 left untouched.

'What's this?' he asks as he gets his book back.

'All the words you spelled correctly, Danny. Now find the others and write them down.'

He picks his pen up quickly and starts searching and jotting. Previously I had written them for him. He'd open his book, cast his eyes over them and sigh. Now he seems more eager, straighter in his chair. Is it that simple? I have a smug moment.

'Oh, Miss, Miss, that's cool, can you do that with mine?' all the others start shouting. My own future presses in on me – endless hours of highlighting.

'No,' I say, 'I was making a point.'

It gives me an idea though. The next time homework is due, I take in a pile of highlighters and dictionaries.

'Check your work before handing it in,' I say, 'and highlight every word you've spelled correctly. Only highlight if you're certain. Check in the dictionary.'

They've never been so keen to self-correct. Highlighters are the future!

(Journal, November 2012)

This moment disappeared into my notes as insignificant until I started to think about motivation and desire linked to past/present/future, at which point it appeared in aionic mode.

For Danny, his mother's *Befindlichkeit* (a state of mind or mood) had transferred to him, creating doubt and fear. It was, is and will be necessary to try to help Danny reframe his world in this area, so that spelling does not become a barrier to attempting to write or feeling that meaning can be successfully conveyed. Already, Danny's pieces of writing are getting longer, and he is exploring more ambitious vocabulary as he worries less about being 'wrong'. He is becoming attuned to other possible states.

I wonder if this moment has created a time fracture, and consider the role that past experiences had to play, as well as the possibility of the opening up of multiple future possibilities. What produced the desire to proofread their work? Was it as simple as novelty? One child, sighing happily as she daubed pink highlighter pen over her work, said: 'It looks lovely now!'

For her, and I suspect others, there was an aesthetic dimension to the proofreading. Perhaps they felt they were making their work more beautiful, more interesting, through the use of colour. Perhaps the pasts of early childhood in which colouring was an enjoyable enterprise are pressing in. Perhaps there was a move away from the notion of writing as labour towards them believing that their writing was art. Perhaps it is all a matter of perception.

Perception has long been thought to be imbued with motivation. For example, in 1947, Bruner and Goodman showed that coins really do look bigger to a hungry child,[27] but The Official Doctrine (TOD) model outlined in Chapter 3 suggests that intelligent people override perception to find truth. To claim this, one would have to say that these children are not intelligent per se, but are, in fact, exhibiting different modes of intelligence – a positive intelligence linked to beauty, hope and art. All but one of these children linked the colour to a positive association with their work – it seemed to have a visceral, emotional impact on them. It may be that the colour is forming a material affect which pierces through habitual assemblages of what writing *is* and making the writing reappear in new form – a form more closely identified with past experiences of play: 'Conventional words or other signs have to be sought for laboriously only in a secondary stage, when the mentioned associative play is sufficiently established and can be produced at will.'[28]

Einstein, of course, is not speaking here of highlighter pens, but the concept of the playful imagination. I am suggesting that the colour acts as a reminder of playful imagination rather than being the thing itself – that it acts as an aionic line of flight from then time to now time. For Einstein, the writing – the communication of that which has been learned – is the laborious element (from an Arendtian view, this is 'work'). For the children, too, the writing up is work – work that some find laborious and others find purposeful. To have this work judged and valued by others carries loaded assemblages of past, present and future possible failures. It reminds me, once again, of the dominance of the Queen of Hearts, who Carroll describes as 'a sort of embodiment of ungovernable passion – a blind and aimless fury'.[29]

It may be useful, if one is to attempt to reframe time within a child's experience of learning, to consider what has been said about the way the human mind experiences time and how it frames identity within an experience of time. Nobel Prize winner Edelman and his partner, Tononi, posit the idea that the human mind has a 'dynamic core' which has a degree of stability – a series of core processes to which our experiences bind themselves and through which events are viewed as significant or not.[30] They argue that there are many layers or states of consciousness which become organised into conscious thought. Those that manifest themselves in language, having moved beyond the inkling stage, are drawn together for one reason or another – largely through habit and repetition but also through resonance and reminder. Whether or not experience binds itself to this core dictates, to a degree, the survival of memory. Edelman, in an earlier text, expands his idea of 'neural Darwinism' – a fight for survival of remembered thought, experience and knowledge.[31] This theory offers an explanation for the appearance of relevance. But there is a problem here. The interpretation is anthropocentric and does not consider the interaction of the human with the other. In addition, a dynamic core suggests that the human mind is constructed around 'sameness' – that memory is built as recollections connect with new experiences which are similar. This has led to a belief in educational practice that repetition, returning, testing and building are the key components from which learning is formed. More recently, neuroscientists, such as Greenfield, have observed that Edelman's view does not fully embrace the level of complexity of the brain as an emergent system.[32] She argues that there is a much more subtle and yet to be understood intra-action between the dominant and emerging synapses relating to memory and conceptions of time and identity.[33]

For Deleuze (and for Derrida and Nietzsche), it is difference, not sameness, that matters. In order to learn, one needs to explore not only what is similar in the return, but also that which is different or altered, because it is in difference that 'becoming otherwise' emerges.[34]

Hence, the notation looks not so much like this:

as this:

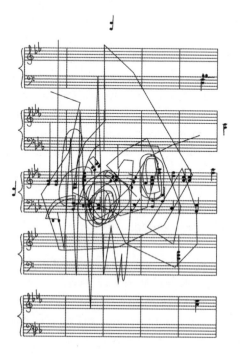

For the children using the highlighters, there seems to be an association between colour and positive experience – sameness – but each one will experience, remember and interpret this differently. We cannot say that colour is the single or most significant correlating factor. There are many ors/ands at work. Nevertheless, the colour serves as an interruption, disrupting the sameness of their experience of writing and imbuing it with difference. In all rhizomatic metaphors, resonance, relevance and recognition form the emerging understandings we create as we meander through the world, but the interest lies in their differences. As we learn of the complexity and the wonder of the mind, the ability to convey its processes become ever more difficult and frustrating. Representing the events that occur in the stop – the aionic interruptions and disruptions – is difficult, perhaps impossible, but we do what we can with the tools we have.

All our past experiences form present preferences to build skills for future competencies. This might be understood in terms of what Husserl calls 'retention' and 'protention'.[35] It is possible that the children in this example have retained past memories and positive associations with colour, and are using this to project into a future skill set. Aionic time, characterised by impersonal verb action such as teaching, learning and doing, is pressing upon the moment, but they are experiencing this as a chronos time – simply being. I am not suggesting that they are consciously aware of the presence of aion, or even fully processing the fullness of the immanence that is chronos. Nevertheless, they are in a smooth space, a 'now' space which is brimming with 'becoming' – the past, present and future are combining to become something. They may only be aware of *Befindlichkeit* but, for me, a lesson is learned about bringing positive, dynamic associations to bear on laborious but necessary tasks.

Time as architect and artisan

The data offered here, in addition to permitting an exploration of time, resonates with Deleuze and Guattari's vision of artisan vs. architect notions of future orientation as explored by Adam and Groves.[36] In the architectonic model, there is a model of the world which, for Deleuze and Guattari, is exemplified in Plato's *Timaeus*, where a god creates a universe from matter based on an idea of a perfect universe.[37] There is a blueprint. There is matter, which is malleable and unstable, but which through careful measuring and crafting can be formed into that which has the appearance of stability and reliability and, providing the architect has the skill, the matter may be commanded and formed.

The current model of education is predicated on an architectonic model. Providing the teacher has the technical skills, the matter (children), who may be unpredictable and unstable but who are malleable, are shaped into that which appears to be useful, productive and knowledgeable. It is possible that the relationship between teacher and children is similar to that of the relationship between materials and forces. Ingold suggests this is about 'the way in which materials of all sorts, with various and variable properties, and enlivened by the forces of the Cosmos, mix and meld with one another in the generation of things'.[38] Deleuze and Guattari insist that whenever we encounter matter, 'it is matter in movement, in flux, in variation'. And the consequence, they go on to assert, is that 'this matter-flow can only be followed'.[39] What Deleuze and Guattari here call a 'matter-flow', I would call a 'material'.

The architect teacher will use disclosure, modelling and practice (pedagogical material) to ensure that the now steps of the future are embedded in the child (formative material). It is this architectural model that is driving the structures of Ofsted criteria. (I return to structures in more detail in the plateau on (r)evolution, Chapter 7.) For now, let's return to the data. My own vision of future was knocked and reshaped by my conversation with a parent. Before this I had been focused on whether or not the writing demonstrated an understanding and engagement with the text. Her state-of-mind affected my focus – it attuned me to another issue and made me look closer at Danny's earlier work and conceptions of self. The architect teacher may have built in some other structures at this point – spelling tests, planned functional literacy sessions and so on – to ensure that the standard of spelling was *seen* to be addressed, that the unpredictable matter was being reformed. But these structures would have reinforced Danny's sense of his future being dependent on his ability to spell and, therefore, this future would be shaped by an inaccurate belief. To resist this, it was necessary to become something other than architect – to navigate a more nomadic space.

In the architectonic model, there is a hierarchical relationship between the mind and the matter it works on – the mind imposes its idea onto the matter. Standing in-between is a worker – someone who carries out the task for the architect in order to realise his/her vision, and this can be passed down. Similarly, in education, there is an imposition of will which is hierarchical, and through which the mind with the idea imposes that vision to shape the matter, setting up a series of 'normalising choices which are both highly repetitive and mutually reinforcing'.[40] This passes down a chain: a minister has an idea and the accountability agents, such as inspectors and writers of syllabi and curriculums, are the artisans. They are then charged with becoming architects by imposing the idea on the deliverers of education – leaders and teachers in schools. They, in turn, create their ideas based on the blueprints offered and shape their own blueprint to mould the children. The children are the matter that matter least, in that they have the least agency to form their own blueprints for learning. But they are human, and for an architectonic model to work there is an assumption that the matter is or can be made to be passive. Active matter is problematic – an issue I explore in 'A Matter of (R)evolution' (Chapter 7). All of this passing is charged with the fear of future possibility.

Plato makes a distinction between architect and artisan by defining the artisan as passive. The artisan takes the blueprint from the architect and then creates – it is a less valid role in terms of power and agency. For Plato, the architect in teaching is the teacher, the artisans are the pupils passively carrying out the work of the teacher, and the matter is the work or output of knowledge (instruction–activity–test). It is this idea of the architect that has informed the TOD model of intelligence, and it is rooted in linear notions of time as well as traditional methodologies – plan/act/do. This implies a linear relationship between subject (knowledge) and object (child), or vice versa, but for Deleuze and Guattari there is no such linearity: 'Subject and object give a poor approximation of thought. Thinking is neither a line drawn between subject and object nor a revolving of one around the other.'[41] For them, the artisan is not merely carrying out the work of the architect, but is, or should be, essential in ensuring that human beings remain connected to the 'futurity immanent in all matter'[42] – that is, an immanence integral to the body without organs. Artisan and matter, matter.

For Deleuze, as outlined by Protevi, the artisan carries 'artisanal sensitivity'[43] – a body of felt awareness and understanding that shapes and moulds the decisions made and responses to the matter. It is a motor-physical and instinctive craft set, not rooted in ideas or mathematic certainty, but in gut feeling, experience and prior knowledge. It is in observation, moulded by fine tuning – by looking for a-tune-meant. And here the notion of sameness and returns comes back into play. Returning to the material of the data is not the same as simply re-presenting that which was. The data is brimming with difference, and the interest lies in its diffractive patterns – a process of following. Hallam and Ingold, in their exploration of matter, state:

> The artist – as also the artisan – is an itinerant, and his work is consubstantial with the trajectory of his or her own life. Moreover the creativity of the work lies in the forward movement that gives rise to things. To read things 'forwards' entails a focus not on abduction but on improvisation.[44]

It is, as Deleuze and Guattari write, 'to join with the World, or to meld with it. One ventures from home on the thread of a tune.' Life, for them, issues along such thread-lines. They call them 'lines of flight', or sometimes 'lines of becoming'.[45]

The multiplicity of these lines demands new understandings of time in the classroom – time needs to stand still while still marching on. It is necessary for the teacher to be able to live in slow time while performing in fast time – to create wormholes. This requires, as I have said elsewhere, a capacity to live in the stop and to read. This is the science of time as nomadic philosophy, bringing with it an acceptance of uncertainty. Practitioners working on these edges, many of them women, are attempting to forge artisanal spaces within a predominantly architectural world. These are chaosmotic spaces, which 'rebound and irrupt on states of things, bodies and the autopoietic nuclei it uses as a support for deterritorialisation … Here we are dealing with an infinity of virtual entities infinitely rich in possibilities, infinitely enrichable through creative processes.'[46] Both Hallam and Ingold and Deleuze and Guattari are setting out the notion of creativity as a 'life', and it is surely the job of the teacher, more than anything else, to provide the conditions in which rich lives can emerge. Joining, melding and creating time for smooth play is the middle work of the artisanal teacher.

Unlike the artisanal approach, the architectural model offers a 'royal' science in which form is imposed from outside and therefore assumes that there is a separate standpoint of higher level consciousness. Nomadic sciences inhabit the form AND the space, folding in and out. There is an opportunity in this model for teachers to refuse or change the imposed expectation that they will be royal architects, and instead become artisans with the children – nomadically inhabiting the form of the learning process. I examine possibilities for these ways of working in Chapter 7.

One might draw a parallel in education to the frustration that MacLure speaks of in her exploration of voice in the realm of social science research: 'the urge to break that voice down: to analyse it until it submits its truths, abstractions or generalisations to the calculations of social science'.[47] It appears that for both the worlds of research and education, 'his fruit is ripe but he is not yet ripe for his fruit'.[48] Even though the realisation that the more we know, the less we know is frustrating, it can also bring liberation. Complexity allows for moments of stopping, inhabiting the void, listening, watching, intra-acting – it opens up the possibility for becoming nomad.

For Deleuze, the nomad uses the traits in the environment to best inhabit the space. The nomadic teacher uses the traits in the children – their prior and present experience and understanding – to best shape the existence of living-in-future; a future which is already present but open to potential, being presently formed while having always lain as a possibility within the matter. In many ways, it is the nomad who is mediating the complex intra-action between chronos and aion time. For the children, the work is their matter – if we return to the example above, using the highlighter pens allows them to discover or craft a form. In the extract 'Postcards from Terezín' (in Chapter 4), the children find form in song. For me, as the teacher, the children are matter, but that matter is not passively awaiting an imposed form; it is already inherently present-in-future. I strive to ensure that they are always making a positive contribution to order.[49] It is a question of discovering, releasing the potentiality within and being mindful of the fact that, even when they appear not to be making such a positive contribution to order (as my example in Eyam in Chapter 6 will demonstrate), it is my duty to find the order they are attempting to show. To try to figure out where they are coming from and how we can merge our interests/moods/potential to shape positive futures. This is not to keep them as they are, but to build capabilities which are based on incremental adaptations to environment, stimulus and the matter with which they (and I) work. To become sensitised.

Deleuze would argue that learning is not about shaping outcomes from fixed capacities – an idea which would suggest that there are limits to ability and intelligence – but about learning capacities that were not there before, while also working with what is there – 'a configuration emerging out of their virtual potential'.[50] Perhaps it is this configuration that Biesta speaks of when he talks of subjectification – the idea that education, in part, carries a duty of emancipation, freedom and building the capacity for responsibility in dealing with both.[51] But these things are not taught, nor are they fixed in an inherent sense – they exist as possibilities and are vulnerable.

Deleuze and Guattari's conception of the word virtual is not tainted with the modern associations that 'virtual reality' has become to suggest – that is, not real at all, but simulated. For them, the virtual future is that which exists already in its potential but the extent of which is unimaginable – imagining it can only limit it. Instead, the future exists in moments of experimentation, play, discovery and openness in which the rhizomes and lines of flight of potential are developed. The crucial aspects of this process are not 'rapid and sustained', as Ofsted would claim, but are characterised by what Groves calls 'hesitation and improvisation'.[52] Improvisation necessitates mistakes. It requires time and trust. It belongs to a pedagogy of hope which emerges from chaos.

Much of what I write does not trouble the rhetoric of educational policy-makers. Much of this rhetoric centres on 'releasing potential' and on 'engaging' learners. On the surface, at least, it seems that a nomadic model – touted as a 'child centred' model – is encouraged. The problem is that this model is not enacted in practice. It cannot thrive when the modes of measurement are linear and limited to examination output and writing skill. The outcome drivers do not match the intentions.

There is a disconnect when a royal assessment model imposes itself upon a nomadic intention. It cannot work, and it is, I believe, bringing education to the brink of crisis. To return to the examples I gave at the beginning of this chapter, the assumed realities of present, dictated by a royal observation schedule, blind the observer to the nomadic tendencies of the teacher, even as the observer claims to seek to look for them.

Future visions, however, can be changed, and as I settle into this relentlessly future-orientated world of education, I am determined to find alternative views, alternative ways of helping children to view time and future differently, to commit small acts of nomadic subversion in the face of a right royal mess.

Notes

1. G. Claxton, Turning Thinking On Its Head: How Bodies Make Up Their Minds, *Thinking Skills and Creativity* 7(2) (2012): 78–84.
2. L. Carroll, *Alice's Adventures in Wonderland* (London: Puffin, 2008 [1865]), p. 115.
3. G. Deleuze quoted in D. Hoy, *The Time of Our Lives: A Critical History of Temporality* (Cambridge, MA: MIT Press, 2009), p. 158.
4. K. Roy, *Teachers in Nomadic Spaces: Deleuze and Curriculum* (New York: Peter Lang, 2003).
5. B. Massumi, *A User's Guide to Capitalism and Schizophrenia: Deviations from Deleuze and Guattari* (Cambridge, MA: MIT Press, 1992), p. 100.
6. Ofsted, Changes to Education Inspections Announced [press release] (30 May 2012). Available at: https://www.gov.uk/government/news/changes-to-education-inspections-announced.
7. F. Guattari quoted in S. O'Sullivan, Guattari's Aesthetic Paradigm: From the Folding of the Finite/Infinite Relation to Schizoanalytic Metamodelisation, *Deleuze Studies* 4(2) (2010): 256–286 at 260.
8. Carroll, *Alice's Adventures in Wonderland*, p. 133.
9. Carroll, *Alice's Adventures in Wonderland*, p. 134.
10. C. Groves, The Living Future in Philosophy. Working paper (2007). Available at: http://www.cardiff.ac.uk/socsi/futures/wp_cg_livingfuture121005.pdf.
11. J. Schostak, *Maladjusted Schooling: Deviance, Social Control and Individuality in Secondary Schooling* [Kindle edn] (London: Routledge, 2012).
12. I. Stronach, Progressivism Against the Audit Culture: The Continuing Case of Summerhill School versus Ofsted. Paper presented to the First International Congress of Qualitative Inquiry, University of Illinois, 4–7 May 2005. Available at: http://core.kmi.open.ac.uk/display/271327.
13. Private correspondence with deputy head teacher.
14. P. Hyman, How I Went From Tony Blair's Adviser to Free School Head, *The Guardian*, 1 September 2013. Available at: http://www.theguardian.com/education/2013/sep/01/free-school-21-stratford-peter-hyman.
15. W. Harlen and R. Deaken Crick, A Systematic Review of the Impact of Summative Assessment and Tests on Students' Motivation for Learning, in *Research Evidence in Education Library* (London: EPPI-Centre, Social Science Research Unit, Institute

of Education, University of London, 2002); R. Webb and G. Vuilliamy, *Coming Full Circle? The Impact of New Labour's Education Policies on Primary School Teachers' Work* (London: Association of Teachers and Lecturers, 2006).

16. M. Bassey, *Education for the Inevitable: Schooling When the Oil Runs Out* (Brighton: Book Guild, 2011).

17. W. James, *The Principles of Psychology*, Vol. 1 (New York: Dover, 1950), p. 609.

18. Hoy, The Time of Our Lives.

19. B. Rosethorn, Undead Temporality, *Critical Fantasies* (21 November 2012). Available at: http://billrosethorn.wordpress.com/2012/11/21/undead-temporality/.

20. G. Deleuze, *The Logic of Sense* (London: Continuum, 2004), p. 164.

21. Deleuze, *The Logic of Sense*, p. 164.

22. K. Robinson, Changing Education Paradigms: RSA Animate [video] (14 October 2010). Available at: http://www.youtube.com/watch?v=zDZFcDGpL4U.

23. E. Burman, Avoid: The Big Society [seminar presentation] (2013). Available at: http://www.slideserve.com/orpah/avoid-the-big-society.

24. N. Rose, *Governing the Soul: The Making of the Private Self*, 2nd edn (London: Free Association Books, 1999).

25. A. Gore, *The Future: Six Drivers of Global Change* (New York: Random House, 2013).

26. M. Heidegger, *The Concept of Time* (Oxford: Blackwell, 1992), p. 67.

27. J. S. Bruner and C. Goodman, Value and Need as Organizing Factors in Perception, *Journal of Abnormal and Social Psychology* 42 (1947): 33–44.

28. A. Einstein quoted in A. Damasio, *Descartes' Error: Emotion, Reason and the Human Mind* (London: Vintage, 2006), p. 107.

29. L. Carroll, *Alice on the Stage* (London: Carson and Comerford, 1887).

30. G. M. Edelman and G. Tononi, *Consciousness: How Matter Becomes Imagination* (London: Penguin, 2000).

31. G. Edelman, *The Remembered Present* (New York: Basic Books, 1989).

32. S. Greenfield, *The Human Brain – A Guided Tour* (London: Basic Books, 1997).

33. S. Greenfield, *You and Me: The Neuroscience of Identity* (London: Notting Hill Editions, 2011).

34. L. Gallacher and M. Gallagher, Methodological Immaturity in Childhood Research? Thinking Through 'Participatory Methods', *Childhood* 15(4) (2008): 499–516 at 511.

35. J. Derrida, *Speech and Phenomena: And Other Essays on Husserl's Theory of Signs* (Evanston, IL: Northwest University Press, 1963), p. 64.

36. B. Adam and C. Groves, *Future Matters: Action, Knowledge, Ethics* (Leiden, NV: Koninklijke Brill, 2007).

37. G. Deleuze and F. Guattari, *What is Philosophy?*, tr. H. Tomlinson and G. Burchell (New York: Columbia University Press, 1994), p. 369.

38. T. Ingold, Bringing Things to Life: Creative Entanglements in a World of Materials. Working Paper 15 (July 2010). Available at: http://www.socialsciences.manchester. ac.uk/medialibrary/morgancentre/research/wps/15-2010-07-realities-bringing-things-to-life.pdf, p. 2.

39. G. Deleuze and F. Guattari, *Difference and Repetition* (New York: Continuum, 2004 [1968]), p. 451.

40. C. Pearce, The Life of Suggestions, *Qualitative Inquiry* 17(7) (2010): 631–638 at 636.

41. Deleuze and Guattari, *What is Philosophy?*, p. 85.

42. Adam and Groves, *Future Matters*, p. 133.

43. J. Protevi, *Political Physics: Deleuze, Derrida and the Body Politic* (London, New York: Athlone, 2001).

44. E. Hallam and T. Ingold (eds), *Creativity and Cultural Improvisation*. ASA Monographs, Vol. 44 (Oxford: Berg Publishers, 2007), p. 3.
45. Deleuze and Guattari, *Difference and Repetition*, p. 344.
46. F. Guattari, *Chaosmosis: An Ethico-Aesthetic Paradigm* (Sydney: Power Publications, 1995), p. 112.
47. M. MacLure, Broken Voices, Dirty Words: On the Productive Insufficiency of Voice, in A. Y. Jackson and L. A. Mazzei (eds), *Voice in Qualitative Inquiry: Challenging Conventional, Interpretive and Critical Conceptions in Qualitative Research* (London and New York: Routledge, 2009), pp. 97–115 at p. 97.
48. F. Nietzsche, *Thus Spoke Zarathustra: A Book for All and None*, tr. W. Kaufman (New York: Modern Library, 1995 [1885]), p. 1.
49. J. Protevi, Larval Subjects, Enaction and E. Coli Chemotaxis, in L. Guillaume and J. Hughes (eds), *Deleuze and the Body* (Edinburgh: Edinburgh University Press, 2011), pp. 29–50.
50. Groves, The Living Future in Philosophy.
51. G. Biesta, *The Beautiful Risk of Education* (Boulder, CO: Paradigm, 2013).
52. Groves, The Living Future in Philosophy.

Chapter 6

A MATTER OF MAKING SENSE AND TAKING RESPONSIBILITY

Virtue lies in our power, and similarly so does vice; because where it is in our power to act, it is also in our power not to act...

Aristotle, *The Nicomachean Ethics*

This plateau is all about sense. All kinds of sense. Making sense, sensing, being sensible, sensibility ... It returns to notions covered in previous plateaus, and contributes to the messy whole relating to time and space, nomads and royals, architects and artisans, but in particular it aims to examine more closely the notion of meaning, sensing and interpreting in order to develop a sense of responsibility both in terms of research and classroom practice. I begin with an exploration of what the word 'sense' might mean, from a Deleuzian perspective, but with a view to exploring how what is sensed forms events and, in turn, how these impact on concepts related to ethical sense (being sensible and responsible). As such, this is a plateau which picks up and connects with others – in particular, in its consideration of justice.

It is my belief that, to educate a child, one must consider notions of justice from the beginning. The just process of education involves the proper balance of control and the preparation of the child for a future in which (s)he will enact and experience justice – making a more just world than the one they were born into. For education should seek to improve, and improvement should be enacted with benevolent intent. One of the difficulties we have in our current technocratic system is a confused sense of purpose in terms not only of education but also of values more broadly. At the moment, in the UK, we are told that we ought to teach 'British values', but these remain hazy. As Biesta points out, our evidence-led system attempts to focus on facts not values, but, at the same time, the rhetoric from those in power and those managing power speaks of values without clearly defining what they are.[1] We are told that British values include 'democracy', as if Britain is the only democratic nation, or as if our democracy is efficient. Yet a comparison of the myriad ways in which democracy can be enacted and understood takes us into a global and historical realm. We are told to act 'ethically', but the ethics we see enacted shift according to the accountability structures placed upon us. Making sense of this is a tricky business, but it is necessary if we are to be sentient professionals and not simply reactive employees following the latest whim.

Becoming sentient requires returning to those notions of 'a-tune-meant' and 'gutterances' – tapping into and recognising the ordinary effects in a classroom – but also stepping back and questioning and deconstructing the way that notions such as justice, values and democratic principles are being presented and foisted upon us. We cannot impose these values on children from the outside; we need to create the conditions in which they can be experienced, understood and assimilated. They need to become part of the child's life, not managed and externally defined concepts that sit outside of the child.

Deleuze and sense

For Deleuze, the notion of sense involved a matting of the immanent potentials in the mode of affect. In *Difference and Repetition*, Deleuze and Guattari distinguish ideational events as a form of sensing,[2] which frees 'images from the sensory apparatus of the human body' through which sensations are too quickly attached to an 'object' in order to classify within 'good sense' and 'common sense'.[3] In neuroscience, these denoting interplays of emotion and thought are called somatic actions. Damasio's work on emotion,[4] and its relation to reason, move Cartesian ideas embedded in the TOD model of the mind forward, but not far enough for Deleuze and Guattari, for whom sensations or emotions are a consequence or product of another, more complex and potent realm – the realm of affect. They reject anthropocentric rationalism and instead explore sense through notions of time and space; being and becoming. Colebrook states that within this frame of reference, 'there could not be mind or consciousness, for example, without the connection between the body, the body's organs and external stimuli',[5] so where these external stimuli are impacting on the data, I explore them in more detail.

In *The Logic of Sense*, Deleuze uses the work of Lewis Carroll to explore immanence, and in *Cinema 1* he uses the work of Orson Welles to explore sense.[6] For him, art creates newness of vision – a new way of sensing and experiencing the world. Carroll's work has not only influenced Deleuze, but physics also borrows the character Alice to theorise an idea called the Alice universe, which conceptualises dimensions as being Mobius-like (or like a Klein bottle) – being both this AND that; here AND there.[7] This theory is not dissimilar to the Deleuzian notion of an event *par excellence* that has a 'double structure' and must be 'followed along two complementary yet mutually exclusive trajectories'.[8] Alice, a fictional artistic entity, inspired by a 'real' human child, finds existence in both organic and inorganic realms. Elsewhere in physics, the famed Large Hadron Collider at CERN contains a heavy ion detector conducting experiments into quark-gluon plasma – the experiment is called ALICE. It is an attempt to make sense of the nano in a minute world that defies our human conceptions of possibility.

In attempting to make sense of these human and non-human worlds, we are, in an allusionary sense, becoming Alice. In art, science and philosophy, there is a desire to slow the fall, to examine the assemblages in the immanent plane, to make sense of. At CERN, this involves firing particles at incredible speed, and then using nano time photography to slow the collision to the point that nano particles can be observed – a slow fall within a fast process. In doing so, they are finding that this nano world is indeed a chaosmos of unpredictability and uncertainty. This cutting edge science is not dissimilar to the Deleuzian theory that sense has the status of a pure ideational *event*, irreducible to propositions and their three dimensions: (1) the states of affairs the propositions denote, (2) the experiences or mental activities (beliefs, desires, images, representations) of persons who express themselves in the proposition, and (3) universals or general concepts – a state in which there is 'lateral sliding' along surfaces.[9] In other words, sense is too fast and disparate to be fully grasped within whole units of meaning (often experienced as beliefs, opinions or universals), but it is possible to dissemble and return to events to examine the assemblage by sliding or relaying between dimensions without trying too hard to fix or reduce.

Immanence (the chaos of sense) exists both outside of and within a proposition, in that while propositional orders may seek to eliminate or exclude chaos, they cannot escape immanence. It is within the fold or pleat. Propositions attempt to form order, and they inform the structures of the education system by assuming that an individual performs deeds in response to demand and instruction. Deleuze explores the cycle of proposition, which is rooted in Cartesian reason, as a circle of movement between 'the denotation to the manifestation to the signification' or from the 'it is this' to the relationship to 'I' leading to 'therefore'.[10] These propositions contribute to the maintenance of the appearance of linearity. The idea of lateral sliding allows Deleuze to use cinema as a means of enabling the actual or real image to coexist alongside its representation. To this end, I ask whether or not this duality (or, perhaps, parallel or Alice existence) could be extended to the classroom. Is it possible for the 'actual' presentation of teaching, as required by Ofsted and senior managers, to coexist alongside a cinematic image of 'potential', and can I manage that effectively? Is there the possibility for becoming-Mobius, being both performer and reformer, being both sides? Throughout this book, I offer some early and tenuous explorations of this idea, which will be ongoing for me as long as I teach. These ideas, I realise, have sat with me for as long as I have been teaching, and have been waiting to be discovered by my possible future self in one potential line of flight.

This plateau, like those around it, is born out of a philosophical position, which accepts that the interesting things happen at the edges, that learning itself is a messy and meandering process, and that planned events and activities are always at the mercy of the unexpected stops of the affective dimension. Two tales are in this place: one of failure and one of faux pas. Like the data in other chapters, they are tales of exploration and possibility – lines of flight. It's just that some lines of flight stay in the air. They relate to instances of difficulty and difference which are separate but connected by notions of responsibility, representation and relationship. As I try to make meaning-sense from them, I also try to interrogate them in terms of their immanence and the points at which connections are made between becoming and being.

Here, the additional element of sense inherent within the word 'sensible' intrudes. My interest in Deleuze has existed alongside a desire to 'do good' – to make choices in which 'a teaching process becomes a dedication to pass on pure and abstract values so lives have a greater potential to be lived well'.[11] This is echoed in the world of research by Denzin, who urges us to create worlds where 'language and performance empower, and humans can become who they wish to be'.[12] This is a world in which 'all inquiry is moral and political',[13] and one where Kemmis argues for the creation of 'moral histories' by action researchers.[14] This leads to an entanglement of sense as moral and ethical (being sensible) with meaning-making (making sense through enquiry and action). This 'return' to 'moral discourse', which Denzin and Lincoln call the 'fractured future',[15] finds echoes in some debate in the political field. But, sadly, this has led only to the empty rhetoric of the 'big society'[16] which, while recognising complexity, has not been enacted at a policy level.[17]

These calls to action appeal to the idealist in me, but my intellectual self baulks. What rights do I have to impose my idealism on others? What assumptions am I making? Whose morality are we talking about? Are there universal measures of 'right' and 'wrong'? Where is my thinking being framed – which lenses/hues/power structures are forming my actions/words/thoughts? This philosophical 'friend' is 'a presence that is intrinsic to thought, a condition of possibility of thought itself, a living category, a transcendental lived reality'.[18] It is simultaneously necessary and debilitating – a challenger and rival who can sometimes induce a sense of hopelessness, from poison to liberation.[19] Or am I hiding in philosophy and thought in order to (a)void (intra-)action? I deal with these thoughts more deeply elsewhere. But for now, I focus on the emerging strands of making sense that grew from these musings and impacted on my practice.

Sense as sensation

One element of immanence is the realm of sensation, which is akin to emotion and feeling. Many aspects of my work and thinking have had emotive connections – they are linked to values and beliefs and a tendency (habit) towards idealism. To keep the idealist in check, but without losing the urge to *do*, I have attempted to re-examine data as a form of action – to go back to the cadaver and pick over the bones again. Where am I positioning myself? If I examine prepositions and adjectives in almost all the data in this work, I see a plethora of 'theys' and 'thems' – objects of curiosity – in relation to the children, and a shifting set of prepositions as I move near to, next to, with and from those I claim to represent. The relationship with the people providing my data (predominantly children) shifts in accordance to how the encounters make me feel – the distancing and moments of togetherness dictated by feelings of acceptance and/or rejection. This ebbing and flowing of emotion in relation to relationships is common in teaching, but rarely analysed and yet it forms some important affective moments which dictate future actions and, in some cases, whole futures.[20]

In the Year 9 options handbook at my last school, there is the following statement:

> Do not make choices based on whether or not you like or dislike your current teacher. You may well have a different teacher next year.

According to the senior management team, there was an assumption, based on many years of anecdotal evidence, that children make important life choices based on their emotional responses to relationships in the classroom. Yet nothing was said in the internal criteria for observation about the relationships in the room. This, asserted the head teacher, was 'inferred'. In their recently published work, Coe et al. listed six characteristics that define great teaching.[21] While some dismissed the work as technocratic and simplistic, it did, in fact, recognise the complexity of teaching; that great teachers create environments that are more than the sum of their parts – in essence, emergent – and that relationships are essential to this. But this ephemeral emergence and the nuances of relationships are still very much misunderstood and undervalued in our school systems.

Elsewhere in my school – echoed, no doubt, in many other schools across the world – conversations are overheard in which children speak of teachers and teachers speak of children:

'They're little shits,' says one experienced teacher …

'I hate her lesson – she's a bitch,' says one child of a different, unknown teacher, as I pass in the corridor. (I hope it's not me.)

Such language is usually formed by a wound – it is a bleed from a cut made when we feel our efforts are not recognised or appreciated or when we feel we have been belittled or slighted. (As we saw from the Year 7 data in Chapter 4, words can be felt and received as a physical wound – 'numpty', 'geek', etc.) For a child, this sits, waiting to be made sense of. But when used to understand or create, a wound can be a positive thing. It is a sign of living and triggers healing. Deleuze talks of an event as a wound: 'my wound existed before me; I was born to embody it'. Understood as an event, 'the wound … hovers above me … non-actualized', yet 'incarnates itself or actualizes itself in a state of things or a lived experience'.[22] It is tempting to pick at the wound, to allow it to fester, but it is healthier to consider it as an aspect of an experience without regret. Here is some data.

Making sense of failure – the wound

It is 2010. I have been asked to help a school develop a new curriculum, and so for some months I have been a regular visitor, teaching children, training staff and co-writing a more contextualised and active curriculum model. In **bold** are notes from my field journal taken from moments in school. In *italics* are notes after a day trip to Eyam in Derbyshire.

> **Monday morning. An inner-city academy. I get out of my car and a group of boys strut towards me. From behind – the angle they can be viewed by their peers – they look threatening. But they are grinning.**
>
> **'Who are you going to be today, Miss?'**
>
> **I shrug and smile back at them.**
>
> **'It must be great being you. Do you wake up and think, "Ooh who shall I be today?" You can be anything you want, can't you?'**
>
> **'Can't we all if we're just pretending?'**

I am sitting on a lawn beside some stocks in the plague village of Eyam with a Year 7 class. We're sort of in a circle which keeps shifting its shape as the children shove and shuffle, pinch and wriggle away from/closer to each other. On a bench about 10 feet away are four elderly people – day visitors to the village – clutching their leaflets and watching with interest a real, live lesson taking place outdoors …

They are very excited. There are lots of wows. Some girls slip out of role to clap their hands like seals. 'Cool' say the boys as I play our time-travel commercials.

'So … we're going to put all that preparation you've been doing into action today … We're going to create our own living museum, here by the information centre, called "Footsteps Through Time".'

/ Can we go to the sweet shop? /

/ Miss what are them camel things up there? /

/ Fuck off Connor, you dick /

/ Miss they're spoiling it /

/ Shut up we're supposed to be learning /

/ Miss are you married? /

/ Do you live here Miss? /

/ I'm freezing /

/ Leo, Shannon fancies you /

/ I found this in the paper today Miss, look /

/ Don't make us do work Miss, we're on a trip /

/ Can we just go to the park? /

The starter takes an hour. When I say it is time to go to the graveyard, they whoop and cheer and rush off … Their form teacher hands me back the video camera. She can't meet my eye.

'You're really engaging them,' says the deputy head as I'm leaving, 'that was brilliant.' I smile and shrug, but I feel smug.

'It's all about the context,' I say.

The same children, with the same teacher, on two different days. One in school, one out of school. As a teacher I am crushed. In the car, on the way home, between blinking back little prickles of tears, I think angrily, 'The little shits'. But all this studying has not been for nothing – my interest as a researcher is piqued. A disaster becomes data. I transcribe the video:

'Miss what are them camel things?'

'What's this bumpy writing?'

'Are you married?'

(Extracts taken from journal, January 2010 and video transcript, April 2010)

Later, back in school, a teacher comments wearily, 'They just weren't interested,' but the fact was that they *were* interested – just not necessarily in the things we wanted them to be interested in. There were too many texts competing for their attention, but the removal of those texts would have limited their experience. Alpacas, sunshine, fields, old people on benches, sweet shops and graveyards. These were the texts imposing on their senses. In the usual constraints of a classroom, the learning may have been managed – the classroom walls acting as an outline within which certain expectations could be established (though, even there, the outline is always an illusion). But here there is no outline – the external physical and non-organic texts crash into the experience. A Deleuzian teacher might have worked with those – 'receiving' children and their conceptualisation of the curriculum and working with them in 'playful exploration'.[23] I pressed ahead. The children lived in and around a large council estate in Bradford. I knew that many of them had never been out of the city, but I hadn't considered their need just to absorb the new environment. I wanted to guide them through it – to signpost what I had decided was important about being there. We were on different tracks and neither took notice of the other's signals. We crashed.

An earlier version of myself might have chalked up the experience to a 'bad day' and discarded it as 'anomalous' data, since the vast majority of the empirical data being collected by the school on these children showed improvements in engagement and achievement. But this was not anomalous – it was interesting, an opportunity, a wound leading to new becomings. At that moment, I faced uncertainty – the possibility (or reality) of failure – not to mention a sensation of shame. But, later, I am reminded of Lather's ideas of how 'being lost' can be reframed positively as the 'stammering knowing'[24] that forms part of the process of becoming. It is this stammering that leads me to attempt, even as the wound is open, to create meaning – to make sense.

Afterwards, I consider the extent to which I was meeting their needs. Semetsky, referring to the work of both Noddings and Deleuze, argues for curriculum and content to be 'based on students' own wants, interests and needs'.[25] But here I found that their needs, wants and interests were almost impossibly divergent – I could not meet them all. They had been content with the content in a classroom where stories of the plague were the most interesting things present, but I was unable to maintain that interest in the face of competition from alpacas, sweet shops and stocks. In attempting to manage the situation, and to impose order on the learning, I stumbled into a power struggle in which the 'hierarchical power structure specific to traditional present-day schooling'[26] became subverted. My attempts to cajole a sense of responsibility from the children was met with a surprising reclamation and declamation of identity:

> *You're behaving disgracefully right now!* (and then, because I'm never one to miss a learning opportunity) *What do you think that means, disgraceful?*
>
> /Bad/
>
> /Like chavs/
>
> /Idiots/
>
> /We're bad/
>
> /We're evil, us, you can't take us anywhere/

These words were spoken with a cheerfulness which, rather than indicating self-loathing, seemed to indicate a delight – a covert form of prestige within the peer group. In the rawness of the wound, I wanted to agree with them: yes, you are – you have injured me! But afterwards (licking my wound) I want to contradict them: you're not idiots/evil. I feel guilty for not saying this at the time, for distancing myself. What happens, I wonder, to the mind of the young person who has absolutely accepted the fact that they are a 'chav' or that they are 'bad', and how does this impact on their views of a future? On their aspirations? Is it possible for a teacher to undo these perceptions – to deterritorialise the assemblages to re-form future identities? Again, I am drawn to CERN's ALICE experiment and the notion of the slow fall. It seems as if these children are hurtling, cheerfully, into collision mode. Is it possible to slow down, to examine possibility? Is it possible that these children, in their cheerfulness, are simply redefining the negatives? Throwing them back at the adult world in an act of resistance and disregard, and hence making sense out of the complexity? Adopting a process of 'chaosmosis' in which complexity and chaos interact in a series of returns? Is it possible that their language marks a return and that, in that return, the insult is reframed as a reclamation of self in a more positive mode? We are different to you. We return to the images of us that we see in the media, and we reclaim and reinvent them. We reject your view of the future. We revel in present. We are chaos.

Nietzsche states:

[W]e falsely experience by perceiving sameness rather than difference. Metaphor, for instance, is useful for survival because it allows us to overlook all the differences in what we perceive in order to pick out objects that resemble one another. We transform Becoming, which emphasizes difference into Being, which fixes multiplicities into identity.[27]

We are different to you. We return to the images of us that we see in the media and we reclaim and reinvent them. We reject your view of the future. We revel in present. We are chaos.

Their cheerfulness and comfort with contradiction (You can't take us anywhere, when we clearly have taken them somewhere), suggests to me both the rejection of a future failure and of a present imposed judgement, which is acting as a deflective practice. You can't take us to your promised/ imagined land of our future. We don't accept or believe you. They are simultaneously accepting and rejecting those notions of self in a process of becoming other; in a process of making sense of who they are and what they might become. But these justifications do not sit well with me. I can accept that potentially they are a form of reclamation, even affirmation. But they represent a turning in and away from society. I worry that I have witnessed a form of 'anti-production, or the power of life to turn against itself, or not express its full power'.[28] While I can see this intellectually as a reclamation of power, I also consider that this will end up being a prison – a 'group fantasy' from which it is difficult to escape.

I am open to the notion of embracing complexity as a potentially positive aspect of learning. Protevi is very clear when he distinguishes between complexity theory and chaos theory, and it seems that we have an example of this difference here. According to Protevi:

Chaos theory treats the growth of unpredictable behaviour from simple rules in deterministic nonlinear systems, whereas complexity theory treats the emergence of relatively simple functional structures from complex interchanges of the component parts of a system.[29]

I am (re)minded of this a year later, as images of them sitting in tracksuit bottoms and hooded tops, haircuts uniformly alike, come back to me as I watch coverage of the summer riots of 2011, which shows, without exception, young people in hooded tops and tracksuit bottoms looting and rioting. These images are a distortion of the reality. In Camberwell Green, for example, only one third of those charged are actually under 18, and nationwide only 22%,[30] yet most of the news coverage focuses on the young. The prime minister speaks of the participants as a 'sick' part of society, refusing to countenance a view that they might instead be symptoms of a sickness in society. *The Telegraph*'s Mary Riddell writes that 'feral kids with no jobs ran amok', though she does warn that to 'heap contempt on the rioters as if they are a pariah caste' is a dangerous and misguided reaction.[31] The assumption that those convicted are young is reinforced as mothers, clutching cigarettes and with jackets over their heads, are filmed running from court with their recently sentenced offspring, and suppositions are made that 'bad parenting' is the cause. 'Jog on' shouts one mother to the photographers, filmed by a BBC North West team. 'Make me look good' shouts another. The media gleefully plays the clips over and over, reinforcing the image of an underclass which is overfed, undereducated, poorly parented and therefore deserving of ridicule and contempt. It seems that the media and government are determined to impose a view of chaos on the public; a view that these chaotic behaviours have emerged from simple beginnings – poor parenting, poor discipline, poor schooling. The government are presenting to us a distortion of the chaos theory model which imposes linearity and denies complexity.

It is a deterministic and simplistic interpretation. A complexity theory view would not seek to find the butterfly wing, the root cause, but would instead look to explore the complex intra-relationships which have led to this outcome (among others) – for example, the image of young people coming out in their hundreds to help clear up. Complexity allows us to connect the event to other assemblages. To make sense.

Fast forward to 2014. Trojan horses, scaremongering about radicalism, Islamophobia running so rife that doors are opened up not only to radical right-wing political parties but also to pockets of thought in the mainstream that an antidote to radical Islam could be an emphasis on the teaching of British values. Elsewhere in the world, other governments make similar attempts to reclaim national identities in the face of perceived terrorist threats. Chaos theory. In my classroom, we learn about the Gunpowder Plot. We look at Guy Fawkes' signature before and after torture. The children debate the means by which Catholic minds were turned to thoughts of terrorism. One 11-year-old says, 'Miss, them plotters were a bit like Al Qaeda – they thought they were freedom fighters, but it can't ever be right to kill people, can it?' It's a 'Je suis Charlie' moment, but these children don't want to mark or commemorate but to understand. In another school, Year 7s are looking at the Israeli–Palestinian conflict straight after a unit of work on the Holocaust. 'Is this another form of genocide?' asks one.

The children are being introduced to complexity. They are not being asked to find simple solutions, to apportion blame or to find certainty. They are being asked to ask questions. They are being asked to consider whether or not there are universal principles that make for a good person, or good actions, regardless of provocation. This is not the simplistic teaching of 'values'; it is not even 'making sense of'. It is simply exposing the frailty of human experience and exploring what is, and what it might be – possibility thinking.

When I see those young people working, thinking, becoming, I return in my mind to the images of the young presented to us in the media in 2011. This is not the only time that such portrayals have been used to define the poor and the young, and it seems to me that the images I am seeing are a culmination of a stereotypical representation – a repetition of sameness in which 'children can never be different, can never escape the enclosure of (repetitive) normativity',[32] even as this normativity functions as a depiction of deviance. These are the images that the young people in Eyam had been party to all their lives, from the imagined worlds of comedy (Harry Enfield's Wayne and Waynetta; Matt Lucas' Vicky Pollard) to the 'real' world of the news. They hear people who look like them being described as 'the violent young [who] ignore civilized boundaries which exist to protect the weak and the vulnerable',[33] when the possibility exists that they are the weak and the vulnerable. Their loyalties are confused and split.

To what extent are their identities being cemented by these overwhelmingly negative representations of young people like them? The boundaries of right/wrong and good/bad are blurred – they *sense* that they are other, and reclaim otherness as a defence. I am at a loss as to what to do. I retreat and think; return and think again. But, in the meantime, the children have moved on into their futures without me, while I come back, again and again, to the past. I don't want to fail in this way again, so I need to 'maximize the potential of that which returns',[34] moving from 'chaos to cosmos' and making 'necessity out of chance' through Deleuze's ethics of '*amor fati* ... the dignity of the event'.[35] When we seek, either in wider societal terms or in educational terms, to reduce difficulties to this point, we create a mode of oppression which seeks to control. As Biesta cautions, complexity reduction can be restraining.[36] And this creates an education system which is deeply uneducational and a society which is quick to blame and slow to learn.

Being sensible

One aspect of sense, explored above, relates to becoming sensitised and to sensing something of significance – a potential becoming. Another aspect revolves around the notion of ethics and responsibility to the subject of enquiry. Viewing data (which invariably involves others) carries responsibilities and can lead to unease. An amorphic researcher is nothing if not opportunistic:

When we take on the deconstructed researcher identity, we are transformed into tricksters who dandle about, questioning, playing, toying with any formulation of reality that stands as the paramount reality.[37]

But an amorphic teacher – an artisan – seizes upon opportunity not simply to 'make sense of' but to provide spaces for sensing to take place. In order for the latter to develop, the work of the former is helpful, but this creates a dissonance between protecting the rights of children and championing their rights by representing their experiences. As a result, I find myself in 'a pedagogical borderland, in the spaces where rhetoric, politics, parody, pastiche, performance, ethnography and critical cultural studies come together'.[38] I find myself somewhere on the edge of teaching, counselling, researching and being human, trying to navigate the ethical spaces of immanence. Much of the data I use is long gone and 'dead' – the flesh is gone, I pick at the bones. Where are the ethics at this late stage of decomposition? Elsewhere, I have described some serendipitous data as blowing in under the door (Finders keepers? Lost property?). Other stories have been carefully transcribed, permissions granted. Here, I recount data that came about due to surveillance, stealth and deception. All the data becomes felted together as matted, condensed, pressed fibres. Normal 'sensible' modes of ethics do not seem to help in deciding what is appropriate to use.

Faux pas

A 'studio' classroom in a secondary school. Pupils are in role as employees of an organisation that has been commissioned to develop an education programme tackling the issue of mental health. Their goal is both to improve their awareness of the complexity of mental health issues and save the NHS money. The 'client' is the Department of Health. I am in role as a junior minister for the department, paying a visit to the company to check on progress. There is a great deal of activity, debate and busy-ness in the room. But one boy is crying. As I enter, he comes up to me, ignoring the 'role'.

'Miss, I'm not doing this any more. It's stupid. They won't listen to me.'

'Who won't listen to you?'

'Them two – they won't let me in. They wouldn't let me hang about with them at break. He's my mate, but since *he* (he points to a third boy) came here they won't let me in.'

He is speaking in sharp bursts, struggling to breathe. He has tears and snot running down his face.

I feel frustrated – I was supposed to be observing the learning. I didn't want to have to deal with little boys falling out with each other. I try to maintain the role as I approach the other two boys.

'Gentlemen, I wondered if we could go to the meeting room to discuss the progress of your group.'

The boys exchange furtive glances – they look at the crying boy. He is still crying and staring at the floor. We walk in silence to the empty room next door. I sit down and take off my costume signifier.

'Might be better to do this out of role?'

They nod.

Boy 2: I don't know why he's crying. We ain't done nuffin.

Boy 1: You won't let me join in.

Boy 2: Cos you mess it up.

Boy 1: I don't.

Boy 2: You do … He does Miss – like we were getting statistics on mental health budget cos, you know, it costs the NHS billions like – and he kept trying to get on YouTube instead. He don't pull his weight.

Me: Why were you trying to go on YouTube?

He shrugs his shoulders, stares at the floor. Sniffs. There is a long silence.

Boy 2: He does it all the time, Miss – dickin' about like. He thinks it's funny, but it's just annoying.

Boy 1: You used to think it were funny an' all until he came.

Boy 2: Yeah, well.

Boy 1: We were mates till he came.

Boy 3: You still are mates. I'm not stopping you being mates.

Boy 1: You are.

Boy 3: I'm not.

Boy 2: He's not.

Boy 1: Yeah, he is – you make me feel .... neglected.

Boy 2: Neglected? Neglected? Don't talk to me about neglected. My mum's gone on holiday and I'm on me own for two weeks. I ain't got enough money for food, I have to go to me dad's, an' he's never there, so I walk all the way there, and then there's no one in, and then I have to walk all the way back, and you don't know what it's like. And I saved up all my bus money for weeks and weeks, and I bought a game, and it doesn't even work, and it was all a waste. And when her baby's born no one's gonna want me. No one wants me now.

Boy 2 starts to sob. The other boys look at him. Boy 1, who was originally crying, stops. Boy 3 puts his hands on the sobbing boy's back.

Boy 3: It's alright, it's alright.

Me: Boys, I think you need to go back to class and let him have a quiet moment.

The other two leave. We sit in silence for a moment.

Shit, I think. Shit. The video camera has been running the whole time.

I get up and stop the camera. I apologise. I get him a glass of water. I fetch the head of year. I explain to both of them that the video was running and recording the conversation, but I will delete it. And I do, but the conversation is alive in my head, and before I delete it I watch it again and then write it down in my field notes. I tell myself that it's alright – it will never see daylight – but a something has been sown.

I keep thinking about it all summer so, in September, when I'm in the school again, I ask if I can see the head of year and the boys again. I explain to them that I have written the story down and show them what I have written (up to 'We sit in silence for a moment') and explain that I would like to use this story in my work. That they and the school will remain anonymous. They all say that's OK – they can't see the harm. Boy 2 says 'I don't mind – everyone knows now, anyway, so I'm not bothered. Can't see why it's interesting though.'

I try to explain that it's not so much what was said, but how it came about – completely unexpectedly. I explain that I am interested in the unpredictable and unexpected. Boy 3 says, 'You've come to't right place then.' The bell goes.

> (Collated notes taken from journal and video,
> July and September 2010)

What was the sensible or responsible course of action? As a result of the unexpected encounter, the school established closer contact with the parents, conversations were brokered with mum and dad, and a proper custody arrangement was put in place. Social services monitored the situation. All this would have been possible without my publishing the story, so these outcomes cannot justify either the collection or the use of the data. I didn't switch the camera on – it had been left running by two pupils recording an interview in the room who had forgotten to turn it off. I did not intend to collect this data – it happened. It burst into being. But I did decide to use it. Is it possible that the consent is informed? I don't know. And what are the ethical boundaries of incidental data?

Bryant would conceptualise the issue as 'a problem based model of ethical composition' in that the event could not have been planned for and that it offered an opportunity for 'inventiveness'.[39] On one hand, I can hope to be open, to respect confidentiality, to ensure that I attempt to apply a 'proportionate reasoning strategy'[40] in which I remain 'intellectually honest',[41] admit mistakes, try to correct them, as far as possible, and move on. Sellers would urge me to ensure that I resist 'slipping into an institutional ethics discourse that relentlessly reduces children in stature and allocates all knowing power to the researcher'.[42] So the data has to matter. It has to elevate the tale from being merely cautionary, or worse, voyeuristic, to saying something of significance. And that burden becomes weighty. Look at how many quotes I have used to appease my guilt! Such is the burden of responsibility.

This is not just the ethical dilemma of the researcher, but also of the teacher. We find ourselves in such moral hinterlands every day – indeed, it is part of human experience. It is linked to loyalty; to the ethics of telling, not telling, retelling; to promises made and broken; to trust. For Deleuze, the matter of ethics is separated from that of morality, which he views as a system of judgements with attendant positions of authority and superiority. Instead, ethics allow for possibility to be explored – how was this possible? What are the implications? Where are the lines of flight?

Here we have an 'accident' – and 'in every event there is an accident: a moment of its actualization'.[43] To ignore the accident is to ignore the potentiality of the event. There is a doubling of meaning. It is both ethical and unethical to use the data/event emerging from the accident, and oscillating in the in-between space (not of 'is it this OR that' but in the acceptance that 'it is both this AND that'), there is the need to be 'sensible'. In this sense, the faux pas can be viewed differently – as a set of assemblages which deterritorialised and reterritorialised an event. Deleuzian ethics are not amoral or nihilistic – they support a notion of justice which is about the responsibility of paying attention to that which occurs. And this justice forces discomfort on me as I flip Mobius-like between feeling that it is OK and it is not OK. I squirm even as I write it – unable to get off the hook of feeling somehow irresponsible in using the data. I squirmed when I saw the light on the camera, and when I asked for permission – knowing it would be granted and knowing that the permission might stem from an inability to say no. I squirmed as I deleted the data in a previous draft and then again when I reinstated it. There has been a physical intra-action between the data and my self – my sense of who I am. It is not possible for me to change what happened, but it is possible to reassemble an 'ongoing practice … for living justly'.[44] In this view, making sense of the responsibility of representation becomes irrelevant: 'all of us are "groupuscules". Representation no longer exists; there's only action.'[45]

In the early days of writing my thesis, I struggled with these questions – feeling guilty that I was taking anecdotes from the classroom and mining them for material in order to achieve a doctoral qualification. And even as it morphed from thesis to book, I worried that, in finding a wider audience, the exploitation might be all the more present. St Pierre writes of this burden as a troubling at the edge of a field of work situated in 'mourning',[46] and I feel this as I carry the burden of these children. The menace of my greedy, data-grabbing researcher self is at odds with the self-image I carried as a teacher, and I got stuck. This dithering at the edges requires working with and using 'practices of failure'[47] that allow me to reposition these concerns and to move – not forwards, but between this ethical space into slippages where I can occupy smooth space. For St Pierre, drawing on Deleuze, this involves 'a tangled responsibility' in which 'either ethics makes no sense at all, or this is what it means and has nothing else to say: *not to be unworthy of what happens to us*'.[48] It is here, then, in attempting not to be unworthy of these and the other children inhabiting this text, that my ethical framework lies.

To be worthy, I need to make the children more than text – more than characters in a story. This is true of the boys described above and the children in Eyam. They become assimilated into me and impact on future children. They have become teacher – living in memory and reminding me that children's experiences, bodies, friendships and expectations all need to be taken into account. They matter. Their stories marked a jolting deterritorialisation for me – a refocusing on the issues of justice surrounding representation. I ask, as I look at their stories, 'is it possible to effect change in the world, if society is only and always a text?'[49] Is it possible to commit to utilising the data, to put it to work in praxis, so that I become a teacher who notices, improvises, acts? I return to the data in a constant movement, toing and froing from past to present, in which I try to reach what Derrida called 'the democracy to come'.[50] I must make it all matter. Doing this requires becoming 'an apprentice to signs',[51] so that I am capable of responding. The two extracts of data I provide above are events, and an event, according to Bogue, 'is an encounter and the essence of learning, as well as thinking, resides in encounters'.[52] As I moved back into teaching, I held these events close so that I could 'work to create encounters' and impact on the lives of young people yet-to-be-met, even if there is little I can do to help those I have left behind.

Denzin and Lincoln posit the idea that the eighth phase of qualitative research (the future) is predicated on a 'pressing need to show how the practices of qualitative research can help change the world in positive ways'.[53] Jun and Smith explore this further through Deleuzian lenses in their book, *Deleuze and Ethics*, in which they consider how the possibilities inherent in the philosophy might provide modes of change and resistance.[54] I share with Biesta a belief that the same is true of education. We need to move away from asking simplistic questions, like 'What works?', and instead be probing and raking for a wider, more meaningful exploration of the values and purposes of education. Biesta issues a clear warning of the reductive nature of such thinking, not denying the role of 'evidence' altogether, but asking important questions about its proper use and limitations.[55]

Braidotti reminds us that while Deleuze rejects morality, he presents 'ethics of forces and affects'. Here, the 'proper object of ethical inquiry is not the subject's moral intentionality or rational consciousness, as much as the effects of truth and power that his or her actions are likely to have upon others in the world'.[56] These effects sit at the edges of experience – in the voids, the split moments, the affective moments – which leave traces. And it is only when attending to, and exploring, the creation and developing meanings of these traces that the nuances and the artistry of teaching can be explored. This involves writing these children's stories into my story; to weave them, and to ask simply, 'Is it safe?' To not be bound by 'morality', which Deleuze conceived as a 'set of constraining rules', but to remain mindful of 'ethics' – 'a set of "facilitative" [facultative] rules that evaluate[s] what we do, say and think according to the immanent mode of existence that it implies'.[57]

This view of the work brings together the idea of sense – of making sense, of sensation – emotion and of being sensible. Ethics and reminds us that, in a Deleuzian frame, all are connected and intra-active. I hope that this, and other data in this thesis, meet that criterion – that they exist as modes of becoming. I hope that they are helping me to be a more literate teacher as I return and return to their tales, and that the worthiness of the retelling will be in my present/past/future practice. For I carry them as I go, and there are miles yet to be travelled.

/Did I do alright boys? Did I make it work?/

/You hardly even mentioned us.
You talked about yersen/

Notes

1. G. Biesta, Why 'What Works' Still Won't Work: From Evidence-Based Education to Value-Based Education, *Studies in Philosophy and Education* 29(5) (2010): 491–503.
2. G. Deleuze and F. Guattari, *Difference and Repetition* (New York: Continuum, 2004 [1968]).
3. C. Colebrook, *Deleuze: A Guide for the Perplexed* (London: Continuum, 2006), p. 115.
4. A. Damasio, *Descartes' Error: Emotion, Reason and the Human Mind* (London: Vintage, 2006).
5. Colebrook, *Deleuze: A Guide for the Perplexed*, p. 115.
6. G. Deleuze, *The Logic of Sense* (London: Continuum, 2004); G. Deleuze, *Cinema 1: The Movement-Image*, tr. H. Tomlinson and B. Habberjam (Minneapolis, MN: University of Minnesota Press, 1986). Available at: http://projectlamar.com/media/Gilles-Deleuze-Cinema-1-The-Movement-Image.pdf.
7. B. McInnis, Methods of Alice Physics, *Journal of Physics A: Mathematical and General* 31(15) (1998): 3607.
8. V. Dukic, The Two-Fold Structure of the Death-Event (2009). Available at: http://artsciweb.concordia.ca/ojs/index.php/gnosis/article/viewFile/83/45.
9. Deleuze, *The Logic of Sense*, p. 11.
10. Deleuze, *The Logic of Sense*, p. 17.
11. I. Semetsky, Deleuze, Edusemiotics and the Logic of Affects, in I. Semetsky and D. Masny (eds), *Deleuze and Education* (Edinburgh: Edinburgh University Press, 2013), pp. 215–235 at p. 216.
12. N. Denzin, The Reflexive Interview and a Performative Social Science, *Qualitative Research* 1(1) (2001): 23–46 at 24.
13. N. Denzin and Y. Lincoln, *Collecting and Interpreting Qualitative Materials* (Thousand Oaks, CA: Sage, 2008), p. viii.
14. S. Kemmis, What Is To Be Done? The Place of Action Research. Keynote address to the Collaborative Action Research Network Annual Conference, Athens, Greece, 29 October to 1 November 2009.
15. Denzin and Lincoln, *Collecting and Interpreting Qualitative Materials*, p. 3.
16. Hansard, HL vol. 719, col. 1006 (16 June 2010). Available at: http://www.publications.parliament.uk/pa/ld201011/ldhansrd/text/100616-0006.htm.
17. E. Burman, Avoid: The Big Society [seminar presentation] (2013). Available at: http://www.slideserve.com/orpah/avoid-the-big-society.

18. G. Deleuze and F. Guattari, *What is Philosophy?*, tr. H. Tomlinson and G. Burchell (New York: Columbia University Press, 1994), p. 3.

19. I. Shor and P. Freire, What is the 'Dialogical Method' of Teaching?, *Journal of Education* 169 (3) (1987): 11–31.

20. But see N. Noddings, *Educating Moral People: A Caring Alternative to Moral Education* (London: Teachers College Press, 2002).

21. R. Coe, C. Aloisi, S. Higgins and L. E. Major, *What Makes Great Teaching? Review of the Underpinning Research* (London: Sutton Trust, 2014). Available at: http://www.suttontrust.com/researcharchive/great-teaching/.

22. G. Deleuze quoted in P. Hallward, *Out of This World: Deleuze and the Philosophy of Creation* (London: Verso, 2006), p. 43.

23. M. Sellers, *Young Children Becoming Curriculum: Deleuze, Te Whāriki and Curricular Understandings* (New York: Routledge, 2013), p. 2.

24. P. Lather, Drawing the Line at Angels: Working the Ruins of Feminist Ethnography, *Qualitative Studies in Education* 10(3) (1997): 285–304 at 299.

25. I. Semetsky, Not by Breadth Alone: Imagining a Self-Organising Classroom, *Complicity: An International Journal of Complexity and Education* 2(1) (2005): 19–36 at 31.

26. Semetsky, Not by Breadth Alone, 31.

27. F. Nietzsche quoted in D. Hoy, *The Time of Our Lives: A Critical History of Temporality* (Cambridge, MA: MIT Press, 2009), p. 162.

28. C. Colebrook, *Deleuze: A Guide for the Perplexed* (London: Continuum, 2006), p. 30.

29. J. Protevi, Deleuze, Guattari and Emergence, *Paragraph: A Journal of Modern Critical Theory* 29(2) (2006): 19–39 at 21.

30. T. Ryall, The Riots Show Why We Need To Listen To Young People, *The Guardian* (15 September 2011). Available at: http://www.guardian.co.uk/society/joepublic/2011/sep/15/radio-1-big-conversation-young-people.

31. M. Riddell, London Riots: The Underclass Lashes Out, *The Telegraph* (8 August 2011). Available at: http://www.telegraph.co.uk/news/uknews/law-and-order/8630533/Riots-the-underclass-lashes-out.html.

32. L. Jones, Becoming Child/Becoming Dress, *Global Studies of Childhood* 3(3) (2013): 289–296 at 290.

33. M. Gove quoted in J. Schostak, *Maladjusted Schooling: Deviance, Social Control and Individuality in Secondary Schooling* [Kindle edn] (London: Routledge, 2012).

34. J. Wallin, Morphologies for a Pedagogical Life, in D. Masny and I. Semetsky (eds), *Deleuze and Education* (Edinburgh: Edinburgh University Press, 2013), pp. 196–214 at p. 208.

35. J. Philippe, Nietzsche and Spinoza: New Personae in a New Plane of Thought, in J. Khalfa (ed.), *An Introduction to the Philosophy of Gilles Deleuze* (London: Continuum, 2003), pp. 50–64 at p. 52.

36. Biesta, Why 'What Works' Still Won't Work, 498.

37. C. Rambo Ronai, Sketching with Derrida: An Ethnography of a Researcher/Erotic Dancer, *Qualitative Inquiry* 4 (1998): 405–420 at 419.

38. D. Conquergood, Ethnography, Rhetoric and Performance, *Quarterly Journal of Speech* 78 (1992): 80–97 at 80.

39. L. Bryant, The Ethics of the Event: Deleuze and Ethics without Αρχή, in N. Jun and D. Smith (eds), *Deleuze and Ethics* (Edinburgh: Edinburgh University Press, 2011), pp. 21–43 at p. 22.

40. M. Angrosino, Recontextualising Observation: Ethnography, Pedagogy and the Prospects for a Progressive Political Agenda, in N. Denzin and Y. Lincoln (eds), *Collecting and Interpreting Qualitative Materials* (Thousand Oaks, CA: Sage, 2008), pp. 161–183 at p. 173.

41. F. Grinnell, The Impact of Ethics on Research, *Chronicle of Higher Education* (The Chronicle Review Section 2) (4 October 2002).

42. Sellers, *Young Children Becoming Curriculum*, p. xx.

43. V. Dukic, The Two-Fold Structure of the Death-Event.

44. K. Barad, *Meeting the Universe Halfway: Quantum Physics and the Entanglement of Matter and Meaning* (Durham, NC and London: Duke University Press, 2007), p. x.

45. G. Deleuze and M. Foucault, Intellectuals and Power, in D. F. Bouchard (ed.), *Language, Counter-Memory, Practice: Selected Essays and Interviews* (Ithaca, NY: Cornell University Press, 1977), pp. 206–207.

46. E. A. St Pierre, Nomadic Inquiry in the Smooth Spaces of the Field: A Preface, in E. A. St Pierre and W. S. Pillow (eds), *Working the Ruins: Feminist Poststructural Theory and Methods in Education* (London: Routledge, 2000), pp. 258–284 at p. 283.

47. P. Lather, Fertile Obsession: Validity after Poststructuralism, *Sociological Quarterly* 34(4) (1993): 673–693 at 683.

48. L. Richardson and E. A. St Pierre, Writing: A Method of Enquiry, in N. Denzin and Y. Lincoln (eds), *Collecting and Interpreting Qualitative Materials* (Thousand Oaks, CA: Sage, 2008), pp. 473–501 at p. 491 (my emphasis).

49. Denzin and Lincoln, *Collecting and Interpreting Qualitative Materials*, p. 27.

50. J. Derrida, *Speech and Phenomena: And Other Essays on Husserl's Theory of Signs* (Evanston, IL: Northwest University Press, 1963), p. 84.

51. G. Deleuze quoted in D. Masny, Multiple Literacies Theory: Exploring Spaces, in I. Semetsky and D. Masny (eds), *Deleuze and Education* (Edinburgh: Edinburgh University Press, 2013), pp. 1–21 at p. 15.

52. R. Bogue, The Master Apprentice, in I. Semetsky and D. Masny (eds), *Deleuze and Education* (Edinburgh: Edinburgh University Press, 2013), pp. 21–37 at p. 33.

53. Denzin and Lincoln, *Collecting and Interpreting Qualitative Materials*, p. viii.

54. N. Jun and D. Smith (eds), *Deleuze and Ethics* (Edinburgh: Edinburgh University Press, 2011).

55. Biesta, Why 'What Works' Still Won't Work.

56. R. Braidotti, *Transpositions: On Nomadic Ethics* (Cambridge: Polity Press, 2006), p. 14.

57. D. Smith, Deleuze and the Question of Desire: Toward an Immanent Theory of Ethics, *Parrhesia* 2 (2007): 66–78 at 67. Available at: http://www.parrhesiajournal.org/parrhesia02/parrhesia02_smith.pdf.

Chapter 7

A MATTER OF (R)EVOLUTION: MACRO, MICRO, NANO RESISTANCE

That sir which serves and seeks for gain,
And follows but for form,
Will pack when it begins to rain,
And leave thee in the storm,
But I will tarry; the fool will stay,
And let the wise man fly:
The knave turns fool that runs away;
The fool no knave, perdy.

King Lear, Act II, sc. iv

Previous plateaus have examined concepts, and through them I have attempted to reframe and reposition myself as a teacher. Here, I consider the impact of that thinking in terms of resistance. The plateau has three views. From a distance, the macro view, I explore the educational landscape within the context of Deleuze's exploration of Foucault's notion of control societies,[1] and I ask what actions might be taken to reframe and reposition our understanding of what we're looking at. In the micro view, standing on the plateau and looking around me, I examine the matter of pedagogy as a means of reframing the curriculum – a reclamation of content and style from within the school. Finally, at the nano level, I attend to the compositional elements of assemblages within the learning process itself, and I explore the possibility of becoming Deleuzian in my own classroom practice. This involves a shifting perspective – tri-focal seeing. To borrow a filmic reference, we are moving from a long shot to a mid shot to a close-up.

To become Deleuzian in the classroom does not, as Roy points out, demand reform or revolution. The difference is to be found in the 'subversive power of the very small and minor "flections"; secret lines of disorientation'.[2] I explore whether these flections can open up spaces for Deleuzian pedagogy, while allowing the teacher to maintain the level of conformity which allows his/her survival within the institution. I examine how such a pedagogy might function as a mode of resistance against the controlling influences affecting both teachers and pupils. These 'modest acts of resistance'[3] take place in the everyday where small acts of becoming can occur. They are not, however, unproblematic. In attempting to find space for the individual to thrive, there is a danger that the overarching system remains intact and unchallenged. It is important to examine the assemblages of those controlling bodies and to ask pertinent macro questions while developing micro and nano practices which seek to build alternative futures, rather than demanding the immediate revolution of current systems.[4] Such noisy actions may only alert authority to the presence of threat and, thereby, cause mobilisation and modulation.

Macro (r)evolution: introduction

I think of resistance as a form of evolution. In biological terms, evolution is linked to Deleuzian notions of desire; the impetus of survival (becoming other) is the ultimate desire of both organic and non-organic material. Evolution is not a conscious process – it is not something that happens in relation to conscious 'will' – and it is external to the individual. It is, however, a manifestation of desire. Here I use it in a metaphorical sense, and ask whether or not it is possible to rise above the self-serving survivalist desires of human nature and, perhaps, conceptualise evolution as a collective, conscious process of improvement which moves beyond the survival of institution, teacher and tradition and into the development of possibility – the potential to 'become other' and to thrive rather than survive. In doing so, we need to do more than evolve. We need to (r)evolve – to keep on reflecting and returning, marking out difference and changing the way we do things.

Brown reminds us that even the freedom to choose a course of action can paradoxically spell the end of freedom in binding us to the choice.

She refers to Foucault's warning that true freedom 'lies neither in institutions nor in ideals and proclamations, but only in practices'.[5] These are perhaps the actions that Arendt describes or Deleuzian actions of effect, described by Cole as that which 'imbues the use of language in pedagogic acts with an intense affective resonance and the multiple traces of becoming that might be present in any teaching and learning context'.[6] Wherever they happen, I contend that they need to be shared and connect with others in order to create networks of resistance that are truly rhizomatic; not necessarily the same – networks of agreement – but connected by autonomy of purpose and a recognition of complexity. This is the intention when I speak of collective (r)evolution. When we view resistance in Deleuzian ways, the notion of 'grassroots movements' takes on new and powerful meaning. I explore some ways that this might take hold through the use of technology in 'A Matter of Hoping' (Chapter 8). But first we need to understand what we are dealing with.

Macro (r)evolution: the curriculum in a control society

It is over 2,000 years since Cicero used the term 'curriculum' to mean a relatively contextualised living and learning process,[7] and since then a great deal has been written on the subject. Egan argues that, in spite of this, little has changed in that the focus remains on the 'what' is to be taught,[8] without attending to the fact that in the intervening 2,000 years there has been such an accumulation of knowledge that it has become practically impossible to cover what Arnold famously asserted was the primary aim of education: to teach 'the best which has been thought and said'.[9] Nevertheless, government rhetoric around the world insists on attempting to fix what should be known, leading to charges that knowledge is 'historically contingent and politically determined' in order to 'maintain social privilege',[10] and that the imparting of that knowledge is managed under a system of control and compliance.[11] Successive governments have conceptualised the curriculum as a noun – a holding place in which all privileged knowledge is contained in a set of objectives. Elsewhere, researchers and teachers alike have questioned this premise and instead argued that the curriculum is a complex system of values and processes, and as such is almost impossible to control and impose.[12] This difficulty in pinning down even the definition of curriculum has led to fierce battles, which are shored up by the belief that the curriculum acts as a container – for some a place of clarity and guidance, for others a place of oppression and control. If we view the curriculum through the concept of a 'disciplinary society', encompassing 'vast spaces of enclosure',[13] then we begin to understand the battle for curriculum as one that is rooted in power.

In England, since 1988 when the first 'national' curriculum model was introduced, many concerns have been raised about the politicisation of the curriculum as a result of successive governments attempting to impose their views about what constitutes valid or desirable knowledge on to the education system.[14] This phenomena has not been unique to this country. Governments in the UK and US have attempted to lay down the core knowledge and skills required of pupils over a period of years – a movement which some have seen as an 'intensification and generalization of normalizing apparatuses of disciplinarity'[15] – which has led to an alienation from creativity and acceptance of difference within school systems. In the UK, the curriculum review of 2011 created a great deal of controversy,[16] and was accused of being 'particularly awkward and poorly managed'[17] by a secretary of state intent on imposing his own preferences in spite of advice offered to him. While that particular secretary of state has gone, his policies live on as part of a global phenomenon in which it is believed that the market can provide solutions to societal needs. The vitriol with which market-led advocates protect their position reminds me of the statement by Deleuze that 'our social system is totally without tolerance'.[18] Detractors are labelled 'The Blob' and their concerns are denied as 'Marxist' by the outriders that Jones proposes exist to protect the interests of the Establishment.[19]

In the UK, it looked like this was a battle over disciplinary structure, but the 2011 curriculum review marked a departure from others that had gone before. For the first time, not all state-funded schools were to be required to teach the national curriculum – academies and free schools would be exempt. This led to accusations that the curriculum was now being used as a punishment for failure to comply with government policy and, in turn, to a questioning of the need to have a curriculum at all.[20]

I would argue that it is not the curriculum itself but the attendant accountability structures which are forming the constraints that are characterised by what Deleuze calls a 'control society'. There is an appearance of freedom – the 'walls' of the curriculum are crumbling – but, in fact, there is even greater control. As such, examinations, progress measures and Ofsted might be viewed as a form of second assemblage as conceptualised by Guattari. These structures sit within what he calls 'a capitalist regime proper',[21] in which impulse and creativity are ordered and reduced to measurable outcomes. This second assemblage seeks to impose structure through 'dualisms' and 'binary opposition'.[22] This can be seen in the language of politicians in both the UK and USA in which the binaries of 'progressive' vs. 'traditional', 'good teachers' vs. 'enemies of promise' emerge, and through which debates about knowledge, curriculum and accountability become entrenched.[23] Advocates of what Sahlberg calls the Global Education Reform Movement (GERM)[24] press these ideas forward in the name of reform, but the very idea of reform is problematic:

The notion of reform is … stupid and hypocritical. Either reforms are designed by people who claim to be representative, who make a profession of speaking for others, and they lead to a division of power, to a distribution of this new power which is constantly increased by a double repression: or they arise from the complaints and demands of those concerned … this latter is no longer reform but revolutionary action that questions the … totality of power and the hierarchy that maintains it.[25]

We have seen in the hyperbolic language of Michael Gove (though he is far from alone and others have taken up his cry), in response to the 'complaints and demands' of teachers and children, a double repression emerging. There is the repression of accountability to data through Ofsted and league tables and the repression of practice through a conflation of curriculum with pedagogy (for example, in September 2014, the teaching of systematic phonics became a legal requirement – the first time a pedagogy has been dictated in law). In conflating curriculum with pedagogy, governments move towards a greater level of control of classroom activity, while at the same time appearing to champion freedom – a process which started under the Labour government in 1997 with the development of the National Strategies. In addition, fragmenting school clusters – which were traditionally geographic under local authorities – into isolated units (free schools) or ideological chains (academies) allows government to privilege one ideology over another and to impose greater levels of control. All of this contributes to a downward pressure on the teacher to comply, even as he/she is told they are being given greater freedom.

In such ways, the oppressive controls of the curriculum are not being removed but merely disguised. To take one example, let's look at the impact of the work of E. D. Hirsch on education policy. Hirsch was greatly admired by Michael Gove, who until his departure from office in 2014 had been the most controversial and long serving secretary of state for education we had known. His ideas have also impacted on US education policy in the form of the Common Core. Under Gove's ministry, Hirsch's profile became significant and his name was used in speeches repeatedly. The central tenet of Hirsch's educational philosophy is the role and importance of a highly prescriptive core knowledge curriculum through which it is believed that cultural capital can be built.[26] Gove stopped short of implementing a core knowledge curriculum as policy, but there was a more subtle imposition. Free schools and academies, such as Toby Young's West London Free School and Conservative minister Lord Nash's Pimlico Academy – both of which follow a Hirschian core curriculum – were frequently praised by Gove.

The curriculum at Pimlico Academy was created by the Core Knowledge Foundation, the director of which was Daisy Christodoulou, a young and inexperienced TeachFirst teacher, who left teaching rather rapidly after qualifying in order to take up a position as a curriculum adviser. She has since been appointed as a member of the Carter Review into what should be done about Initial Teacher Training in the UK. Christodoulou was also frequently praised by Gove as an 'excellent teacher',[27] in spite of the fact that she was not a teacher, and her book, which was highly critical of 'progressive' teaching methods, received high praise in the USA from Hirsch himself.[28] There was a clear message on both sides of the Atlantic: schools following the 'right' curriculum would receive approval from government. Christodoulou's book was swiftly followed by two more in the same vein. The first, *Prisoners of the Blob*, was written by Toby Young and published by Civitas, the think tank pushing the Core Curriculum.[29] The second, *Progressively Worse*, was written by Robert Peal, an NQT at Toby Young's school and a former education spokesperson for Civitas.[30] There was suddenly a great deal of noise coming from a small corner, setting out a clear belief that a certain set of curriculum values and pedagogies were preferable to others. As a result, a specific range of knowledge is privileged over broader offers.

The EBacc measurement in the UK, which ensures that schools are judged on the numbers of children passing five or more GCSEs (including English, maths, science, a modern foreign language and either history or geography), led to other subjects immediately being relegated to second-class status. A report by the Education Select Committee in 2011 reported an alarming drop in arts subjects as a direct consequence of the EBacc,[31] and others have noted its negative impact.[32] As such, we see a potential movement from the 'moulding' of the vast spaces of disciplinary societies (i.e. the national curriculum enacted in schools) to the 'modulation' of the control society. Those attempting to retain power are engaging in supposed reform while, in fact, they are simply recasting the system in a modulating form designed to take on the appearance of freedom when it is in fact simply another weapon. There is no longer a need for government to prescribe the curriculum (although it wishes to be seen to do so); the curriculum becomes controlled by accountability measures – it has become a modulating cast.[33] The content of SATs, GCSE and A level papers dictate the enacted curriculum. This form of control allows for swift change without consultation. Why spend time and money on curriculum consultation when a rapid adjustment of an accountability measure will impact on the curriculum directly? In such ways, control becomes 'like a sieve whose mesh will transmute from point to point'.[34] The same mode of thinking extends to the demand for evidence, which as Biesta warns leads to a 'democratic deficit' in which the supposed outcomes of the evidence override and undermine the professional integrity of the individual teacher.[35]

Macro (r)evolution: the problems with resisting the control society

Advocates of the GERM ideology argue that core knowledge should sit at the heart of the curriculum. They consider the curriculum to be a way of ensuring wider inclusivity by allowing all children to access the knowledge base of the ruling classes. However, their approach is reductive because while they resist narrow goals of providing purely functional skills, they remain tied into an 'attempt to homogenize and limit the signs and processes of learning, for example, to functioning within representationalist ideologies and specific needs such as those of the market'.[36] They propose a pedagogy of 'direct instruction' in order to ensure that the knowledge is embedded in the mind of the child, and contest the role of 'nature' in the formation of the 'intellect'. In short, they position themselves firmly within oppositional concepts of 'natural' and 'intellectual', 'discovery' and 'instruction'.

Within a capitalist assemblage, the notion of the individual succeeding, but only as an economic unit, is predominant – O'Sullivan cites the Nike slogan, 'Just Do It!', as an example of this.[37] But it is inherent in education policy too. In his statement to parliament on the new national curriculum, Michael Gove stated:

These changes will reinforce our drive to raise standards in our schools. They will ensure that the new national curriculum provides a rigorous basis for teaching, provides a benchmark for all schools to improve their performance, and gives children and parents a better guarantee that every student will acquire the knowledge to succeed in the modern world.[38]

This language, which is to be found in the mouths of politicians across the globe, situates the learner as a passive recipient in whose best interests learning is delivered to them. Both learner and teacher follow the instructions issued to them in a world suffering from a 'systematic lack of imagination [characterised by] the hopeless acquiescence of the powerless to those in power, coupled with the latter's insistence that everything is the way it is because, in some sense, it could not be otherwise'.[39] This world removes the agency of learning from both child and teacher, standing in direct opposition to a Deleuzian concept of learning 'with'. Outcomes are categorised in terms of 'performance' in which 'standards' are 'driven'.[40] All of these words conceptualise learning as linear and out of the control of the learner/passenger.

Wallin, taking Deleuze's interpretation of Nietzsche's *Thus Spoke Zarathustra* as a model for understanding the imposition of the curriculum on the pedagogical life of the teacher and child, argues that the curriculum becomes 'a power of stratification'.[41] Hence, learning becomes work, and 'work has become our foe'.[42] It is not only the structures of controlled accountability that bind us, but also the language of educational discourse. When MacLure points to the use of language in policy-making, we might envisage Nietzsche's camel, navigating his desert and adapting to the climate by taking on dominant discourses in order to perform better:

Like any discourse therefore, these policies impose structures, levels and taxonomies on the flux of experience. They set limits on the ways that the world can be viewed and construed, determine what can and can't be said, and establish what will count as truth. They institute orders of importance amongst entities and concepts, and assert which ones 'belong' together. Most significantly of all, they define what kind of subject – teacher, student, inspector, researcher – it is possible to be. Those who speak the language of the National Strategies, or of Ofsted inspection, or the Research Assessment Exercise, necessarily bend themselves into the new shapes afforded by their disciplinary syntax and hierarchies of significance.[43]

The fact that these discourses transmute so frequently makes the camel's life even more difficult. The camel-teacher knows that it is necessary to carry some of the discourses forward, but it is difficult to know which ones are necessary and which are not (it is always more difficult to discard knowledge than it is to acquire it). As such, teachers become overloaded with extras which make their jobs impossible to achieve. In the face of impossibility, we tend to cling to what we know or, at least, what we feel we understand, because this gives us the appearance of being in control of a process. We see this when teachers worry about changes such as the abolition of levels (Levels are dead! Long live levels!). Deleuze and Guattari point out this inherent contradiction in their work on desire – the subject desiring freedom from capitalism is also the subject who desires the products that keep capitalism alive. The teacher who desires freedom from Ofsted is also the teacher who desires to be told what to do. The child who desires freedom from the test also desires to know what mark they got and how they compare with their peers. These contradictions are human, but they make resistance difficult. The challenge is to find alternative ways of meeting desire without capitulating to the system. Not an easy or straightforward task, and even less so when the landscape is shifting and fragmenting so rapidly.

The pervading influence of Ofsted drives many camel-teachers into a set of gaming behaviours which undermine the credibility of the profession:

The vast majority of teachers went into teaching for one of two reasons, and often for both; they loved children or they loved a subject. But for many, within a year or two, the focus of their effort is neither what children need, or what they could do to improve and develop their own knowledge. The focus is Ofsted. It is as if we, as a profession, are engaged in a game of football where we are all running around after the referee instead of the ball.[44]

These gaming behaviours are, of course, not common to all. There has been a long tradition of resisting such controls, notably at the Summerhill School, but also through the pedagogical models of Steiner and Montessori and the many resistant projects that have been documented throughout the previous century.[45] There has always been innovation. But it seems to me that we are in a new era in which innovation itself is being appropriated as a tool of control. The fracturing of local authority networks, the globalisation of the curriculum debate (fuelled by international test comparisons), and the dismantling of the education sector into independent networks and chains of private enterprise and sponsorship are new and make innovation the privilege of the elite. Only the independent sector has freedom to innovate on a macro level.

Academies and free schools (or charter schools in the USA) may be told that they are 'free', but they are still accountable to Ofsted or school districts. In the UK, there are echoes in Ofsted's treatment of some of the more innovative free schools to its treatment of Summerhill in 2000. In 2013, the Discovery Free School in West Sussex failed its inspection having been described by Ofsted as having 'serious shortcomings' because 'too many pupils are in danger of leaving the school without being able to read and write properly.' Inspectors concluded that, as a result, 'pupils are unlikely to flourish in their secondary schools and future lives'.[46] It was a case of 'progressive intentions subverted by a reactionary regime'.[47] The school's ethos that children should be allowed to develop at their own rates did not correspond with the expectations of Ofsted (a similar disconnect had led to the perceived failure of Summerhill). But there is no one championing the Discovery School. Few schools have the courage, resources or media attention that were available to Summerhill, and discomfort with the ideology of free schools has left the Discovery School with no friends on the left – a by-product of the confusions caused by the modulating cast.

Some free schools, such as the Family School and School 21 in London, have established themselves as democratic or innovative schools in order to step out of or resist the mould, but they are all ultimately held accountable to Ofsted. If the examination results are poor, the school is in trouble. And even where there are no exam results to measure – when schools are too new to have produced them – the perception of what is deemed to be acceptable, in terms of leading to good examination results, drives Ofsted judgements. In other words, state-funded schools are free to roam in chains.

Micro (r)evolution: resisting simplicity

To think more subversively, we need to shift our view to the micro – here we see another picture. If we conceptualise the macro as a set of what Guattari calls 'royal roads',[48] then what weapons do we have at our disposal to fracture or disrupt them? And is it possible to do so without placing our schools (and ourselves) in the firing line? When even pedagogy is dictated by 'what Ofsted wants', rather than 'what children need', what course of action is open to us? Pleasing Ofsted has become a matter of survival for teachers and schools, and it has become hugely distracting. Subverting this practice requires the creation of 'optional rules',[49] and a series of personal and ethical codes that allow teachers to coexist within the dominant power schema. O'Sullivan describes this as a 'folding in of the outside – by the subject on his or her own terms – that constitutes a freedom of sorts from subjection'.[50] To do so requires confidence and a belief that there is value in what is taking place, regardless of the judgement placed upon it. This is not a question of arrogantly pressing ahead with our own agenda regardless of what others think, but attending to detail and recognising complexity – sitting in the AND space.

If we view the process of a lesson observation through the lens of multiple literacy theory as a series of assemblages, then we can get a sense of the complexity of moving from macro to micro to nano in terms of accountability structures. The observer arrives with a complex set of criteria stemming from their understanding of their training and the agenda of their organisation, a preconceived idea of the school based on data, and the multiply layered personal and professional experiences which have constituted the perception that they are, have been or would be capable of being 'good' teachers. It is this latter complexity that leads to the many reported incidents of inconsistency between inspectors during inspections. Also add to that macro complexity – the series of assemblages when an inspector enters the room. I have taken the following example from a personal experience, and it is remembered rather than having been recorded at the time. The point of view of the inspector and child are, of course, fictionalised – I could not read their minds. Note, also, that only the words in bold were actually spoken. This data 'happened' almost a decade ago – what you read are traces of memory, the residue.

Teacher: **Could you open the boxes on your desks and have a look inside.** This is not 'my classroom' – is he looking at the displays? They're not mine. I don't like that poster. It's not mine. What on earth is Dylan doing?

Dylan: **Why are we not in the drama studio?** That's not fair, we're going to have to do work. There's a fly on my desk. Is it dead? No, its legs are twitching. Cool.

Inspector: Nice, orderly room, like the displays. Children are interested in the box. I'm interested in the box – what's inside? Ooh, hang on, what's that one doing?

Caitlin: (screaming) **Urgh, urgh, he squashed a fly with his ruler.**

Teacher: Not now, not now, please God, not now. Give me the ruler, Dylan, give me the f***ing ruler. Smile, smile. **Back in your seats – it's just a dead fly. Now, there are far more interesting things in that box – what have you found, Dylan?**

There is an intensity of chronos in this exchange. This is all about *now* – what happens now is crucial. But aion is impinging all the time. The fly carries with it a threat to my future. The inspector brings in assumptions from the past. The habits of the past are impacting on Dylan who wants to be in the studio. But time slows in the present. Managing the present becomes all, while simultaneously picking up speed in the potential future impact of the fly. There is a throb of immanence as the assemblages compete.

I fall

Sharp suit – tradition/judgement

Blobs of discarded adhesive tack

Twee cutsy kitten poster

Billy looks thin

Buzz

Chit-chat

Chairs scraping

Don't sit there – sit there

Thirst

Heat – is this room too warm?

Buzz

Ooh – relief

Ooh – panic

Gathering, heads closing in

Shriek

Heart beating faster

Face feels hot

Sick

Breathe, breathe, smile

It is a moment of infinites – lines of flight. The lesson will now have shot off in multiple directions. For many of the children, the content of the box is forever linked with the dead fly, but whether they experience that as excitement, disgust, distraction or curiosity will be individualised. For me, the image of a dead fly forever links to a stressful classroom experience. The inspector may have no recollection of fly or box, because to her, the assemblage of fly, fear, disappointment, hope may not have been evident. The inspector can never know what assemblages are taking place and how these impact on learning. What they seek to evidence is at best tokenistic. But every element has been eventful:

[T]he world is made of events, and nothing but events: happenings rather than things, verbs rather than nouns, processes rather than substances. Becoming is the deepest dimension of Being. Even a seemingly solid and permanent object is an event; or, better, a multiplicity and a series of events.[51]

The fly, the ruler, they were not nouns – objects – but events taking on actions – the distracting, enticing, repulsing fly flying; the swooshing, squashing ruler ruling over matters of life and death. All are momentarily becoming other. Does the inspector note and assess the complexity of this? Does he / she consider its impact on the learning / communicating / negotiating intra-actions of the classroom? Of course not, but these things impact and matter. They affect in significant ways.

There is no AND space in an Ofsted inspection, although there are movements towards flexibility in the reforms proposed by the former national director for inspection reform, Michael Cladingbowl. For example, it seems that Ofsted have accepted the unreliability of graded snapshots of individual lessons and have dropped this as a practice from 2014. Elsewhere, the problems with making snap, value-based judgements are beginning to emerge. There are voices insisting, finally, that something is done and shifts are beginning to take place.[52] But the dependency on data – on the belief that evidence of learning can be reliably found on paper or in books – remains. (We can see from the examples of Summerhill and Discovery that there is little room for alternative thinking, and the fear of being *too* different pushes schools towards data-driven compliance.)

Learning takes place in the mind, heart and body. It does not take place in books. Yet, there is an increased emphasis on book and work scrutiny and on final results. Even as inspectors accept that it is not possible to see learning in a lesson observation, few management teams are willing to let go of this power over their staff. It is possible, however, to slip between the spaces. To put pressure on senior leaders in-between inspections to maintain a focus on the children and the context of the school, and not on the imagined world of what the external assessors might want. To teach to the subject and not to the test (the criteria for which can change even in the middle of a course, as English teachers found to their cost in 2013). To retain a degree of integrity and dignity. These are all small and doable acts of resistance which open up possibilities for new becomings. Moreover, they model for children alternative possibilities and worlds in which the end test is not the be-all and end-all.

We may have a system in which the 'public schools dare not say no to those machines of State thought from which its critique automatically follows',[53] but resistance is possible by becoming Mobius. For me, as an AST who was employed to model good practice, it required painstaking conversations with colleagues about what 'good' practice might be – a gentle butting at the assumptions they may have carried with them for many years. This meant situating myself within and between senior managers and fellow teachers, butting both ways. I was both questioner AND enforcer – both present as Mobius. Performing AND resisting performance – again, both parts of the same whole, not contradictions. It is exhausting work because it requires constant returning – why did that happen? Why do we act this way? Where are the differences? Where are the possibilities? The constant nudging attempts to bring us closer to Deleuze and Guattari's 'ritournelle' (refrain)[54] – a place that marks points of stability in a field of chaos, the beginnings of order in chaos, sparking encounters in time and space that lies 'elsewhere'.

Even now, working more freely as a consultant, the butting and buffering role is the same. In doing so, I push teachers towards improvisation, and I owe it to them to find examples of schools which are managing to do so and still keep the inspectors satisfied. The problem for these schools (and for me) is in making apparent to the inspector that the improvisation is masterful and not chaotic. This is a path that Bealings Primary School in Suffolk seems to have navigated successfully. The school uses a model of pedagogy called 'mantle of the expert', in which the content of the curriculum is delivered through the medium of purposeful role play, and the children adopt the role of experts engaged in a process of solving a problem.[55] According to Ofsted:

Bealings is an outstanding school. Pupils become confident and competent learners and are highly motivated because they experience an exciting, memorable curriculum and are expertly taught ... Within the context of imaginative situations that are made real to pupils, teachers are highly adept at inspiring pupils so that they want to find out and do more and more.[56]

Such an approach may be viewed as a lionisation of a Trojan pedagogy in which children are empowered to encounter possible imaginary futures in the world of work. In one term they can be operating as landscape gardeners, in the next as marine biologists. The teachers ask questions such as, 'What are the implications of this choice?' or 'What might happen if ...?', to guide the children through the notion of possibilities. Assemblages are created to suit the imagined environment – 'What equipment would our lab need?' These form texts which are understood by the group to represent reality, such as the cardboard box covered in tinfoil on the wall which the children 'accept' as a fingerprint scanner and which they must pass to enter the lab. The mode is improvised play, but the learning is serious stuff. It is possibility orientated. The child is not conned into belief but complicit in the process of building belief. The teacher will ask, 'Can we agree that this might be or represent ...?' rather than 'Let's pretend ...' or 'This is ...' The subtle but important shift of language allows the children to begin to navigate the fact that there are other possibilities at the edge of reality or belief. They are being allowed to critique the world in a way that enables them not to be governed so much.[57] They can begin to imagine, through experience, the kinds of permeations and differences that might exist in the future. Like the teacher who may not be 'aware' but is nevertheless 'sensitive',[58] the Ofsted inspector may know that significant happenings are occurring which lead to an 'outstanding' judgement but may not be entirely sure how these events are being assembled. It is essential, then, that the teacher learns to trust in his/her pedagogy, to take control of the curriculum and to let go of fear.

In doing so, it is possible to engage with Guattari's notion of schizoanalysis, which attempts to 'proliferate models and also to combine models, or parts thereof, which might otherwise be seen as non-compatible'.[59] Guattari views schizo fracture as a means by which the unconscious (or affective dimension) might be accessed by a 'royal road', so schizoanalysis requires not only the rupturing of royal roads but also the identification of the lines of flight of desire as possible modes of enquiry. As such, I wonder if these ruptures might exist in micro actions and whether, when shared collectively, these micro actions can combine to create macro (r)evolution.

Micro (r)evolution: reclaiming curriculum

For the teacher feeling overwhelmed by the mixed and frightening messages of the macro world, it may be useful to look at what Deleuze says about the relationship between the learner, the teacher and that which is to be learned. This is best understood through his analogy of the child learning to swim. If the curriculum is reduced to the study of the wave and the test is to swim, then the 'modern world' that Gove alludes to is the sea. Deleuze points out that 'the movement of the swimmer does not resemble that of the wave'[60] – that is, the enactment of the learning will not necessarily replicate the knowledge that has been acquired. The knowledge of the wave may be one factor which could be used to propel the swimmer, but the child will need more than this to navigate the water. Furthermore, the instruction from the teacher – the demonstration – will not be enough to make the child a swimmer either. The learning is a much more complex process. Williams clarifies:

Knowledge alone is insufficient. Knowledge also requires an apprenticeship to evolving practice. This practice is not a matter of knowledge. It is a matter of experimental doing and acting, when knowledge is not enough, when knowledge fails. A gardener on a new hill in changing climate. A cyclist going beyond her limits on a hill taken too fast. A teacher in front of a new class each new day ... A writer essaying the next sentence ... The first day without a loved one ... and the hundredth. A scientist with new results.[61]

The teacher has to get in the water, to feel the current pull and to assist as the child adapts. It is no use standing on the edge. But the teacher also needs to recognise that her effect is limited – the child will need to apply judgement, to adjust, modify, balance, choose. So, it is essential to open up pedagogical space for experimentation; setting up safe, playful but challenging places in which knowledge can fail is a matter of improvisation. Curriculum needs to be more than just a body of knowledge.

Arendt describes as labour those experiences that 'leave nothing behind ... the result of its effort is almost as quickly consumed as the effort is spent'.[62] One might see teaching as labour, if the process feels like a never-ending conveyer belt of children heading for SATs or GCSEs (the hidden curriculum-as-plan). This interpretation reflects the curriculum as a process of 'ends-means, instrumental or transcendent production',[63] which creates the 'fixture of sameness' which Aoki notes is a feature of a curriculum-as-plan model.[64] Sellers, on the other hand conceives and enacts the curriculum within her early years setting as a 'processual ... lived in experience ... less of a thing and more about happening'.[65] Working in New Zealand, without Ofsted, Sellers finds an element of curriculum wriggle room – a freedom that is enshrined within the Te Whāriki model, which might be considered a model of curriculum-as-lived. Curriculum-as-plan, on the other hand, is an imposed model which assumes a preferable future and which has the needs of the economic state as a key function. This model 'territorialises pedagogical life in an image of arboreality ... by transposing upon it a molar grid of objectives and outcomes that prescribe what teachers and students should do'.[66] But is it possible to resist this plan with (r)evolutionary curriculum? To reframe the way we look? As Stronach says, 'being radical in a doctoral space is easy enough',[67] but it is entirely different to try out radical actions in the workplace.

In 2012, I was approached by the head teacher of a school in Oldham who wondered if I would be willing to set up and run a 'new' curriculum for Key Stage 3. His key aims were to engender a love of reading in children, to foster confidence and self-awareness and to create a subject which would allow each child to have a teacher with whom they would spend a significant amount of time and who would 'know' them. We met several times and together created a new subject / curriculum area called 'English and Philosophy'. The premise was that the English and philosophy course would allow several subjects to be brought together (English, drama, religious education (RE), personal, health and social education (PHSE)) to create an intensive block of time. Each half-term would focus around a novel (reading), underpinned by enquiry questions (context and philosophical thinking), and the contexts of the novels would open up access to content normally delivered in RE and PHSE. The prospect excited me and tempted me back into teaching. It was not a new idea – other schools have done similar things[68] – but it was the first opportunity I'd had to work on such a project from within, instead of either evaluating as a researcher or working as a visiting practitioner.

It seemed to me that here was a possibility for slippage. On the surface, the priorities of government policy were being upheld. As Cole points out, Deleuzian teaching and learning practice is 'pragmatic' in that it seeks not to overthrow systems, but instead to work within them, 'making changes in education that will work in terms of improving the reality of thought'.[69] Children were reading regularly and writing regularly. But they were also talking, doing, making, enquiring and questioning. We were working as a community in which the teacher 'is keeping things open so that the event of the subjectivity may arise … in which being is brought into life – a life shared with others in responsiveness and responsibility'.[70] The questions underpinning each text were designed to disrupt assumptions: is the world a fair place? What is a good person? To what extent am I a product of my environment? What is justice? I deliberately chose questions with no easy answers – where multiplicity was necessary – and pedagogy was developed to push this. Teachers were asked to probe – to ask 'And so …', 'And what if?', 'And is it possible?' – so that instead of coming to conclusions, children were encouraged to see the complexity underpinning key concepts or ideas such as justice, love and democracy. The (r)evolving curriculum centred around these concepts. The public curriculum demonstrated compliance. As such, it was hoped that the experience that Key Stage 3 children were getting might open up a potential movement between what was *expected* and what was radical; not a revolution but a space for evolving ideas to relay back and forth:

How would we think and act if we could imagine a justice that was pure, infinite and uncorrupted? The concept is, therefore, the power of thinking to survey *the movement of life, not being located within the lived, but grasping a certain aspect of the lived all at once: what is thinking as such, justice as such, reason as such?*[71]

Exploring these concepts through literature and drama enables the children to view a concept in multiple ways, as well as to grapple with it from their own experience and understanding. For example, in one lesson, the children had been exploring democracy as a preamble to reading *The Boy in the Striped Pyjamas*. They were told that the word democracy has its roots in the Greek words 'demos' and 'kratos' (people and power/ rule), and were asked the question, 'If democracy means "rule of the people", do we live in a democratic society?' A discussion raged which resulted not in clear answers but in multiple flights:

'We have democratic rights once every five years ...' (fact AND ...)

'Children don't really have a democratic voice' (observation AND ...)

'We're luckier than some people, some people don't get any choice at all' (empathy AND ...)

'We could do better' (intention AND ...)

'Is it easy to become a politician or do you have to be posh?' (possibility AND ...)

AND (unspoken multiplicities ad infinitum ...)

Such questions and observations were necessarily embedded into the core of our curriculum. Even where citizenship still exists, there is not enough time to linger in the edges of these ideas when the subject takes place for one hour every fortnight. By placing notions of justice and democracy at the heart of 'English', it is placed in the core of the curriculum and given time to ferment. It is an evolution of the idea of what it is to do/be 'English' – a pedagogical and curriculum (r)evolutionary act. Achieving this aim requires a commitment to introduce children to the notion of the idea – one which, 'with its novel concepts, does not solve a problem. It expresses it as a challenge to find solutions, but also with the critical power to call back any into question.'[72] For Deleuze, 'it is the excess in the Idea which explains the lack in the concept'.[73] Consider the following piece of writing from a Year 7 pupil which emerged after this discussion about democracy:

> Democracy comes from the Greek words Demos and Kratos which mean people and power so democracy means people power. In some ways we have a democracy because people over the age of 18 can vote for a government, but once they are in power they can do what they like and they might not even keep their promises so this is not a real democracy. In some countries, people vote on the laws through a referendum so this is more of a democracy because it is a direct democracy so I would prefer this kind. I also think that children in our country don't really have a democratic voice because we can't vote. We are people but we have no power.

Taking as its point of departure the very 'idea' of democracy realised through this text, perhaps what is interesting is what exceeds traditional/usual educational interest/focus and escapes the grasp of the conceptual forms that vocabulary, structure and spelling have previously taken. Despite attention on vocabulary, structure and spelling as important educational concepts in the development and progress of pupils' writing, we asked, when planning the concepts in the curriculum, what ideas could support those textual conventions, releasing whatever else exists to leak out from all sides and open up possibilities for pedagogical innovation – a pedagogical life. In this way, we attempted not simply to make our teaching more 'democratic' or to build aspects of citizenship into the curriculum, but to bring forward an element of transcendental materialism into the work. We were finding ways to lay down future possible escape routes from the forces of corporate process and political discourse. This is not to brainwash the children with ideology, but to lay out the idea of alternative ways of looking at and experiencing concepts. This child's writing has taken the AND aspects of the discussion and brought them together, so that this is not so much a linear text – though it attempts to follow the conventions of linearity demanded by the assessment criteria – but it is layered with multiple flights (this place/that place, this age/that age, this definition/that definition, this time/that time) and routes of possibility.

Over the weeks, I worked to ensure that these kinds of explorations and discussions became the dominant experience for the children, so that working with uncertainty became usual for them. The children who were certain that we lived in a democracy became more conditional about how they defined and understood that term and began to see themselves as within the idea of democracy. Initially, as one child said, 'democracy is when you grow up and get to vote'. Now it is something they talk about with the pronoun 'we' instead of 'you'. But on its own this is not enough. Simply 'doing' democracy does not make the process of learning more democratic – a point that Biesta makes in his exploration of Dewey's notion of the 'idea' as something that has to be experienced.[74]

A visit from children from a democratic free school in Denmark impacted on this shift in thinking when they told our children that they chose what they would study. There are pilot schemes in this area taking place in other schools in the UK – for example, at King Edward VI Grammar School in Essex and at the London Nautical School. Teachers in these schools are finding room to develop democratic processes not only in the way that schools are run but also in the way the curriculum is organised by and with the children. This is an element of (r)evolution that we pedagogical activists need to develop, partly by linking into the wide online network of teacher and learner bloggers exploring co-construction. In such ways, we move towards addressing some of the educational challenges that Biesta puts forward when he asserts that education is as much about knowledge of 'relationships, and, more specifically, about relationships between (our) actions and (their) consequences'[75] – viewing education as a transactional process and not a static one.

In my previous school, the evolving pedagogy appears to be working, even as I have moved on – ideas are continuing to permeate the culture. Staff teaching other subjects in the school report that Year 7 and Year 8 students are 'more open', 'engaged', 'willing to take risks', 'willing to have a go', 'articulate', 'independent', even 'outperforming Year 9'.[76] But while I was there, the data showed a narrower picture. The school collection of 'data', like those in many other schools, is a tool designed to provide 'evidence' to Ofsted of children's progress. This progress is measured against achievement at Key Stage 2 through to SATs, but SATs only measure the child's writing and reading ability. There is no way, in the school system, to record and evidence progress in the acquisition of knowledge, confidence, speaking and listening skills, metacognitive skills, research skills – in fact, in any of the areas that the children have been most successful. While there have been trends of improvement in reading and writing, these have followed a similar trajectory to previous years in which these were the sole aims of the curriculum. On these measures, then, there is little evidence that what is in place now is an improvement on what went before. Suggestions for modifying this assessment collection model were met with resistance (It's what Ofsted want). And even as national reform came in and the requirement to record progress in levels was removed, the school clung to the old system like flotsam.

As a result, the teachers who remain are always stuck in conjunctions. They work to ensure that children make progress roughly in line with what is expected AND they accept that the notions of linearity are flawed. They deliver the curriculum AND work with the lines of flight in areas which are not measured but which they know are important, such as self-management, initiative, confidence, articulacy and creativity. They deliver the official curriculum AND they enact a hidden curriculum. We are always working between positions, trying to find the small possibilities for movement.

In their written and spoken work, the children are demonstrating multiple literacy skills. In their analysis of the images in Shaun Tan's book *The Arrival* for example, they write words like 'waiting' next to a packed suitcase, 'territorial' next to a hat on a peg … they are reading intention into the images, predicting possible lines of past and present and understanding how the physical world imposes meaning on the emotional world.

The annotations described above show children demonstrating multiple literacy skills. They are able to understand that the physical world imposes upon and interacts with the emotional. They are linking notions of desire, working with symbol and making connections. They are not familiar with Deleuze or Masny, but they are nevertheless becoming multiply literate. This may not be measured, but it fires the imagination, giving depth and purpose to work so that they are able to conform when required.

DAY 1

Today I left behind my beloved family and friends, I had no choice. I must find work in this cruel, dark place I have come to- a new world without warmth or love or comfort. If I don't work my family will be turned out of their home and will starve to death on the streets. I find that I have swapped one world of tyranny and corruption for another equally bad place of ugliness, hard labour and solitude. I desperately miss my precious family and feel like I'm going to collapse with exhaustion and the burden of responsibility that I'm carrying. I'm terrified when I think about what will become of us all- if I don't get this right then everything will go wrong...

The idea that there needs to be a pedagogy of possibility underpinning the creation of this work is something that is not properly considered in curriculum development models, but pedagogy working in partnership with curriculum – AND slipping between the two – is an important element of this work. In such ways, we develop 'wave action' which may erode over time 'aspects of practice that have remained ... due to previous formations of power'.[77]

Rather than seeing contradictions and constraints between dominant and resistant models of the curriculum, it is possible to look at the former as a necessary construct in order to maintain the survival of a hidden curriculum (at least in the current political climate). It is important to maintain the status quo in order to be able to disrupt it – to be both sides so that there can be a breach or fracture in the 'existing regime', so that 'the imagination then may function as a powerful political force: the power of making and breaking, concealing and revealing, learning and burning'.[78] In order for this curriculum to be nurtured, and to survive, it is necessary for it to keep slipping between the dominant and radical models, taking off in lines of flight which are necessarily 'unpredictable'[79] but also safe from interference because it is performing normatively. However, the multiplicities and opportunities for becoming are inherent, not only in the curriculum model or in the macro pedagogy but also, crucially, in the nano world of human interactions both with other humans and with the non-organic world.

Nano (r)evolution: pedagogical edgework

For Deleuze, teaching is an act done in intra-active partnership with students. Bogue suggests that the teacher is an emitter of signs – a producer of texts which can enhance or inhibit that which is intended to be taught.[80] But signs travel both ways – she needs not simply to emit, but to receive, interpret and adapt. In this view, the teacher is emitting and receiving; she is both radar and radio, signal and sensor. As she slips between the two, learning does not stop – it is not static. But in constant movement, and without attending to signs, the teacher may unwittingly send the learning in an unintended direction. In *Difference and Repetition*, Deleuze notes that learning 'takes place in the relation between a sign and a response (encounter with the Other)'.[81] This learning theory suggests that it is the immediate environment and inter-/intra-action that has most impact on learning. It opens up the possibility that curriculum, policy and accountability might be subverted or circumvented through relationships, environment and pedagogy; that the small singularities created in that space might be conceived of as acts of occupation – each one leading to lines of flight of potentiality.

Developing curriculum models as vehicles for pedagogical exploration is one mode of resistance, but I have argued throughout this book for the need to pay attention to the nano. If pedagogy within curriculum is micro, then edgeworking pedagogy is nano. In this final section, I will be attending to the detail – the small, seemingly insignificant evolutionary changes that can impact on the micro and macro worlds. Not to do so would be to ignore the complexity of pedagogy, interaction and time.

Wallin argues that to move from curriculum-as-plan to a pedagogical life, there needs to be a rethinking of 'pedagogy as the task of founding a compositional plane' and as a process 'becoming unanticipated by an antecedent being'.[82] As such, pedagogical life shifts from a notion of controlling the content and processes in the classroom to releasing potential 'becomings'. This is not a linear process but is situated in a series of returns – the revolving element of (r)evolution. The classroom is a 'highly differentiated environment'[83] in which texts jostle for attention. These texts can be distracting, and it is always necessary to pay attention to those that matter. If we accept the idea that children are minors – in the Deleuzian sense of being within a minority, politicised by the majority – then the teacher can guide these returns towards 'becoming-minoritarian'.[84] This is more than simple empathy. It is a process of intra-actively becoming child in order to open up possibilities of empowerment. This requires opening smooth spaces for exploration of self, but to do so requires being *present* – that is, within the complexity – and not attempting to limit the complexity in order to guide it to a predefined conclusion. As Roy puts it, teaching in this way requires us to be 'able to see learning opportunities in irregular spaces and moments and in discontinuous flashes rather than in continuities'.[85] This is highly challenging for a teacher who is measured in terms of the linear progress the children are deemed to have made.

The selection of text is an important micro element that allows this nano work to take place. If we seek to empower children, then it makes sense for them to be engaging with characters and narratives which open up explorations of congruence with their own experience – leading perhaps to Neil's 'becoming immigrant' in Chapter 3. In our selection of texts in Year 7 and 8, there was a deliberate choice of books which would allow for explorations of minority positions through dramatic enquiry. *The Arrival* by Shaun Tan, for example, allowed us to explore the experience of immigrant communities through an assemblage of signs. There are no words in the text, only images, from which the children extracted meaning, emotion and value systems in order to explore possibilities for these characters in dramatic action.

Williams argues that whenever a teacher makes a decision to group a class in order to release a different potential – or chooses content or form to achieve the same effect – then the act not only 'challenges and destroys a given order', but also 'experiments with a different one'.[86] It is this 'different order' that I have been most keen to explore in my new role, and doing so has required subversive acts. Drama forms an important part of this pedagogy because it offers possibility and lines of flight. Deleuze closely explores the arts – he is drawn to their transformational capacities which produce 'fragments, allusions, strivings, investigations' which create 'affirmative junctions'.[87] When the children enact an event or become other in role, they are in slippage between two selves and multiple possibilities.

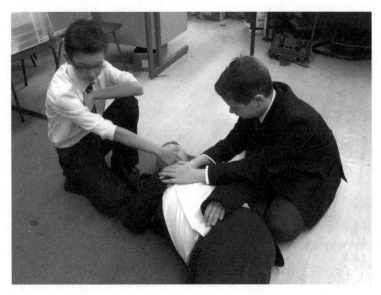

Reading life and death: the children were asked to show why the protagonist fled his country, setting up a pre-text to that within the text. They chose to show the effects of an oppressive state. They decided not to show a point of death, but of near-death – a possibility of death rather than the actual. There is interaction with life (pulses and heartbeats); attempts to revive. Pupils are showing textual knowledge, political knowledge, biological knowledge and emotional knowledge. They are *doing* drama but they are *demonstrating* multiple aspects of knowledge and facilitating possibility. Telling it would be differently experienced and remembered – no heartbeat under the hand, no touch, no resistance from the cold floor on the back, no ache in the legs when forced to kneel for a period of time, no breath. The intra-action between what is known, what is felt and what might yet be is crucial.

Our work tends not to focus on re-enactment of pre-existing scripts ('is' work), but on the creation of possibilities through devising ('and' work). Small groups of children work with situations and questions, and present them back. None is the 'right' answer; all are possible lines of flight forming minor literacies:

A minor literature has three features: the language used is affected by deterritorialisation, that is, a smoothing out of space or a stripping out of syntax so that it loses all symbolism and signification; everything is political (and individuals are connected to a political immediacy); and everything has a collective value.[88]

It is almost impossible to get children (or indeed anyone) to smooth out symbol so that there is no signification – they constantly revert to symbolic image. If we look at the image above, we see signification of life/death – for example, the pulse, CPR. But the boys are nevertheless working in smooth space where they are exploring the conditions that might lead to leaving home. None of their explorations are 'truth', simply possibility, each interpretation deterritorialising the next. There is political action underpinning everything and they are more than capable of exploring it without it limiting their capacity to act in the future. The dramatic frame allows for slippage between the adult/child world that forms the discussion of Arendt's work in Biesta's interpretation.[89] The children are not fed these possibilities. They are working within a political realm in response to the question, 'Why might someone leave the people they love?' Crucially, they are also accepting a collective value – the value of love – and working with the potential disruptions to that value. We explore duality through complex questions (Do you have to have suffered tyranny in order to understand freedom?) in order to try to open up the idea that there are complexities within what seem to be oppositions – the AND space. Are tyranny and freedom connected? Are they really opposites? Such conversations abound in this curriculum, but there are no 'right' or 'wrong' answers. I do not teach the children Deleuze, but I do expose them to the idea of complexity, and each time we return to that idea it 'is coloured by its passage through the Second Assemblage'.[90]

There are echoes here to Dewey's pragmatic approach to education:

What [a person] gets and gives as a human being, a being with desires, emotions and ideas, is ... a widening and deepening of conscious life – a more intense, disciplined and expanding realization of meanings ... And education is not a mere means to such a life. Education is such a life.[91]

This realisation of meanings is created productively – 'setting fire to the unjust state of things instead of burning the things themselves and restoring life to primary life'.[92] And it is done collectively. In recent years, there has been a denigration of Dewey's work. He has been reduced to an icon of progressive thinking in a way which suggests that he advocated an entirely child-led form of discovery learning in which neither adults nor knowledge had any part to play. This is an irresponsible interpretation, but one which has been seized upon by GERM advocates in order to justify their policies. Instead, as Biesta points out, Dewey's philosophy was not so much child led as communication led.[93] It was about adults and children moving in joint exploration without ever undermining the role of the adult (or, crucially, the child) in that process. I view this way of learning as 'becoming-natal' – that is, allowing children to politically engage without imposing a political view upon them, enabling them to deconstruct what they accept as norms by walking in another's shoes, by becoming 'other'. In this light, I return to and reconsider the data that has permeated this book, seeing again resonant moments as acts of (r)evolution: Neil's evolution from an immigrant into an agentive, coping self; Danny's evolution into a speller; a group of children evolving into those who are heard and others into those who are understood. All acts of political agency. I matter; I can be other.

In this sense, then, rows about curriculum content, school structures and pedagogical impositions are irrelevant if one can find (r)evolutionary means to circumvent them. That is not to reduce these matters to insignificance, or to ignore them altogether, but to facilitate an educational life that can thrive in spite of the transmuting impositions of the control society. By this I mean the kind of education which examines 'how best to approach the singularity of the living present with all its problems, intensities, resonances and repetitions',[94] and which fractures the assumption of propositions. The propositional structures of school accountability and the curriculum are not dismissed from the present assemblages of the event of learning; they are forcefully present, even as they are subverted. Control and freedom become Mobius, locked together in (r)evolutionary conjunctions. Williams makes clear that this is a difficult balancing act – that teaching is largely a 'destructive' process which has a duty to 'run counter to establishment and to smash icons'[95] – but he is clear that there is the matter of dosage in such acts. A balance must be struck between conservatism and the bloodthirsty rush to destroy – in the same way that Deleuze and Guattari remind us that burning injustice is preferable to burning the things that are unjust themselves. We must decide, he argues, 'which past lines [we] must carry forward' and 'which future lines must be sacrificed'. He goes on to say that the teacher 'is on the cusp of history and in a singular situation, having to divine what the future might hold while nurturing the present thanks to the past'.[96] I have argued above that while striving for change is important, we need to find ways, in the moment, of working within and through existing structures – resisting either/or notions. This is not about sitting on a fence, but rather sliding across it, under it, in and out of the knots and bumps.

In this view of education, the emerging identity of the child forces returns and projections. We cannot simply see the child as 'learner'. We need to see the child as seen by him/herself at different points of time. We need to open up the vulnerability of the act of creation to the child (the risk that Biesta speaks of). Together, teacher and child must return to previous moments to consider what is now different, what has altered and how are we changed, and they must project possibilities onto the future. This is the real meaning of assessment: sitting beside a child and examining what has been done and what is yet to do. This can mean returning to all the different interpretations or ideas created and exploring how they are differently understood and created. It also involves returning to work through redrafting, presenting, summarising, reflecting and explaining to teachers and parents, 'This is what I was, and this is how I am changed.' In such ways, we move between smooth and striated spaces, between aion and chronos time; being nomad while attending to the demands of the royals.

For Wallin, there are parallels here to 'becoming lion' – the move from compliance with curriculum to a recognition that the 'educational orthodoxy known as the curriculum-in-plan must be differentiated in kind from its immanent encounter with the living multiplicity of the classroom'.[97] Becoming lion involves taking control of the environment, recognising that the structures the camel sees as a burden are navigable, even integral, to the process of both surviving and thriving. For example, the lion-teacher may challenge the validity of data collection within a school while recognising the value of the labour of marking children's work. It may be desirable to oppose (opposition is a responsible course of action), but it is still possible to work within the existing system – for example, shifting the emphasis of curriculum content from 'what' to 'why' and 'what if' is one way to become more lion-like. This allows for slippage between camel (doing what needs to be done) AND lion (doing what is desirable) AND child (opening up possibilities).

As such, the teacher has to be attuned to possibilities and aware of the future in terms of bringing both the 'concrete and actual'[98] of the present into a series of multiple possibilities which are present and becoming at the moment of encounter; to be aware that there is not 'one' predictable path. For those working within complexity models of pedagogy, this suggests a view of teaching and learning as improvisation, with all its attendant risks and weaknesses. Wallin argues that in a classroom, 'no amount of planning will be sufficient', and that the goal of the teacher is to become a skilled improviser.[99] The improviser must always be on the lookout for signs that are the 'immanent production of untimely connections, the introduction of new problems',[100] which become the matter of pedagogical life. To improvise is 'to follow the ways of the world, as they unfold'.[101] It is, as Deleuze and Guattari write, 'to join with the World, or to meld with it. One ventures from home on the thread of a tune'.[102] It is our role as teachers, then, not only to ensure that our antennae are ready for these unexpected interactions, but that children learn, in part, to recognise and explore them as well. Much of the data throughout this book have explored this mode of improvisation, whether conscious or not. Why? Because the alternative is a future in which our children have been taught that the most important thing in life is to comply. To not question. To accept that those in power know what they are doing. In a properly functioning, healthy society, it may be possible for the vast majority of the population to thrive under benign rule. But in an unequal or unfair society – or worse, under a radically cruel system of governance – such compliance is dangerous. In his 2014 EBOR lecture, Professor Richard Pring read out the famous letter by Holocaust survivor Haim Ginott to demonstrate the dangers of intelligence without wisdom:

Dear Teacher:

I am the survivor of a concentration camp. My eyes saw what no man should witness: gas chambers built by learned engineers; children poisoned by educated physicians; infants killed by trained nurses; women and babies shot and burned by high school and college graduates. So I am suspicious of education.

My request is: Help your students become human. Your efforts must never produce learned monsters, skilled psychopaths, educated Eichmanns.

Reading, writing, arithmetic are important only if they serve to make our children more humane.[103]

We need to begin to see teaching as an evolutionary process, not as a fixed set of ideas and practices – evolution itself is a mode of improvisation. But to (re)turn to the theme of this plateau, (r)evolution, it is not the aim of an evolving organism to become a final definitive thing, but to push forward in possibility of otherness. Evolution pushes blindly forward, but (r)evolutionary practice requires revolving, moving back and round again and again, to see what other possibilities we might find, what conjunctions there might be. I have attempted to explain the need for the teacher to be both telescopic and microscopic in her vision. To demonstrate that all kinds of resistance are possible. In the final plateau I ask, what now? What next? What then?

Notes

1. G. Deleuze, Postscript on the Societies of Control, *October* 59 (Winter 1992): 3–7. Available at: http://pages.akbild.ac.at/kdm/_media/_pdf/Gilles%20Deleuze%20 -%20Postscript%20on%20the%20Societies%20of%20Control.pdf.
2. K. Roy, *Teachers in Nomadic Spaces: Deleuze and Curriculum* (New York: Peter Lang, 2003), p. vii.
3. B. Massumi, *Parables for the Virtual: Movement, Affect, Sensation* (Durham, NC: Duke University Press, 2002), p. 2.
4. D. Cole, *Educational Life Forms: Deleuzian Teaching and Learning Practice* (Rotterdam: Sense, 2011).
5. W. Brown, *Edgework: Critical Essays on Knowledge and Politics* (Princeton, NJ: Princeton University Press, 2005), pp. 83–97.
6. D. Cole, The Power of Emotional Factors in English Teaching, *Power and Education* 1(1) (2009): 57–70 at 61.
7. See M. Sellers, *Young Children Becoming Curriculum: Deleuze, Te Whāriki and Curricular Understandings* (New York: Routledge, 2013), p. 27.
8. K. Egan, What is Curriculum?, *Curriculum Inquiry* 8 (1978): 65–72.
9. M. Arnold, *Culture and Anarchy* (Cambridge: Cambridge University Press, 1971 [1869]), p. 6.
10. W. Reynolds and J. Webber, Introduction: Curriculum Dis/positions, in W. Reynolds and J. Webber (eds), *Expanding Curriculum Theory: Dis/positions and Lines of Flight* (Mahwah, NJ: Lawrence Erlbaum, 2008), pp. 1–18 at p. 4.
11. See T. Aoki, Teaching as Indwelling Between Two Curriculum Worlds, in W. Pinar and R. Irwin (eds), *Curriculum in a New Key: The Collected Works of Ted A. Aoki* (Mahwah, NJ: Lawrence Erlbaum, 2005 [1986]), pp. 159–165; and J. Wallin, Morphologies for a Pedagogical Life, in D. Masny and I. Semetsky (eds), *Deleuze and Education* (Edinburgh: Edinburgh University Press, 2013), pp. 196–214.
12. W. F. Pinar, W. M. Reynolds, P. Slattery and P. M. Taubman, *Understanding Curriculum: An Introduction to the Study of Historical and Contemporary Curriculum Discourses* (New York: Peter Lang, 1995).

13. Foucault quoted in Deleuze, Postscript on the Societies of Control, 3.

14. R. J. Alexander, *Culture and Pedagogy: International Comparisons in Primary Education* (Oxford: Blackwell, 2000); J. Baer, The Impact of the Core Knowledge Curriculum on Creativity, *Creativity Research Journal* 15(2&3) (2003): 297–300; Cole, *Educational Life Forms*; and M. Waters, *Thinking Allowed: On Schooling* (Carmarthen: Independent Thinking Press, 2013).

15. M. Hardt and A. Negri, *Empire* (Cambridge, MA: Harvard University Press, 2000), p. 23.

16. R. J. Alexander, Neither National Nor a Curriculum?, *Forum* 54(3) (2012): 369–384. Available at: http://www.robinalexander.org.uk/wp-content/uploads/2012/11/Alexander-Neither-national-nor-a-curriculum-Forum.pdf.

17. See Waters, *Thinking Allowed*, p. 284.

18. G. Deleuze and M. Foucault, Intellectuals and Power, in D. F. Bouchard (ed.), *Language, Counter-Memory, Practice: Selected Essays and Interviews* (Ithaca, NY: Cornell University Press, 1977), p. 209.

19. O. Jones, *The Establishment and How They Get Away With It* (London: Penguin, 2014).

20. E. Morris, The National Curriculum: Why Have One If It's Not for Everyone?, *The Guardian* (23 January 2012). Available at: http://www.theguardian.com/education/2012/jan/23/national-curriculum-review.

21. F. Guattari, *Chaosmosis: An Ethico-Aesthetic Paradigm* (Sydney: Power Publications, 1995), p. 103.

22. S. O'Sullivan, Guattari's Aesthetic Paradigm: From the Folding of the Finite/Infinite Relation to Schizoanalytic Metamodelisation, *Deleuze Studies* 4(2) (2010): 256–286.

23. Reynolds and Webber, Introduction: Curriculum Dis/positions, p. 4.

24. P. Sahlberg, Global Education Reform Movement is Here!, *Pasi Sahlberg Blog* (2013). Available at: http://pasisahlberg.com/global-educational-reform-movement-is-here/.

25. Deleuze and Foucault, Intellectuals and Power, p. 209.

26. E. D. Hirsch, *The Knowledge Deficit: Closing the Shocking Educational Gap for American Children* (New York: Houghton Mifflin, 2007).

27. M. Gove, Education Reform: Schools. Written Statement to Parliament (8 July 2013). Available at: https://www.gov.uk/government/speeches/education-reform-schools.

28. D. Christodoulou, *Seven Myths About Education* (Abingdon: Routledge, 2014).

29. T. Young, *Prisoners of the Blob: Why Most Education Experts are Wrong About Nearly Everything* (London: Civitas, 2014).

30. R. Peal, *Progressively Worse: The Burden of Bad Ideas in British Schools* (London: Civitas, 2014).

31. House of Commons Education Committee, The English Baccalaureate: Fifth Report of Session 2010–12, Volume I (19 July 2011). Available at: http://www.publications.parliament.uk/pa/cm201012/cmselect/cmeduc/851/851.pdf.

32. The Design and Technology Association, Education Select Committee Raises Serious Concerns Over the EBacc (31 January 2013). Available at: https://www.data.org.uk/news/education-select-committee-raises-serious-concerns-over-the-ebacc/.

33. Deleuze, Postscript on the Societies of Control, 4.

34. Deleuze, Postscript on the Societies of Control, 4.

35. G. Biesta, Why 'What Works' Still Won't Work: From Evidence Based Education to Value-Based Education, *Studies in Philosophy and Education* 29(5) (2010): 491–503 at 494.

36. Roy, *Teachers in Nomadic Spaces*, pp. 4–5.

37. O'Sullivan, Guattari's Aesthetic Paradigm.

38. Gove, Education Reform: Schools.
39. N. Jun, Deleuze, Values and Normativity, in N. Jun and D. Smith (eds), *Deleuze and Ethics* (Edinburgh: Edinburgh University Press, 2011), pp. 89–107 at p. 93.
40. W. G. Spady and K. Marshall, Beyond Traditional Outcome-Based Education, *Educational Leadership* 49(2) (1991): 67–72.
41. Wallin, Morphologies for a Pedagogical Life, p. 198.
42. J. Bell, Whistle While You Work: Deleuze and the Spirit of Capitalism, in N. Jun and D. Smith (eds), *Deleuze and Ethics* (Edinburgh: Edinburgh University Press, 2011), pp. 5–21 at p. 5.
43. MacLure, Entertaining Doubts, p. 3.
44. D. Kidd, Teachers, Let's Get Behind the Education Spring, *The Guardian* (23 April 2013). Available at: http://www.guardian.co.uk/teacher-network/teacher-blog/2013/apr/23/michael-gove-education-spring-teacher-protest.
45. L. Stenhouse, Case Study and Case Records: Towards a Contemporary History of Education, *British Educational Research Journal* 4(2) (1978): 21–39.
46. R. Adams, Pioneering Free School Fails, Awarded Lowest Ofsted Grades, *The Guardian* (19 June 2013). Available at: http://www.theguardian.com/politics/2013/jun/19/free-school-fails-ofsted-gove.
47. I. Stronach, (B)othering Education: An Autobiography of Alternatives, *Other Education: The Journal of Educational Alternatives* 1(1) (2012): 171–174 at 171.
48. Guattari, *Chaosmosis*, p. 64.
49. M. Foucault, On the Genealogy of Ethics: An Overview of Work in Progress (1994). Available at: http://sfbay-anarchists.org/wp-content/uploads/2012/12/Foucault-On-the-Genealogy-of-Ethics-An-Overview-of-Work-in-Progress.pdf.
50. O'Sullivan, Guattari's Aesthetic Paradigm, 262.
51. S. Shaviro, Deleuze's Encounter with Whitehead (n.d.). Available at: http://www.shaviro.com/Othertexts/DeleuzeWhitehead.pdf, p. 1.
52. Demos, Demos: Scrap Ofsted Inspections to Tackle 'Target-Obsessed Culture' in Schools (2013). Available at: http://www.demos.co.uk/press_releases/demosscrapofstedinspectionstotackletargetobsessedcultureinschools.
53. Wallin, Morphologies for a Pedagogical Life, p. 200.
54. G. Deleuze and F. Guattari, *A Thousand Plateaus: Capitalism and Schizophrenia*, tr. B. Massumi (London: Athlone, 1987), p. 281.
55. D. Heathcote and G. Bolton, *Drama for Learning: Dorothy Heathcote's Mantle of the Expert* (Oxford: Heinemann Drama, 1995).
56. Ofsted, Bealings School Inspection Report (10–11 July 2012). Available at: http://www.bealings.org.uk/wp-content/uploads/2008/06/Ofsted-2012-1.pdf, p. 4.
57. M. Foucault, What is Critique?, in S. Lotringer and L. Hochroth (eds), *The Politics of Truth* (New York: Semiotext(e), 1997), pp. 23–82.
58. J. Williams, Time and Education in the Philosophy of Gilles Deleuze, in D. Masny and I. Semetsky (eds), *Deleuze and Education* (Edinburgh: Edinburgh University Press, 2013), pp. 242–243 at p. 242.
59. O'Sullivan, Guattari's Aesthetic Paradigm, 262.
60. G. Deleuze, *The Logic of Sense* (London: Continuum, 2004), p. 23.
61. Williams, Time and Education in the Philosophy of Gilles Deleuze, p. 247 (emphasis in original).
62. H. Arendt, *The Human Condition*, 2nd edn (Chicago, IL: University of Chicago Press, 1998 [1958]), p. 87.
63. Wallin, Morphologies for a Pedagogical Life, p. 200.

64. Aoki, Teaching as Indwelling Between Two Curriculum Worlds, p. 161.
65. Sellers, *Young Children Becoming Curriculum*, p. 1.
66. Wallin, Morphologies for a Pedagogical Life, p. 198.
67. Stronach, (B)othering Education, 172.
68. M. Fautley, E. Millard and R. Hatcher, *Re-making the Secondary Curriculum* (Stoke-on-Trent: Trentham Books, 2011); and D. Kidd, Creating Partnerships, *English in Education: Journal of the National Association for Teachers of English* 42 (2007).
69. Cole, *Educational Life Forms*, p. 110.
70. G. Biesta, *The Beautiful Risk of Education* (Boulder, CO: Paradigm, 2013), p. 24.
71. C. Colebrook, *Deleuze: A Guide for the Perplexed* (London: Continuum, 2006), p. 94 (emphasis in original).
72. Williams, Time and Education in the Philosophy of Gilles Deleuze, p. 243.
73. G. Deleuze, He Stuttered, in C. V. Boundas and D. Olkowski (eds), *Gilles Deleuze and the Theatre of Philosophy* (London: Routledge, 1994), p. 273.
74. Biesta, *The Beautiful Risk of Education*.
75. Biesta, Why 'What Works' Still Won't Work, 495.
76. Responses to email request for information in preparation for a curriculum review.
77. Cole, *Educational Life Forms*, p. 109.
78. J. Jipson and N. Paley, *Daredevil Research: Recreating Analytic Practice* (New York: Peter Lang, 1997), p. 8.
79. Jipson and Paley, *Daredevil Research*, p. 165.
80. R. Bogue, The Master Apprentice, in D. Masny and I. Semetsky (eds), *Deleuze and Education* (Edinburgh: Edinburgh University Press, 2013), pp. 21–37 at p. 21.
81. G. Deleuze and F. Guattari, *Difference and Repetition* (New York: Continuum, 2004 [1968]).
82. Wallin, Morphologies for a Pedagogical Life, p. 205.
83. Roy, *Teachers in Nomadic Spaces*, pp. 4–5.
84. Deleuze and Guattari, *A Thousand Plateaus*, p. 303.
85. Roy, *Teachers in Nomadic Spaces*, pp. 4–5.
86. Williams, Time and Education in the Philosophy of Gilles Deleuze, pp. 242–243.
87. G. Deleuze quoted in J. Allan, Staged Interventions: Deleuze, Arts and Education, in D. Masny and I. Semetsky (eds), *Deleuze and Education* (Edinburgh: Edinburgh University Press, 2013), pp. 38–40 at p. 38.
88. Deleuze quoted in Allan, Staged Interventions, pp. 38–40.
89. Biesta, *The Beautiful Risk of Education*, pp. 101–118.
90. O'Sullivan, Guattari's Aesthetic Paradigm, 261.
91. J. Dewey quoted in I. Semetsky, *Deleuze, Education and Becoming* (Rotterdam: Sense, 2006), p. xxiii.
92. G. Deleuze and F. Guattari, *Kafka: Toward a Minor Literature*, tr. D. Polan (Minneapolis, MN: University of Minneapolis Press, 1986), p. 108.
93. Biesta, *The Beautiful Risk of Education*, pp. 25–42.
94. V. Dukic, The Two-Fold Structure of the Death-Event (2009). Available at: http://artsciweb.concordia.ca/ojs/index.php/gnosis/article/viewFile/83/45, p. 245.
95. Williams, Time and Education in the Philosophy of Gilles Deleuze, p. 245.
96. Williams, Time and Education in the Philosophy of Gilles Deleuze, p. 246.
97. Wallin, Morphologies for a Pedagogical Life, p. 198.
98. Williams, Time and Education in the Philosophy of Gilles Deleuze, p. 242.
99. Wallin, Morphologies for a Pedagogical Life, p. 204.
100. Wallin, Morphologies for a Pedagogical Life, p. 198.

101. T. Ingold, Bringing Things to Life: Creative Entanglements in a World of Materials. Working Paper 15 (2010). Available at: http://www.socialsciences.manchester.ac.uk/medialibrary/morgancentre/research/wps/15-2010-07-realities-bringing-things-to-life.pdf, p. 10.

102. Deleuze and Guattari, *Difference and Repetition*, p. 244.

103. H. Ginott, *Teacher and Child: A Book for Parents and Teachers* (New York: Scribner, 1993), p. 317, quoted by R. Pring, What Counts As An Educated Person In This Day and Age?, EBOR Lecture, York St John University (17 September 2014).

Chapter 8

A MATTER OF HOPING: A RETURN TO THE MIDDLE

Gatsby believed in the green light, the orgastic future that year by year recedes before us. It eluded us then, but that's no matter – tomorrow we will run faster, stretch out our arms farther ... And then one fine morning –

So we beat on, boats against the current, borne back ceaselessly into the past.

F. Scott Fitzgerald, *The Great Gatsby* (1925)

Hoping

It is easy, in times such as these, to lose heart. The acts of resistance I explore in 'A Matter of (R)evolution' (Chapter 7) are attempts to take heart, to move to the heart of the matter. This plateau, coming last in terms of page numbers is *lateau* ('late water'), an attempt to resist concluding by returning to the middle. It is late but still mid. It is *eau* – the water of the spring that swells in the middle of the rhizome. It is (not) an end. It is concerned with hoping, and hope is not easily won. Hope is not an end point but an ongoing state of mind affected by a series of events which, even when destabilising, can be reframed to offer new lines of resistance and resolve. It is that vital element 'which depends on an imagination that can be forged from the daily fabric of existence whilst having a capacity to endure and sustain'.[1] To hope is to arm oneself for a battle against perceptions of inevitability and fear of complexity. Indeed, Deleuze states that 'there is no need to fear or hope, but only to look for new weapons',[2] and so it marks a movement between resistance and resilience. And because this is a continuous looping process, I add the suffix 'ing' – hope is always in the process of becoming. This plateau therefore asks 'So what?' of my attempts to better understand my experiences through Deleuzian lenses. It asks 'So what?' of my modes of resistance. It asks 'How will/do you make it all matter?' and 'How do you keep on keeping on?'

Hoping is a movement – it requires returning to the past, attempting to learn and finding those in-between spaces where differences can be made. This involves engaging with difficulty and challenge. For example, Wendy Brown, questioning the wisdom of small acts of subversion, asks whether it is 'a mistake to value this resistance too highly, for it is, like most rights claims, a defense in the context of domination, a strategy for negotiation, domination rather than a sign of emancipation from it'.[3] Her statement could lead me to despair – are my small acts of resistance, my attempts to create a living pedagogy, merely a strategy for coping (rather than hoping)? How do I make these understandings and actions 'other', eventful and worthy? Having left teaching for the moment, these questions are all the more pertinent. Did I fail? Now a travelling teacher, working with children and adults in other schools, this activism seems even more important. Time is limited; the subversion can only be small and it must be quickly enacted.

Brown's are important considerations, but to be Deleuzian is not to ask or look for the grand gestures of revolutionary reform, but to recognise that impact can be felt in small but accumulative (r)evolutionary ways. To be rhizome is not to commit large acts that seek to change the world, but to find small quiet spaces in which to question and explore. Change is inevitable and unpredictable. Seeking to trigger small disruptions is enough to start the oscillations that will lead to change, but one can never control the direction the lines will take. Accepting this, while seeking to contribute towards a 'better' life, is part of the mess we live with. One needs to be full of care(ing), of hope(ing). Making small quiet spaces to contemplate and move is part of the process of (r)evolution. It is to recognise that one is connected and always in the middle of something. Rather than becoming despondent at the smallness of my contributions, I have to keep moving, sowing seeds. As I continue travelling, I find myself 'in a shape or element that tears us apart but also propels us into a hitherto unknown and unheard of world of problems'; in the inter-world between 'not knowing and knowing – the living passage from one to the other'.[4] It is not what one seeks to do that matters, but what one seeks to be.

Remembering

I consider the plateaus I have presented on this journey in and out of rabbit holes. There has been a growing acceptance of uncertainty and the struggle to find a language to represent it; a movement towards conceptualising an amorphodology not only as a method of researching but of living and teaching. I look back at my early writings and notice how much more willing I am now to speak of this uncertainty – to write about it and share it publicly in meetings and online. I consider how much more comfortable I am sitting in and opening up void spaces. I observe how the richness of the void space is impacting on the teachers and pupils I work with, who are becoming less passive and less likely to deflect tasks with the learned helplessness of 'I don't get it' or 'I can't' – or, in the case of adults, 'Ofsted won't like it'. Instead, the 'I don't knows' are becoming more playful – explorations rather than excuses. I can see how I am visualising and conceptualising time in the classroom; considering the impacts and flights into the future and past of my language, and how this might open up present possibilities. I try to create chronos spaces, in the moment, in order to allow children to oscillate in the possibility of smooth spaces as often as I can. I think how much more attendant I am to what children might be, might have been, are. How committed I am to providing opportunities which are eventful and present. I consider how important teaching is to me – even though I am really a nomadic teacher now, travelling from school to school – and how much it all matters. How the nonsense makes sense. I can see the gathering elements that are shaping me as geological forces will shape the plateau. But I am in the middle of being shaped; always in the middle of the event. So I cannot conclude. Nevertheless, I can see how becomings are becoming, even if I cannot yet see what they will be.

Teaching, even witnessing teaching, is a deeply emotional experience, but I have learned here that so is writing the teacher into being. Some argue that where broken heartedness, guilt, disappointment and joy are encountered and felt, where it is found, the channels forged by the mining can lead to change.[5] As such, if this writing was ever to be more than a means to an end of a doctoral qualification – if it was to be more than 'work' – then it had to lead to *vita activa*, a life which is not simply 'active' or 'productive' but which leads to affirmative actions and deeds. This life lies in the complex interplay of those rhizomatic elements which combine to become more than a sum of their parts. I write, I learn, I act, I share. Others read, they learn, they act, they share. The writing is an element of the rhizome. But I know that *this* writing is not going to be widely read. What is its contribution? In its embodiment in my (and your) future actions and practices, it is a carrier. A (r)evolutionary mutation.

Communicating

Pasi Sahlberg has conceptualised the Global Education Reform Movement as a GERM – a virus, effectively infecting education systems across the world, so perhaps the resistance to that infection is in mutation. Books will do some of the work, but it has been online where many of these thoughts have taken hold and been discussed. For me, it has been possible to do all of this from the quiet space of my home – sitting in pyjamas, blogging about the complexity of teaching and learning. David Cole argues that the act of blogging is to use the internet as a form of immanent materialism, as a means of subverting dominant discourses to create smooth space: 'It is a space where virtual multiplicities may form and break free, move over and shape opinion through previously unforeseen connections.'[6] I attempt to use this space to encourage others to resist simplicity, to ask awkward questions, to uncover absurdity. I encourage us to connect, to form networks and alliances, to speak out and up. In this way, our disquiet, our thoughts, become other – a rhizomatic network of immanent materialism which allows teachers and students to engage in an exploration of educational life forms without having to 'slavishly' read the theory underpinning the ideas.[7] It allows hope to spring up through the cracks.

These online networks bring with them the possibility of positive disruption, and they are not entirely virtual. For example, a trend towards TeachMeets has emerged through Twitter. TeachMeets take place all across the country. They are free and function as continuing professional development (CPD), but the participants are the invited speakers. They are not forced upon teachers as INSET and organised by management, but instead come from a grassroots network of teachers sharing their best ideas. Other educational events, like Northern Rocks, have also sprung up with the intention of reclaiming the profession for those most invested in it – teachers and children. It seems to me that technology and networking in tandem offers the possibility for what Charles Leadbeater calls 'disruptive liberation'[8] – a potential for technology to bring together communities in shared goals and visions, giving them a medium through which they can be heard. In such ways are teachers self-organising to manage their own CPD, using their own practices and networks. I like the fact that these are hailed as 'grassroots movements' – they are rhizome.

Cole would argue that this is a Deleuzian flight, even if Deleuze himself suggested that computers were simply a part of the modulation of the control society network.[9] He was, of course, writing before the internet became the world wide web, which Cole frames within the concept of a 'body without organs',[10] and his concerns centred around the idea of computers as isolating tools of state, controlling the flow of information. While scientists point out that the internet is an architectural and algo-rithmical system, and therefore not emergent,[11] this does not account for the complexity emerging from the intra-action with and between human users. In this way, technology functions as an assemblage of multiplicity and contradiction, and I suggest that it can act as a derivative force of the mass collection of monad and can lead to positive change. While it is a tool of capitalism (online shopping, cookies, adverts), it is also a place of resistance (online campaigns, political blogs). The internet is both an instrument of the control society – a virtual 'vast space of enclosure' AND a smooth space in which something can become. It is Mobius – both architect and artisan – and can be utilised as an instrument of hope/desire and fear. This duplicitous nature of the internet has led Buchanan to caution against conceptualising it as Deleuzian,[12] but I would argue that it is not whether the internet is or isn't this or that, but what it has offered in terms of putting ideas to work that matters. Certainly, it has allowed me and many other teachers to take their small, subversive practices to a wider audience.

Returning – the ceaseless past

I'm almost done, but some things just don't leave you alone …

The following data is taken from 'The Mantle of Macbeth',[13] which was written as an ethnodramatic presentation of a curriculum intervention. I was observing a session in an 11–16 secondary school which had recently been placed in National Challenge. We had been exploring whether or not a creative pedagogy could help the school to improve English GCSE results. I was working as an external evaluator of the process on behalf of Creative Partnerships.

Scene 7 (extract): *A small meeting room. Hannah, in role as Martha, is sitting at a round table opposite three of the boys – Wayne, Dean and Craig. The boys, GCSE pupils in a school placed in National Challenge, are in role as employees of a theatre company. She stands to greet them.*

Hannah (as Martha): We have a little mock-up of the set here and some blocks and figures – they're a bit rough and ready but you can use them to explain your ideas if you like.

Immediately the boys pick up the pipe cleaner figures and the wooden boxes.

Hannah (as Martha): I thought you might want to start by explaining to me what the scene is and what your concept has been. To be honest, gentlemen, it seems a bit of a tough one this – making *Macbeth* accessible to 15-year-olds. Not really their thing is it?

> Their world/our world … the boys are imposing their understanding of 'reality' onto the text but positioning themselves in role outside of both. They are in AND space, occupying a conjunction. The inhabited space of the professional adult AND the 15-year-old AND Macbeth.

The boys nod sagely.

Dean: I think they'll like our idea though – we've set it in modern day and we thought that maybe the play takes place in a gang – the fighting at the beginning could be a battle with another gang.

Wayne: It's something that'll appeal to 15-year-olds, we think – it's their world, drugs and violence – and then they'll see that it's a good play really. That *Macbeth* – it's like it has a lesson in it. He does something really bad and thinks he can get away with it, but it teaches you – like it teaches you that the consequences – the guilt – it's in his head. He's haunting himself. He can't get away from his own conscience. I think that's something that 15-year-olds might need to hear.

Hannah (as Martha): That's really powerful. I think I can see how it might work. So let's focus in on this scene then – what's going on?

Dean: Macbeth has just killed Duncan – stabbed him when he was asleep – and now he's come back with the daggers and blood all over his hands, and Lady Macbeth goes schitz with him.

Hannah (as Martha): Schitz?

Dean: She's really angry with him, has a go at him – what have you brought these daggers here for? You should have left them. She gives him a hard time.

Hannah (as Martha): How is he feeling, do you think?

Wayne: He's sick. It's one thing being in battle, being a hero – like at the beginning of the play, he's a real warrior – but here, he's betrayed his king – the person he should be most, I don't know, like loyal to, you know? And he's done it while he's asleep, stabbed him when he couldn't do anything about it. Macbeth knows that's wrong – cowardly – and I think he feels sick about it – even now.

Hannah (as Martha): OK, so how are we staging this – what is Macbeth wearing?

Craig: Black.

Hannah (as Martha): Can you expand on that?

Craig: He's in black and he's walking in the shadows. He doesn't want to be seen – he's just killed someone and like, when you're out robbin', you wear black so you're less noticeable.

There is a pause as everyone takes in what Craig has said.

> The norms of Craig's life are pushing into the text of *Macbeth* – the play is being framed as an extension of his own life, informing his understanding. Craig is not just taking on Macbeth, Macbeth is taking on Craig – a becoming-Craig.

Hannah (as Martha): Anything else?

Dean: It's dark, it's late – we were talking about it earlier, at dinnertime, and we thought we'd have it lit in like a low blue light – cold and dark and lots of shadow.

Hannah (as Martha): Why, what time is it?

Wayne: About 3 in the morning. You know, that time when every-one's drunk so much they've passed out, been sick – and no one's likely to notice Macbeth skulking about.

They all nod in agreement.

Hannah (as Martha): And how tense is this scene, do you think?

Craig: What does tense mean?

Wayne: Like stress – an atmosphere – I don't know how to describe it. Like this would be low tension (he leans back in his chair, relaxed and sighs contentedly). And this would be high tension (sits up bolt upright, fists clenched, ready to punch).

Craig: Oh right, yeah – pretty tense then. He don't seem that happy with what he's done, does he, and his missus is giving him a well hard time now.

Just as we thought it was over, we're borne back into pedagogy; into signage, effect and notions of becoming. This is the data I have not been able to put down. I remember holding my breath when Craig spoke of robbing – it seemed like a void had opened up that no one rushed to fill. I did not 'know' Deleuze at the time but I sensed a 'something', and returns brought the feeling that I had witnessed a process of becoming. A role was opening up a smooth space where Craig was neither one thing nor another. Craig-becoming-Macbeth-becoming-Craig; the slip-pages from one time and space interacted. In this moment, I had a peep through a window into his system of values and way of living as Craig out of school, while he was at the same time enacting an alternative – a future professional self. We were simultaneously in chronos and aion – a pressing present but one in which past events and future possibilities were throbbing. Craig's statement 'when you're out robbin', you wear black' folds in on itself and out again – the costume denotes hiding, shad-ows, criminal activity; Craig's knowledge and experience; my discomfort at his confession; my excitement at his confession; his awareness of his connection to Macbeth; his potential to change OR to remain the same. Past/present/future in folds of literature and social justice.

There have been many stories in this book, but this was the 'scene' or extract I came back to again and again – each return driven by difference. I returned to it when I heard Craig had been expelled, and mourned the loss of a possibility. I returned as I started to write my doctorate, newly acquainted with Deleuze, and saw time and event differently. I returned as I edited and removed other analyses because it was all about Craig. I have continuously moved this extract of data from plateau to plateau, never quite knowing where to put Craig, until I now realise that I cannot put him down. I am becoming-Craig. I am becoming them all. Only having written this do I see the consistent stories of failure – having not quite got it 'right'. The failure I feel in not picking up on and pursuing his revelation sits like baggage on my shoulder. I carry him and the others – Neil, Danny, the children in Eyam, children unheard. I carry them all as a reminder to do better. Not to be 'good' but to be mindful.

For Deleuze, education is not a process in which there is a pursuit for 'higher' values, such as goodness, but a recognition of the multiplicity of the notion in the first place. This is beautifully exemplified in *The Boy in the Striped Pyjamas* by John Boyne. In the novel, 9-year-old Bruno, the son of a concentration camp commandant, desperate for a playmate, clambers under the fence into the camp and joins his friend, Shmuel. To fit in, he puts on a pair of the striped pyjamas that all the prisoners wear. Pulling them over his head, he makes the 'mistake' of breathing in. The pyjamas smell. Bruno does not make the connection, but the reader does – he is donning the clothes of a dead man. It is an act of foreshadowing. But it is more than this – it is a Deleuzian multiplicity. The pyjamas simultaneously hold the promise of play for Bruno, humiliation for Shmuel, horror for the reader, a suggestion of a life of pain and suffering for the previous owner(s). They carry the future potentiality of Bruno's own death and his past loneliness and naivety. They carry all the prior knowledge we have of the Holocaust, and for the reader bring together the past, present and future in the moment. Folds upon folds of meaning in a smell. And these folds extend so that my Year 7s, and Craig, and the children in Eyam, and all the other children present in the data in this book become part of one whole and complex system of folds. They are all, past, present and future, folded into a whole idea of child as I work through this dilemma. Not to find solutions, but to explore the edges of the dilemma. Standing at the edge of the plateau and looking at the formations.

The plateaus in this book were conceived to act as a series of 'larval subjects' – a 'developing structure ... until it emerges as it is'[14] – and the emergence of them has given me a sense of agency, which Hoy describes as 'the double of a contemplative self that surveys the thousands of interactions required to integrate tiny actions within a more complex apparent action'.[15] I have presented some of those actions here, without glossing over their complexity. Like St Pierre, I can find no 'facile comfort of a beginning and an end [that] slips carelessly over the spectacular trajectories in the middle that demand our most rigorous attention'.[16] There is no end. But there is resistance. It is edgework. It is the slow fall of multiple acts of remembrance. And acts of remembrance are what teachers do.

/She called me a numpty/

/We're evil, us/

/When you're out robbin'/

/I've learned I can cope/

Notes

1. C. Pearce, The Life of Suggestions, *Qualitative Inquiry* 17(7) (2010): 631–638 at 635.
2. G. Deleuze, Postscript on the Societies of Control, *October 59* (Winter 1992): 3–7 at 4. Available at: http://pages.akbild.ac.at/kdm/_media/_pdf/Gilles%20Deleuze%20-%20Postscript%20on%20the%20Societies%20of%20Control.pdf.
3. W. Brown, *Edgework: Critical Essays on Knowledge and Politics* (Princeton, NJ: Princeton University Press, 2005), p. 95.
4. G. Deleuze, *The Logic of Sense* (London: Continuum, 2004), p. 215.
5. See P. Golde (ed.), *Women in the Field: Anthropological Experiences* (Chicago, IL: Aldine Publishing, 1970); and E. S. Junqueira, Feminist Ethnography in Education and the Challenges of Conducting Fieldwork: Critically Examining Reciprocity and Relationships between Academic and Public Interests, *Perspectives on Urban Education* (Spring 2009): 73–79.
6. D. Cole, Matter in Motion: The Educational Materialism of Gilles Deleuze, *Educational Philosophy and Theory* 44(1) (2011): 3–17 at 12. Available at: http://www.academia.edu/536560/Matter_in_Motion_The_Educational_Materialism_of_Gilles_Deleuze.
7. See D. Cole, *Educational Life Forms: Deleuzian Teaching and Learning Practice* (Rotterdam: Sense, 2011).
8. C. Leadbeater, Technology in Education: The Past, Present and Future. Speech delivered at the Sunday Times Festival of Education, Wellington College, Berkshire, 21–22 June 2013.
9. Cole, *Educational Life Forms: Deleuzian Teaching and Learning Practice*; G. Deleuze, Postscript on the Societies of Control, *October 59* (Winter 1992): 3–7. Available at: http://pages.akbild.ac.at/kdm/_media/_pdf/Gilles%20Deleuze%20-%20Postscript%20on%20the%20Societies%20of%20Control.pdf. See also: I. Buchanan, Deleuze and the Internet, *Australian Humanities Review* 43 (December 2007): 1–19.

Available at: http://www.australianhumanitiesreview.org/archive/Issue-December-2007/Buchanan.html.

10. Cole, *Educational Life Forms: Deleuzian Teaching and Learning Practice*.

11. J. Crowcroft, Internet Failures: An Emergent Sea of Complex Systems and Critical Design Errors?, *Computer Journal* 53 (2009): 1752–1757. Available at: http://www.cl.cam.ac.uk/~jac22/out/bcs.pdf.

12. Buchanan, Deleuze and the Internet.

13. D. Kidd, The Mantle of Macbeth: Life Made Conscious – The Drama of English, *English in Education* 45(1) (2011): 72–85.

14. G. Deleuze quoted in D. Hoy, *The Time of Our Lives: A Critical History of Temporality* (Cambridge, MA: MIT Press, 2009), p. 159.

15. Hoy, *The Time of Our Lives*, p. 159.

16. E. A. St Pierre, Nomadic Inquiry in the Smooth Spaces of the Field: A Preface, in E. A. St Pierre and W. S. Pillow (eds), *Working the Ruins: Feminist Poststructural Theory and Methods in Education* (London: Routledge, 2000), pp. 258–284 at p. 262.

BIBLIOGRAPHY

Adam, B. and C. Groves (2007). *Future Matters: Action, Knowledge, Ethics* (Leiden, NV: Koninklijke Brill).

Adams, R. (2013). Pioneering Free School Fails, Awarded Lowest Ofsted Grades, *The Guardian* (19 June). Available at: http://www.theguardian.com/politics/2013/jun/19/free-school-fails-ofsted-gove.

Alexander, R. J. (2000). *Culture and Pedagogy: International Comparisons in Primary Education* (Oxford: Blackwell).

Alexander, R. J. (2012). Neither National Nor a Curriculum?, *Forum* 54(3): 369–384. Available at: http://www.robinalexander.org.uk/wp-content/uploads/2012/11/Alexander-Neither-national-nor-a-curriculum-Forum.pdf.

Alhadeff-Jones, M. (2008). Three Generations of Complexity Theories: Nuances and Ambiguities, *Educational Philosophy and Theory* 40(1): 66–82.

Allan, J. (2013). Staged Interventions: Deleuze, Arts and Education, in D. Masny and I. Semetsky (eds), *Deleuze and Education* (Edinburgh: Edinburgh University Press), pp. 38–40.

Amorin, A. and C. Ryan (2005). Deleuze, Action Research and Rhizomatic Growth, *Educational Action Research* 13(4): 581–593.

Anderson, P. (1972). More is Different, *Science* 177(4047): 393–396.

Angrosino, M. (2008). Recontextualising Observation: Ethnography, Pedagogy and the Prospects for a Progressive Political Agenda, in N. Denzin and Y. Lincoln (eds), *Collecting and Interpreting Qualitative Materials* (Thousand Oaks, CA: Sage), pp. 161–183.

Aoki, T. (2005 [1986]). Teaching as Indwelling Between Two Curriculum Worlds, in W. Pinar and R. Irwin (eds), *Curriculum in a New Key: The Collected Works of Ted A. Aoki* (Mahwah, NJ: Lawrence Erlbaum), pp. 159–165.

Aoki, T. (2005 [1991]). Sonare and Videre: A Story, Three Echoes and a Lingering Note, in W. Pinar and R. Irwin (eds), *Curriculum in a New Key: The Collected Works of Ted A. Aoki* (Mahwah, NJ: Lawrence Erlbaum), pp. 367–376.

Applebaum, D. (1995). *The Stop* (New York: SUNY Press).

Arendt, H. (1998). *The Human Condition*, 2nd edn (Chicago, IL: University of Chicago Press).

Arnold, M. (1971 [1869]). *Culture and Anarchy* (Cambridge: Cambridge University Press).

Badiou, A. (2007). The Event in Deleuze, *Parrhesia* 2: 37–44. Available at: http://www.parrhesiajournal.org/parrhesia02/parrhesia02_badiou02.pdf.

Baer, J. (2003). The Impact of the Core Knowledge Curriculum on Creativity, *Creativity Research Journal* 15(2&3): 297–300.

Bahnisch, M. (2003). Deleuze and Guattari's Political Ontology of Desire, in P. Corrigan (ed.), *Proceedings of the TASA 2003 Conference* (Armidale: University of New England), pp. 1–12.

Barad, K. (2007). *Meeting the Universe Halfway: Quantum Physics and the Entanglement of Matter and Meaning* (Durham, NC and London: Duke University Press).

Barthes, R. (1985). The Third Meaning, Research Notes on Some Einsteinian Skills, in *The Responsibility of Forms: Critical Essays on Music, Art and Representation*, tr. R. Howard (Berkeley, CA: University of California Press).

Bassey, M. (2011). *Education for the Inevitable: Schooling When the Oil Runs Out* (Brighton: Book Guild).

Bearn, G. (2000). The University of Beauty, in P. Dhillon and P. Standish (eds), *Educating After Lyotard* (London: Routledge), pp. 230–268.

Bell, J. (2011). Whistle While You Work: Deleuze and the Spirit of Capitalism, in N. Jun and D. Smith (eds), *Deleuze and Ethics* (Edinburgh: Edinburgh University Press), pp. 5–21.

Bergson, H. (2011 [1896]). *Matter and Memory* (London: Lightning Source).

Berlant, L. (2010). Cruel Optimism, in M. Gregg and G. J. Seigworth (eds), *The Affect Theory Reader* (Durham, NC: Duke University Press), pp. 93–117.

Biesta, G. (2010). Why 'What Works' Still Won't Work: From Evidence-Based Education to Value-Based Education, *Studies in Philosophy and Education* 29(5): 491–503.

Biesta, G. (2013). *The Beautiful Risk of Education* (Boulder, CO: Paradigm).

Birke, L., M. Bryld and N. Lykke (2004). Animal Performances: An Exploration of Intersections between Feminist Science Studies and Studies of Human/Animal Relationships, *Feminist Theory* 5(2): 167–183.

Boal, A. (1992). *Games for Actors and Non-Actors* (London: Routledge).

Bogue, R. (2003). *Deleuze on Literature* (New York: Routledge).

Bogue, R. (2013). The Master Apprentice, in D. Masny and I. Semetsky (eds), *Deleuze and Education* (Edinburgh: Edinburgh University Press), pp. 21–37.

Bohr, N. (1998). Causality and Complementarity, *Philosophy of Science* 4 (1937). Reproduced in J. Faye and H. Folse (eds), *The Philosophical Writings of Niels Bohr*, Vol. 4 (Woodbridge: Ox Bow Press).

Braidotti, R. (2001). Becoming-Woman: Rethinking the Positivity of Difference, in E. Bronfen and M. Kavka (eds), *Feminist Consequences: Theory for the New Century* (New York: Columbia University Press), pp. 381–414.

Braidotti, R. (2006). *Transpositions: On Nomadic Ethics* (Cambridge: Polity Press).

Brown, W. (2005). *Edgework: Critical Essays on Knowledge and Politics* (Princeton, NJ: Princeton University Press).

Bruner, J. S. and C. Goodman (1947). Value and Need as Organizing Factors in Perception, *Journal of Abnormal and Social Psychology* 42: 33–44.

Bryant, L. (2011). The Ethics of the Event: Deleuze and Ethics without Αρχή, in N. Jun and D. Smith (eds), *Deleuze and Ethics* (Edinburgh: Edinburgh University Press), pp. 21–43.

Buchanan, I. (2007). Deleuze and the Internet, *Australian Humanities Review* 43 (December): 1–19. Available at: http://www.australianhumanitiesreview.org/archive/Issue-December-2007/Buchanan.html.

Burman, E. (2013). Avoid: The Big Society [seminar presentation]. Available at: http://www.slideserve.com/orpah/avoid-the-big-society.

Butler, J. (1993). *Bodies that Matter: On the Discursive Limits of 'Sex'* (New York: Routledge).

Butler, J. (2005). Burning Acts – Injurious Speech, in A. Parker and E. Kosofsky Sedgwick (eds), *Performativity and Performance* (New York: Routledge), pp. 197–228.

Carroll, L. (1887). *Alice on the Stage* (London: Carson and Comerford).

Carroll, L. (1998 [1865]). *Alice's Adventures in Wonderland* (London: Penguin Classics).

Christodoulou, D. (2014). *Seven Myths About Education* (Abingdon: Routledge).

Clark, A. (1998). Where Brain, Body, and World Collide, *Daedalus* 127(2): 257–280.

Claxton, G. (1997). *Hare-Brain, Tortoise-Mind* (London: Fourth Estate Press).

Claxton, G. (2012). Turning Thinking On Its Head: How Bodies Make Up Their Minds, *Thinking Skills and Creativity* 7(2): 78–84.

Coe, R. (2013). Improving Education: A Triumph of Hope Over Experience. Inaugural lecture to the Centre for Evaluation and Monitoring, Durham University, 18 June. Available at: http://www.cem.org/attachments/publications/ImprovingEducation2013.pdf.

Coe, R., C. Aloisi, S. Higgins and L. E. Major (2014). *What Makes Great Teaching? Review of the Underpinning Research* (London: Sutton Trust). Available at: http://www.suttontrust.com/researcharchive/great-teaching/.

Cole, D. (2009a). MLT as a Minor Poststructuralism of Education, in D. Cole and D. Masny (eds), *Multiple Literacies Theory: A Deleuzian Perspective* (Rotterdam: Sense), pp. 167–180.

Cole, D. (2009b). The Power of Emotional Factors in English Teaching, *Power and Education* 1(1): 57–70.

Cole, D. (2011a). *Educational Life Forms: Deleuzian Teaching and Learning Practice* (Rotterdam: Sense).

Cole, D. (2011b). Matter in Motion: The Educational Materialism of Gilles Deleuze, *Educational Philosophy and Theory* 44(1): 3–17. Available at: http://www.academia.edu/536560/Matter_in_Motion_The_Educational_Materialism_of_Gilles_Deleuze.

Cole, D. (2013). Affective Literacies: Deleuze, Discipline and Power in Spaces, in I. Semetsky and D. Masny (eds), *Deleuze and Education* (Edinburgh: Edinburgh University Press), pp. 94–102.

Colebrook, C. (2002). *Understanding Deleuze* (London: Unwin).

Colebrook, C. (2006). *Deleuze: A Guide for the Perplexed* (London: Continuum).

Colebrook, C. and J. Bell (eds) (2008). *Deleuze and History* (Edinburgh: Edinburgh University Press).

Conquergood, D. (1992). Ethnography, Rhetoric and Performance, *Quarterly Journal of Speech* 78: 80–97.

Crowcroft, J. (2009). Internet Failures: An Emergent Sea of Complex Systems and Critical Design Errors? *Computer Journal* 53: 1752–1757. Available at: http://www.cl.cam.ac.uk/~jac22/out/bcs.pdf.

Dahlberg, G. and P. Moss (2013). Contesting Early Childhood – Series Editor's Introduction, in M. Sellers, *Young Children Becoming Curriculum: Deleuze, Te Whāriki and Curricular Understandings* (New York: Routledge), pp. x–xiv.

Damasio, A. (2000). *The Feeling of What Happens: Body, Emotion and the Making of Consciousness* (New York: Vintage).

Damasio, A. (2006). *Descartes' Error: Emotion, Reason and the Human Mind* (London: Vintage).

Dekker, S., N. Lee, P. Howard-Jones and J. Jollies (2012). Neuromyths in Education: Prevalence and Predictors of Misconceptions Among Teachers, *Frontiers in Psychology* 3: 429. Available at: http://www.ncbi.nlm.nih.gov/pmc/articles/PMC3475349/.

Deleuze, G. (1986). *Cinema 1: The Movement-Image*, tr. H. Tomlinson and B. Habberjam (Minneapolis, MN: University of Minnesota Press). Available at: http://projectlamar.com/media/Gilles-Deleuze-Cinema-1-The-Movement-Image.pdf.

Deleuze, G. (1992). Postscript on the Societies of Control, *October* 59 (Winter): 3–7. Available at: http://pages.akbild.ac.at/kdm/_media/_pdf/Gilles%20Deleuze%20-%20Postscript%20on%20the%20Societies%20of%20Control.pdf.

Deleuze, G. (1994). He Stuttered, in C. V. Boundas and D. Olkowski (eds), *Gilles Deleuze and the Theatre of Philosophy* (London: Routledge), pp. 23–28.

Deleuze, G. (1995). *Negotiations 1972–1990* (London: Continuum).

Deleuze, G. (2001). *Pure Immanence, Essays on a Life*, tr. Anne Boyman (New York: Zone Books, 2001). Available at: http://projectlamar.com/media/Pure_Immanence.pdf.

Deleuze, G. (2004). *The Logic of Sense* (London: Continuum).

Deleuze, G. (2006). *The Fold* (London: Continuum).

Deleuze, G. and M. Foucault (1977). Intellectuals and Power, in D. F. Bouchard (ed.), *Language, Counter-Memory, Practice: Selected Essays and Interviews* (Ithaca, NY: Cornell University Press), pp. 205–218.

Deleuze, G. and F. Guattari (1986). *Kafka: Toward a Minor Literature*, tr. D. Polan (Minneapolis, MN: University of Minneapolis Press).

Deleuze, G. and F. Guattari (1987). *A Thousand Plateaus: Capitalism and Schizophrenia*, tr. B. Massumi (London: Athlone).

Deleuze, G. and F. Guattari (1994). *What is Philosophy?*, tr. H. Tomlinson and G. Burchell (New York: Columbia University Press).

Deleuze, G. and F. Guattari (2004 [1968]). *Difference and Repetition* (New York: Continuum).

Deleuze, G. and C. Parnet (1987). *Dialogues* (London: Athlone).

Demos (2013). Scrap Ofsted Inspections to Tackle 'Target-Obsessed Culture' in Schools. Available at: http://www.demos.co.uk/press_releases/demosscrapofstedinspectionstotackletargetobsessedcultureinschools.

Denzin, N. (2001). The Reflexive Interview and a Performative Social Science, *Qualitative Research* 1(1): 23–46.

Denzin, N. (2003). *Performing (Auto)ethnography: The Politics and Pedagogy of Culture* (Thousand Oaks, CA: Sage).

Denzin, N. and Y. Lincoln (2008). *Collecting and Interpreting Qualitative Materials* (Thousand Oaks, CA: Sage).

Derrida, J. (1963). *Speech and Phenomena: And Other Essays on Husserl's Theory of Signs* (Evanston, IL: Northwest University Press).

Derrida, J. (1967). *Writing and Difference* (New York: Routledge).

Design and Technology Association (2013). Education Select Committee Raises Serious Concerns Over the Ebacc (31 January). Available at: https://www.data.org.uk/news/education-select-committee-raises-serious-concerns-over-the-ebacc/.

Dewey, J. (1925). *Experience and Nature* (New York: Dover).

Dukic, V. (2009). The Two-Fold Structure of the Death-Event. Available at: http://artsciweb.concordia.ca/ojs/index.php/gnosis/article/viewFile/83/45.

Edelman, G. M. (1989). *The Remembered Present* (New York: Basic Books).

Edelman, G. M. and G. Tononi (2000). *Consciousness: How Matter Becomes Imagination* (London: Penguin).

Egan, K. (1978). What is Curriculum?, *Curriculum Inquiry* 8: 65–72.

Egan, K. (2008). *The Future of Education – Reimagining Our Schools from the Ground Up* (New Haven, CT and London: Yale University Press).

Einstein, A. and N. Rosen (1935). The Particle Problem in the General Theory of Relativity, *Physical Review* 48(73). Available at: http://prola.aps.org/abstract/PR/v48/i1/p73_1.

Ellis, C. and A. P. Bochner (2000). Autoethnography, Personal Narrative, and Reflexivity: Researcher as Subject, in N. Denzin and Y. Lincoln (eds), *The Handbook of Qualitative Research* (Thousand Oaks, CA: Sage), pp. 733–769.

Fautley, M., E. Millard and R. Hatcher (2011). *Re-making the Secondary Curriculum* (Stoke-on-Trent: Trentham Books).

Fels, L. (2010). Coming into Presence: The Unfolding of a Moment, *Journal of Educational Controversy* 5(1). Available at: http://www.wce.wwu.edu/Resources/CEP/eJournal/v005n001/.

Feynman, R. (1998). *Six Easy Pieces: The Fundamentals of Physics Explained* (London: Penguin).

Feynman, R., R. Leighton and M. Sands (1963). *The Feynman Lectures on Physics*, Vol. 1 (Boston, MA: Addison–Wesley).

Foucault, M. (1994). On the Genealogy of Ethics: An Overview of Work in Progress. Available at: http://sfbay-anarchists.org/wp-content/uploads/2012/12/Foucault-On-the-Genealogy-of-Ethics-An-Overview-of-Work-in-Progress.pdf.

Foucault, M. (1997). What is Critique?, in S. Lotringer and L. Hochroth (eds), *The Politics of Truth* (New York: Semiotext(e)), pp. 23–82.

Foucault, M. (2002). *The Archaeology of Knowledge* (New York: Routledge).

Furedi, F. (2013). Scientism in the Classroom: Opinion Masquerading as Research. Paper presented at ResearchEd, Dulwich College, London, 7 September.

Gallacher, L. and M. Gallagher (2008). Methodological Immaturity in Childhood Research? Thinking Through 'Participatory Methods', *Childhood* 15(4): 499–516.

Gardner, H. (1999). *Intelligence Reframed* (New York: Basic Books).

Gardner, M. (1974). *The Annotated Snark* (London: Penguin).

Ginott, H. (1993). *Teacher and Child: A Book for Parents and Teachers* (New York: Scribner).

Goksun, T., S. Goldin-Meadow, N. Newcombe and T. Shipley (2013). Individual Differences in Mental Rotation: What Does Gesture Tell Us?, *Cognitive Processing* 14: 153–162.

Goldacre, B. (2013). *Building Evidence into Education* (London: DfE). Available at: http://media.education.gov.uk/assets/files/pdf/b/ben%20goldacre%20paper.pdf.

Golde, P. (ed.) (1970). *Women in the Field: Anthropological Experiences* (Chicago, IL: Aldine Publishing).

Goldin-Meadow, S. and M. W. Alibali (2013). Gesture's Role in Speaking, Learning, and Reading Language, *Annual Review of Psychology* 123: 448–453.

Goldin-Meadow, S. and S. Wagner (2005). How Our Hands Help Us Learn, *Trends in Cognitive Science* 9(5): 234–241.

Goodchild, P. (1996). *Deleuze and Guattari: An Introduction to the Politics of Desire* (London: Sage).

Gore, A. (2013). *The Future: Six Drivers of Global Change* (New York: Random House).

Goswami, U. (2006). Neuroscience and Education: From Research to Practice?, *Nature Reviews Neuroscience* 7: 406–413.

Gove, M. (2013a). Education Reform: Schools. Written Statement to Parliament (8 July). Available at: https://www.gov.uk/government/speeches/education-reform-schools.

Gove, M. (2013b). I Refuse to Surrender to the Marxist Teachers Hell-Bent On Destroying Our Schools, *Daily Mail* (23 March). Available at: http://www.dailymail.co.uk/debate/article-2298146/I-refuse-surrender-Marxist-teachers-hell-bent-destroying-schools-Education-Secretary-berates-new-enemies-promise-opposing-plans.html.

Gove, M. (2013c). Keynote address at the Sunday Times Festival of Education, Wellington College, 21 June.

Greene, M. (1988). *The Dialectic of Freedom* (New York: Teachers College Press).

Greenfield, S. (1997). *The Human Brain: A Guided Tour* (London: Basic Books).

Greenfield, S. (2011). *You and Me: The Neuroscience of Identity* (London: Notting Hill Editions).

Grinnell, F. (2002). The Impact of Ethics on Research, *Chronicle of Higher Education* (The Chronicle Review Section 2) (4 October).

Grossberg, L. (2010). Affect's Future: Rediscovering the Virtual in the Actual (An Interview with Gregory J. Seigworth and Melissa Gregg), in M. Gregg and G. J. Seigworth (eds), *The Affect Theory Reader* (Durham, NC: Duke University Press), pp. 309–339.

Grosz, E. (2008). *Chaos, Territory, Art: Deleuze and the Framing of the Earth* (New York: Columbia University Press).

Groves, C. (2005). The Living Future in Philosophy. Working paper. Available at: http://www.cardiff.ac.uk/socsi/futures/wp_cg_livingfuture121005.pdf.

Guattari, F. (1995). *Chaosmosis: An Ethico-Aesthetic Paradigm* (Sydney: Power Publications).

Hallam, E. and T. Ingold (eds) (2007). *Creativity and Cultural Improvisation*. ASA Monographs, Vol. 44 (Oxford: Berg Publishers).

Hallward, P. (2006). *Out of This World: Deleuze and the Philosophy of Creation* (London: Verso).

Haraway, D. (1997). *Modest_Witness@Second_Millennium.FemaleMan_Meets_OncoMouse: Feminism and Technoscience* (New York: Routledge).

Hardt, M. and A. Negri (2000). *Empire* (Cambridge, MA: Harvard University Press).

Harlen, W. and R. Deaken Crick (2002). A Systematic Review of the Impact of Summative Assessment and Tests on Students' Motivation for Learning, in *Research Evidence in Education Library* (London: EPPI-Centre, Social Science Research Unit, Institute of Education, University of London).

Hattie, J. (2009). *Visible Learning: A Synthesis of Over 800 Meta-Analyses Relating to Achievement* (London: Routledge).

Hayden, P. (1998). *Multiplicity and Becoming: The Pluralist Empiricism of Gilles Deleuze* (New York: Peter Lang).

Heathcote, D. and G. Bolton (1995). *Drama for Learning: Dorothy Heathcote's Mantle of the Expert* (Oxford: Heinemann Drama).

Heidegger, M. (1992). *The Concept of Time* (Oxford: Blackwell).

Higgins, C. (2011). *The Good Life of Teaching: An Ethics of Professional Practice* (Chichester: Wiley-Blackwell).

Hirsch, E. D. (2007). *The Knowledge Deficit: Closing the Shocking Educational Gap for American Children* (New York: Houghton Mifflin).

Holmes, R. (2010). Risky Pleasures: Using the Work of Graffiti Writers to Theorize the Act of Ethnography, *Qualitative Inquiry* 16 (10): 871–882.

Holmes, R. (2013). Fresh Kills: To (De)Compose Data, *Qualitative Inquiry*. Special issue: Analysis After Coding. Guest co-editors E. St Pierre and A. Jackson.

House of Commons Education Committee (2011). The English Baccalaureate: Fifth Report of Session 2010–12, Volume I (19 July). Available at: http://www.publications.parliament.uk/pa/cm201012/cmselect/cmeduc/851/851.pdf.

Hoy, D. (2009). *The Time of Our Lives: A Critical History of Temporality* (Cambridge, MA: MIT Press).

Hyman, P. (2013). How I Went From Tony Blair's Adviser to Free School Head, *The Guardian* (1 September). Available at: http://www.theguardian.com/education/2013/sep/01/free-school-21-stratford-peter-hyman.

Ingold, T. (2010). Bringing Things to Life: Creative Entanglements in a World of Materials. Working Paper 15 (July). Available at: http://www.socialsciences.manchester.ac.uk/medialibrary/morgancentre/research/wps/15-2010-07-realities-bringing-things-to-life.pdf.

Jackson, A. Y. and L. A. Mazzei (2008). Experience and 'I' in Autoethnography: A Deconstruction, *International Review of Qualitative Research* 1(3): 299–318.

James, W. (1950). *The Principles of Psychology*, Vol. 1 (New York: Dover).

Jipson, J. and N. Paley (1997). *Daredevil Research: Recreating Analytic Practice* (New York: Peter Lang).

Jones, L. (2013). Becoming Child/Becoming Dress, *Global Studies of Childhood* 3(3): 289–296.

Jones, M. G. and L. Brader-Araje (2002). The Impact of Constructivism on Education: Language, Discourse and Meaning, *American Communication Journal* 5(3). Available at: http://ac-journal.org/journal/vol5/iss3/special/jones.pdf.

Jones, O. (2014). *The Establishment and How They Get Away With It* (London: Penguin).

Jun, H. (2011). Deleuze, Values and Normativity, in N. Jun and D. Smith (eds), *Deleuze and Ethics* (Edinburgh: Edinburgh University Press), pp. 89–107.

Jun, N. and D. Smith (eds) (2011). *Deleuze and Ethics* (Edinburgh: Edinburgh University Press).

Junqueira, E. S. (2009). Feminist Ethnography in Education and the Challenges of Conducting Fieldwork: Critically Examining Reciprocity and Relationships between Academic and Public Interests, *Perspectives on Urban Education* (Spring): 73–79.

Kemmis, S. (2009). What Is To Be Done? The Place of Action Research. Keynote address to the Collaborative Action Research Network Annual Conference, Athens, Greece, 29 October to 1 November.

Kidd, D. (2007). Creating Partnerships, *English in Education: Journal of the National Association for Teachers of English* 42.

Kidd, D. (2011). The Mantle of Macbeth: Life Made Conscious – The Drama of English, *English in Education* 45(1): 72–85.

Kidd, D. (2013). Teachers, Let's Get Behind the Education Spring, *The Guardian* (23 April). Available at: http://www.guardian.co.uk/teacher-network/teacher-blog/2013/apr/23/michael-gove-education-spring-teacher-protest.

Kidd, D. and R. Patterson (2009). 'Something of Nothing' – A-Voiding Action in Action Research. Presentation at the Collaborative Action Research Network Annual Conference, Athens, Greece, 29 October to 1 November.

Kirby, J. (2014). The Research-Practice Paradox, *Pragmatic Reform* (29 March). Available at: https://pragmaticreform.wordpress.com/2014/03/29/research-practice-paradox/.

Kitchin, R., C. Perkins and M. Dodge (2009). Thinking about Maps, in M. Dodge, R. Kitchin and C. Perkins (eds), *Rethinking Maps: New Frontiers in Cartography Theory* (Abingdon: Routledge), pp. 1–25.

Krietemeyer, B. and G. Prouty (2003). The Art of Psychological Contact: The Psychotherapy of a Mentally Retarded Psychotic Patient, *Person Centred and Experiential Psychotherapies* 2(3): 151–161.

Lather, P. (1993). Fertile Obsession: Validity after Poststructuralism, *Sociological Quarterly* 34(4): 673–693.

Lather, P. (1997). Drawing the Line at Angels: Working the Ruins of Feminist Ethnography, *Qualitative Studies in Education* 10(3) (1997): 285–304.

Leadbeater, C. (2013). Technology in Education: The Past, Present and Future. Speech delivered at the Sunday Times Festival of Education, Wellington College, Berkshire, 21–22 June.

Lenz Taguchi, H. (2012). A Diffractive and Deleuzian Approach to Analyzing Interview Data, *Feminist Theory* 13: 265–281.

Lyotard, J. F. (1986). *The Postmodern Condition: A Report on Knowledge* (Manchester: Manchester University Press).

MacLure, M. (2006). Entertaining Doubts, on Frivolity as Resistance, in J. Satterthwaite, W. Martin and L. Roberts (eds), *Discourse, Resistance and Identity Formation* (London: Trentham). Available at: http://www.esri.mmu.ac.uk/respapers/papers-pdf/frivolity.pdf.

MacLure, M. (2009). Broken Voices, Dirty Words: On the Productive Insufficiency of Voice, in A. Y. Jackson and L. A. Mazzei (eds), *Voice in*

Qualitative Inquiry: Challenging Conventional, Interpretive and Critical Conceptions in Qualitative Research (London and New York: Routledge), pp. 97–115.

MacLure, M. (2011). Where Are the Ruins?, *Qualitative Inquiry* 17(10): 997–1005.

MacLure, M., R. Holmes, L. Jones and C. Macrae (2010). Silence as Resistance to Analysis. Or, On Not Opening One's Mouth Properly, *Qualitative Inquiry* 16(6): 492–500.

Marcussen, L. (2008). *The Architecture of Space: The Space of Architecture* (Copenhagen: Danish Architectural Press).

Masny, D. (2006). Learning and Creative Processes: A Poststructural Perspective on Language and Multiple Literacies, *International Journal of Learning* 12(5): 147–155.

Masny, D. (2010). Rhizoanalysis: Nomadic Pathways in Reading, Reading the World and Self. Paper presented at the 3rd International Deleuze Studies Conference, Amsterdam, July. Available at: http://www.youtube.com/watch?v=CNTcuhdVeek/.

Masny, D. (ed.) (2013a). *Cartographies of Becoming in Education* (Rotterdam: Sense).

Masny, D. (2013b). Multiple Literacies Theory: Exploring Spaces, in I. Semetsky and D. Masny (eds), *Deleuze and Education* (Edinburgh: Edinburgh University Press), pp. 1–21.

Massumi, B. (1992). *A User's Guide to Capitalism and Schizophrenia: Deviations from Deleuze and Guattari* (Cambridge, MA: MIT Press).

Massumi, B. (2002). *Parables for the Virtual: Movement, Affect, Sensation* (Durham, NC: Duke University Press).

Maturana, H. and F. Varela (1992). *The Tree of Knowledge: The Biological Roots of Human Understanding* (Boston, MA: Shambala).

Mazzei, L. (2010). Thinking Data with Deleuze, *International Journal of Qualitative Studies in Education* 23(5): 511–523.

McDermott, R. and M. McDermott (2010). 'One aneither': A Joycean critique of Educational Research, *eJournal of Educational Controversy* 5(1). Available at: http://www.wce.wwu.edu/Resources/CEP/eJournal/v005n001/a018.shtml.

McInnis, B. (1998). Methods of Alice Physics, *Journal of Physics A: Mathematical and General* 31(15): 3607.

McLeod, J. (2007). *Counselling Skill* (Berkshire: Open University Press).

Morris, E. (2012). The National Curriculum: Why Have One If It's Not for Everyone?, *The Guardian* (23 January). Available at: http://www.theguardian.com/education/2012/jan/23/national-curriculum-review.

National Literacy Trust (2012). *Boys' Reading Commission: the Report of the All-Party Parliamentary Literacy Group Commission* (London: National Literacy

Trust). Available at: http://www.literacytrust.org.uk/assets/0001/4056/Boys_Commission_Report.pdf.

Nesbitt, N. (2005). The Expulsion of the Negative: Deleuze, Adorno and the Ethics of Internal Difference, *SubStance* 34(2): 75–97.

Nietzsche, F. (1994). *On the Genealogy of Morals*, tr. C. Diethe (Cambridge: Cambridge University Press).

Nietzsche, F. (1995 [1885]). *Thus Spoke Zarathustra: A Book for All and None*, tr. W. Kaufman (New York: Modern Library).

Noddings, N. (2002). *Educating Moral People: A Caring Alternative to Moral Education* (London: Teachers College Press).

Norris, C. (1987). *Derrida* (Cambridge: Harvard University Press).

O'Sullivan, S. (2010). Guattari's Aesthetic Paradigm: From the Folding of the Finite/Infinite Relation to Schizoanalytic Metamodelisation, *Deleuze Studies* 4(2): 256–286.

Olkowski, O. E. (2012). *Postmodern Philosophy and the Scientific Turn* (Bloomington, IN: Indiana University Press).

Peal, R. (2014). *Progressively Worse: The Burden of Bad Ideas in British Schools* (London: Civitas).

Pearce, C. (2010). The Life of Suggestions, *Qualitative Inquiry* 17(7): 631–638.

Pearce, C., D. Kidd, R. Patterson and U. Hanley (2012). The Politics of Becoming ... Making Time ..., *Qualitative Inquiry* 18(5): 418–426.

Perec, G. (2008). *A Void* (London: Random House).

Philippe, J. (2003). Nietzsche and Spinoza: New Personae in a New Plane of Thought, in J. Khalfa (ed.), *An Introduction to the Philosophy of Gilles Deleuze* (London: Continuum), pp. 50–64.

Pinar, W. F., W. M. Reynolds, P. Slattery and P. M. Taubman (1995). *Understanding Curriculum: An Introduction to the Study of Historical and Contemporary Curriculum Discourses* (New York: Peter Lang).

Plant, R. (2013). *Analytic Review: Data Systems* (London: Department for Education). Available at: https://www.gov.uk/government/uploads/system/uploads/attachment_data/file/193912/00047-2013PDF-EN-02.pdf.

Plotnitsky, A. (2006). Chaosmologies: Quantum Field Theory, Chaos and Thought in Deleuze and Guattari's *What is Philosophy?*, *Paragraph: A Journal of Modern Critical Theory* 29(2): 40–56.

Prigogene, I. (1978). Thermodynamics of Evolution, *Physics Today* 25(12): 38.

Prigogene, I. (1984). *Order out of Chaos* (New York: Bantam).

Pring, R. (2014). What Counts As An Educated Person In This Day and Age?, EBOR Lecture, York St John University (17 September).

Protevi, J. (2001). *Political Physics: Deleuze, Derrida and the Body Politic* (London and New York: Athlone).

Protevi, J. (2006). Deleuze, Guattari and Emergence, *Paragraph: A Journal of Modern Critical Theory* 29(2): 19–39.

Protevi, J. (2011). Larval Subjects, Enaction and E. Coli Chemotaxis, in L. Guillaume and J. Hughes (eds), *Deleuze and the Body* (Edinburgh: Edinburgh University Press), pp. 29–50.

Rambo Ronai, C. (1998). Sketching with Derrida: An Ethnography of a Researcher/Erotic Dancer, *Qualitative Inquiry* 4: 405–420.

Resnick, L. (1999). Making America Smarter, *Education Week Century Series* 18(40): 38–40.

Reynolds, W. and J. Webber (2008). Introduction: Curriculum Dis/positions, in W. Reynolds and J. Webber (eds), *Expanding Curriculum Theory: Dis/positions and Lines of Flight* (Mahwah, NJ: Lawrence Erlbaum), pp. 1–18.

Ricca, B. (2012). Beyond Teaching Methods: A Complexity Approach, *Complicity: An International Journal of Complexity and Education* 9(2): 31–51.

Richardson, L. (1997). *Fields of Play: Constructing an Academic Life* (New Brunswick, NJ: Rutgers University Press).

Richardson, L. and E. A. St Pierre (2008). Writing: A Method of Enquiry, in N. Denzin and Y. Lincoln (eds), *Collecting and Interpreting Qualitative Materials* (Thousand Oaks, CA: Sage), pp. 473–501.

Riddell, M. (2011). London Riots: The Underclass Lashes Out, *The Telegraph* (8 August). Available at: http://www.telegraph.co.uk/news/uknews/law-and-order/8630533/Riots-the-underclass-lashes-out.html.

Robinson, K. (2010). Changing Education Paradigms: RSA Animate [video] (14 October). Available at: http://www.youtube.com/watch?v=zDZFcDGpL4U.

Rose, N. (1999). *Governing the Soul: The Making of the Private Self*, 2nd edn (London: Free Association Books).

Rosethorn, B. (2012). Undead Temporality, *Critical Fantasies* (21 November). Available at: http://billrosethorn.wordpress.com/2012/11/21/undead-temporality/.

Roy, K. (2003). *Teachers in Nomadic Spaces: Deleuze and the Curriculum* (New York: Peter Lang).

Ryall, T. (2011). The Riots Show Why We Need To Listen To Young People, *The Guardian* (15 September). Available at: http://www.guardian.co.uk/society/joepublic/2011/sep/15/radio-1-big-conversation-young-people.

Sahlberg, P. (2013). Global Education Reform Movement is Here!, *Pasi Sahlberg Blog*. Available at: http://pasisahlberg.com/global-educational-reform-movement-is-here/.

Schostak, J. (2012). *Maladjusted Schooling: Deviance, Social Control and Individuality in Secondary Schooling* [Kindle edn] (London: Routledge).

Sellers, M. (2013). *Young Children Becoming Curriculum: Deleuze, Te Whāriki and Curricular Understandings* (New York: Routledge).

Semetsky, I. (2005). Not by Breadth Alone: Imagining a Self-Organising Classroom, *Complicity: An International Journal of Complexity and Education* 2(1): 19–36.

Semetsky, I. (2006). *Deleuze, Education and Becoming* (Rotterdam: Sense).

Semetsky, I. (2013). Deleuze, Edusemiotics and the Logic of Affects, in D. Masny and I. Semetsky (eds), *Deleuze and Education* (Edinburgh: Edinburgh University Press), pp. 215–235.

Serres, M. with B. Latour (1995). *Conversations on Science, Culture and Time* (Ann Arbor, MI: University of Michigan Press).

Shaviro, S. (n.d.). Deleuze's Encounter with Whitehead. Available at: http://www.shaviro.com/Othertexts/DeleuzeWhitehead.pdf.

Shor, I. and P. Freire (1987). What is the 'Dialogical Method' of Teaching?, *Journal of Education* 169(3): 11–31.

Shouse, E. (2005). Feeling, Emotion and Affect, *M/C Journal* 8(6). Available at: http://journal.media-culture.org.au/0512/03-shouse.php.

Slavin, R. E. (2002). Evidence-Based Educational Policies: Transforming Educational Practice and Research, *Educational Researcher* 31(7): 15–21.

Smith, D. (2007). Deleuze and the Question of Desire: Toward an Immanent Theory of Ethics, *Parrhesia* 2: 66–78. Available at: http://www.parrhesiajournal.org/parrhesia02/parrhesia02_smith.pdf.

Spady, W. G. and K. Marshall (1991). Beyond Traditional Outcome-Based Education, *Educational Leadership* 49(2): 67–72.

St Pierre, E. A. (2000). Nomadic Inquiry in the Smooth Spaces of the Field: A Preface, in E. A. St Pierre and W. S. Pillow (eds), *Working the Ruins: Feminist Poststructural Theory and Methods in Education* (London: Routledge), pp. 258–284.

St Pierre, E. A. (2011). Qualitative Data Analysis after Coding. Paper presented at the AERA Annual Meeting, New Orleans, April.

Stenhouse, L. (1978). Case Study and Case Records: Towards a Contemporary History of Education, *British Educational Research Journal* 4(2): 21–39.

Stewart, K. (2007). *Ordinary Affects* (Durham, NC and London: Duke University Press).

Stronach, I. (2005). Progressivism Against the Audit Culture: The Continuing Case of Summerhill School versus OfSTED. Paper presented to the First International Congress of Qualitative Inquiry, University of Illinois, 4–7 May 2005. Available at: http://core.kmi.open.ac.uk/display/271327.

Stronach, I. (2012). (B)othering Education: An Autobiography of Alternatives, *Other Education: The Journal of Educational Alternatives* 1(1): 171–174.

Tobin, K. (ed.) (1993). *The Practice of Constructivism in Science Education* (Washington, DC: AAAS Press).

Trinh, T. (1989). *Women, Native, Other: Writing Postcoloniality and Feminism* (Bloomington, IN: Indiana University Press).

Trinh, T. (1992). *Framer Framed* (London: Routledge).

Turner, D. (2009). *Theory and Practice of Education* (London: Continuum).

Vazquez, A. S. (1977). *The Philosophy of Praxis* (Atlantic Highlands, NJ: Humanities Press).

Visser, M. (1995). *Lorentzian Wormholes: From Einstein to Hawking* (New York: American Institute of Physics Press).

Walby, S. (2003). Complexity Theory, Globalisation and Diversity. Paper presented to the British Sociological Association, University of York. Available at: http://www.leeds.ac.uk/sociology/people/swdocs/Complexity%20 Theory%20realism%20and%20path%20dependency.pdf.

Walker, M. G. (2011). On Dark Matter in Dwarf Spheroidal Galaxies, *EAS Publications Series* 48: 425–434.

Wallin, J. (2013a). Get Out From Behind the Lectern: Counter-Cartographies of the Transversal Institution, in D. Masny (ed.), *Cartographies of Becoming in Education* (Rotterdam: Sense), pp. 35–52.

Wallin, J. (2013b). Morphologies for a Pedagogical Life, in D. Masny and I. Semetsky (eds), *Deleuze and Education* (Edinburgh: Edinburgh University Press), pp. 196–214.

Waters, M. (2013). *Thinking Allowed: On Schooling* (Carmarthen: Independent Thinking Press).

Webb, R. and G. Vuilliamy (2006). *Coming Full Circle? The Impact of New Labour's Education Policies on Primary School Teachers' Work* (London: Association of Teachers and Lecturers).

Wiliam, D. (2014). Why Education Will Never Be a Research-Based Profession. Paper presented at ResearchEd, London, 6 September.

Williams, J. (2013). Time and Education in the Philosophy of Gilles Deleuze, in D. Masny and I. Semetsky (eds), *Deleuze and Education* (Edinburgh: Edinburgh University Press), pp. 235–243.

Young, T. (2014). *Prisoners of the Blob: Why Most Education Experts are Wrong About Nearly Everything* (London: Civitas).

Zizek, S. (2012). *Organs without Bodies* (London: Routledge).

INDEX